HOW THIN THE VEIL

*Originally published by Greenberg
Publishing Company in 1952.*

Published by Mission Point Press
2554 Chandler Lake Road, Traverse City, MI, 49696
MissionPointPress.com

No part of this book may be reproduced, stored in a retrieval
system, or transmitted in any form or by any means electronic,
mechanical, photocopying, recording or otherwise, without the
prior consent of the publisher.

ISBN: 978-1-943995-19-6
Library of Congress Control Number: 2016917112

Printed in the United States of America.

HOW THIN THE VEIL

A Memoir of 45 Days
in the Traverse City
State Hospital

BY JACK KERKHOFF

with an introduction by
Ray Minervini

MISSION POINT PRESS

INTRODUCTION

Like Jack Kerkhoff, my life has been changed immeasurably by the old Traverse City State Hospital. I too, was drawn to this place of grand Victorian-Italianate architecture, towering trees and stately lawns—but for different reasons. He and I are separated by many decades, but we are connected by what many regard as a sacred place.

The Northern Michigan Asylum, as it was first known, opened in 1885 to serve the mental and physical health needs of the citizens of northern Michigan. It was built on the "Kirkbride Plan," which was the state-of-the-art design of 19th century asylums. It prescribed large hospital structures with segregated wards, high ceilings, tall windows (for fresh air and light), central heat and ventilation, landscaped lawns and hundreds of acres of farm land for self-sufficiency. The primary Traverse City hospital was nearly 400,000 square feet, and was later designated as "Building 50."

Similar facilities were built around the country, in the days before psychoactive medications. These asylums were designed to serve the philosophy of the Moral Treatment movement to care for the health, comfort and safety of patients in the most therapeutic environment possible.

Asylum literally means "sanctuary." Some people call Kirkbride Asylums "cathedrals of care," and like cathedrals, these were massive facilities built of brick, stone and timbers, intended to serve a useful life of hundreds of years.

By the time Jack came to the TCSH after World War II, the hospital had served thousands of patients over the preceding seven decades. It was no longer a modern facility, but the aging buildings and the dedicated staff served a critical role. And while not every patient was a success story, the hospital saved lives and provided some level of safety and comfort. Many families in Michigan may have deep memories and anecdotes related to patient experiences in the asylum—perhaps a parent, aunt or grandfather was once a patient. Jack's story is rare, because he was generous and brave enough to share it with the world in these pages.

While Jack committed himself to the hospital to save his life, I committed myself to save Building 50. I love old buildings. I love seeing the craftsmanship that goes into our historic structures, probably because I grew up in the building trades, helping my father work with bricks, cement and plaster from a young age. We lived in Detroit when it was considered one of America's great cities, and I watched with sadness over the years as many of its grand buildings were slowly "demolished by neglect."

I moved to Traverse City in 1990, the year after the State of Michigan permanently closed the TCSH facility. While busy with my construction company in the years soon after, I was eventually invited to participate in a community effort to preserve and reuse the now shuttered buildings. The community had renamed the campus the Grand Traverse Commons, due to the fact that nearly 300 acres of the campus was now dedicated as public park land. While the trials and tribulations of the various adaptive reuse efforts in the 1990s could be its own book, one outcome was that I had become enamored with the place, especially Building 50. The Committee to Preserve Building 50 was a grassroots organization in the truest sense of the word, and I took a seat on the board of the public redevelopment corporation as the Committee's representative.

The task of finding new uses for nearly 1,000,000 square feet of historic buildings in a city of 15,000 people proved a very difficult task. For every would-be developer that came forward, months would be spent considering proposals while the old buildings continued to leak and decay. As my dad always said, "After all is said and done, there's a lot more said than done." In 2000 I came to realize that if Building 50 was going to be saved, it might have to be me.

I had renovated many historic buildings in the past, but never one of nearly 400,000 square feet, and I certainly never had been in the role of developer either. With the help of employees and others we formed an ad hoc redevelopment group to see how we could do it. It turns out no one had ever adaptively re-used a Kirkbride asylum before. It was around this time that I was given an old copy of *How Thin the Veil*. Jack's story gave me another reason to fight to save the buildings.

So I put forth a redevelopment proposal. After the laughter died down, people realized I was serious. In short, with a tremendous amount of effort, perseverance and community support, we were given a chance to embark on this huge undertaking of "saving Building 50." Since 2002 we have been actively preserving and reusing our 63-acre portion of the old TCSH property, which we call The Village at Grand Traverse Commons. One bite at a time, we have converted buildings to condominiums, apartments and small businesses—"the butcher, the baker, the candlestick maker"—and in doing so we have preserved the historic buildings and given rise to a neighborhood. Many of the people who live, work and do business at the old state hospital are here with an appreciation of what this place once was.

It's hard to believe today, but 20 years ago many people just wanted to tear down Building 50, often citing that it was a place of sadness and despair. I've always believed that kind of thinking ignores the happiness and hope that often flourished here, and the noble intent that compelled our state to build a "sanctuary" to care for our fellow human beings.

It is my hope that as we work to preserve and re-use the historic structures of the TCSH. We not only save buildings, we save the birthplace of countless stories: the dramas, comedies and tragedies of the human condition in a grand place of healing.

As we often say, we are only the stewards of this historic campus. We look forward as it is reborn but we embrace its past, and create opportunities, hopefully with a future museum on the Building 50 grounds, to honor the people who were patients and caregivers here.

And like Jack Kerkhoff, we can help share their stories.

Thank you,
Ray Minervini

HOW THIN
THE VEIL

The names of all state hospital patients who appear as characters in this book have been changed. The names of doctors, with the exception of the Superintendent, have been omitted at their request for professional reasons. Registered nurses and attendants on D-3 have given permission to use their names.

**to
Jackie and Mac**

*"Ah, to think how thin the veil that lies between
the pain of Hell and Paradise!"*

— George W. Russell ("A.E.")

the
FIRST
day

So this is my homecoming. This is my return to the town where I spent the happiest days of my youth.

Much is changed; much is not. Through the swirling flakes of snow I can glimpse the same bay, a dead slate color this late in November. The drifts are piled high on Front Street, and the automobiles slip and slide. There are different store fronts, different names on the signs swaying in the wind. All of Front Street, so noisy and exciting when I was young, seems hushed by the snow. Even a big trailer-truck, plowing its way still farther north, is as muffled as a baby's toy.

I look, without thinking, for the patient farm horses and the sleighs, and then I remember: That was many years ago. That was when they played *Over There* at the high school dances. And we ate hamburgers and banana splits after the dances, and lived to see another day. That was when we went to Liberty Loan rallies and damned the Kaiser without knowing why.

The little car that had brought me back lurched into a wide, white driveway lined by five-foot drifts. How many times I had scampered up that driveway with my gang, fearful yet curious. How many times we had wandered outside the bleak, tower-topped buildings that had iron bars at the windows, and shouted at the men and women behind the bars and giggled over the obscenities they tossed back at us.

So this is my return to Traverse City, Michigan. Not to the sprawling white house on Washington Street, which all of us loved, but to Traverse City State Hospital, in other days bluntly called an insane asylum.

The young doctor in Receiving Hospital pretended for a few minutes that this was a social call. We talked of this person and that, of his wife who had grown up with my sisters. We talked of the snowstorm and of my trip from Grand Rapids, 150 miles to the south.

"And now," he said, "what's the trouble?"

No point in beating about the bush. I told him in a rush of words. How, a year ago, I cut my wrists with a razor blade. How, a month ago, I swallowed an overdose of sleeping pills.

"That almost did it," I said. "But they pumped out my stomach. The urge keeps coming back; it came back last night. I'm going to be successful next time or I'm going to be straightened here."

He was not alarmed. "You'll come in as a voluntary patient?"

"Yes."

"As a voluntary, you may leave at any time. We cannot hold you."

"I'll stay," I promised, "until I am told I may go."

He took me down the hall and left me with a psychologist, another man, who said cheerfully, "Go ahead and smoke: this won't hurt."

The psychologist took ten pasteboard cards from a desk

drawer. "This is the Rorschach test," he said, "a projective technique."

"Oh!"

"You simply look at these cards and tell me what you see on each. That's all there is to it."

On each card was what resembled an ink blob. I looked at Number One and saw nothing but the blob and different colors. Then slowly figures began to emerge—skeletons, a king wearing a crown, prehistoric monsters, bats, fish swimming among coral.

"I must be crazy to see such things," I said as I laid down card Number Ten. He smiled and told me to draw a figure of a man or woman.

"I can't draw a straight line," I protested, but he continued to smile, and I drew the figure of a man that any first-grader could have bettered.

"Now draw a house." But what I drew resembled a steamboat more than a house.

The psychologist left, telling me to wait. I waited an hour or more and then was taken back to the doctor's office.

"Well," he said, "the Rorshach indicates that perhaps you will be better off staying here for a few days."

"What does it show? Or shouldn't I ask that?"

He laughed, "I won't try to explain it in detail. Don't know if I could. But what you saw on the cards is symbolic. What you saw indicates to the psychologist that you are impetuous, which comes as a surprise to me."

"I'm impetuous all right, but why are you surprised?"

"You always struck me as a deliberate sort of person, looking before you leaped."

"I do all my leaping wearing a blindfold!"

"The test also shows that at the moment you are depressed."

As a paying patient I would be charged $2.40 a day, the doctor said.

"That covers everything? That's remarkable!"

"It covers everything. It is the figure set by the state."

"And it will take only a few days?"

"Well, that will be up to your ward doctor. I think you'll like him. He has been here eleven years and he knows his business. You'll be on D-3, I imagine. That's a nice floor, here in Receiving."

We went to another office where a nurse took my pedigree and I signed a paper stating that I had entered voluntarily. The nurse spoke briefly into the telephone, and in a few minutes a slight young man in white appeared.

"Your attendant on D-3 tonight will be Mr. Ammidon," the nurse said. "This is Mr. Ammidon."

Mr. Ammidon said hello and I said hello. We went into an elevator, which stopped at the floor marked D-3. "It's about time for supper," Mr. Ammidon said. "You'd better eat, and we'll fix you up later.

He unlocked a door, also marked D-3, and we were met by thirty to thirty-five men, all crowded around the door. They stared at me. One laughed shrilly. "He's a big one! Ho, ho! Must weigh two hundred!"

"Pipe down!" ordered Mr. Ammidon, making a passage-way for me. We went into a room marked "Bath." The ward doctor was there, talking to one of the patients. The doctor had on his overcoat and hat.

"What!" he said, "another one?" He twisted his red face in mock dismay.

I liked him immediately. He had an Irish name and he looked Irish. There was a slight white stubble on his chin and his close-cropped hair was white. Behind his glasses his eyes seemed tired, but they looked through one, not in a hypnotic way, but with penetration and, it seemed to me, understanding. Apparently he had heard about me from the young doctor.

"Feel lousy?"

"Not too bad."

"Been drinking?"

"Last night."

"Shaky?"

"No."

"Want anything?" He grinned. "A shot, maybe?"

"Don't need it."

He turned to Mr. Ammidon. "The usual pill at bedtime. Another later if he wants it."

Mr. Ammidon nodded. The doctor patted me on the shoulder. "Take it easy. See you tomorrow."

"There's the supper bell," said Mr. Ammidon. "Feel like eating?"

I shook my head.

"Better try," he urged.

Mr. Ammidon unlocked the door leading into the "neutral space," where the elevators, the laundry chute, and the incinerator are. The men rushed across the space and into the dining room just vacated by the women patients on C-3, the ward adjoining the men's. A woman attendant in white and several women patients in "state clothes" stood at the steam table filling plates as the men filed by cafeteria-style. I took some creamed potatoes, a piece of bread spread with apple butter, and a glass of milk, but I had no appetite. The liquor I had drunk the night before had worn off; I was dismayed by the step I had taken and thought for a moment of leaving. I'm a voluntary, I said to myself; I can leave any time.

Mr. Ammidon seemed to guess my thoughts. "You'll get used to the place in a few days," he said. "It's not so bad."

I smiled feebly. "What I need, Mr. Ammidon, is bed."

"Call me Art. I'll give you a room after supper. Bedtime is nine o'clock; the rooms are locked until then, but we can side-step a rule tonight, I guess."

I was listless, paid little attention to the other patients who paused in eager eating, as their stomachs filled, and darted curious glances at me. In twenty minutes all had finished. Art passed around a large metal basin into which the patients dropped their knives, forks, and spoons.

"Too many kleptomaniacs among us," he explained.

We filed by the steam table again, and a woman patient scraped our plates. She joked with the men, and some of them laughed and teased her.

"How's your sex life, Mary?" bawled one.

"Static!" she said. "Extremely static!" She had beautiful cheekbones and complexion, but her hair was done up with rag curlers and most of her front teeth were missing.

Art unlocked the dining room door, and the men filed out across the neutral space and through the door marked D-3. There Art stood with a package of matches, lighting cigarettes and pipes. The first to receive lights waited and gave lights to those trailing behind.

"Patients aren't permitted to have matches or lighters," he said. "You have to get your fire as we call it here, from an attendant, nurse, or patient who is smoking. Now and then an arsonist gets in here, and we can't be too careful."

All the patients hurried to the Day Room while Art took me again to the room marked "Bath." He explained that I would have to wear state clothes until my clothes were checked and tags bearing my name affixed to them. "You can keep your belt and your shoes," he said.

I stripped, took a shower, was weighed, and then got into the state clothes—thick socks, shorts, a pair of work trousers, and a shirt that was too small. Art also found a nightshirt in the clothes room and gave it to me. "Most of the men sleep in their underwear," he said.

I gave up my money and several packages of matches. I had a carton of cigarettes, which Art said he would lock up in the Treatment Room. "Just ask for a pack when you want one."

We went into the Treatment Room, down the long hall that led to the Day Room. On one side of the hall were the private bedrooms and the Treatment Room: on the other were two wards, the tiny "office" with a grille front, where sat the attendant or nurse on duty, Bath, Clothes Room, Supply Room, Utility Room, and a kitchen for the attendants and nurses. In the Treatment Room Art gave me a pill.

Then he unlocked bedroom Number 5. It was a small room with one screened window and contained a single bed, a small chest of drawers, a chair, and a throw-rug. The room had a scrubbed look.

"Sit around for awhile if you want," said Art. "Or you can get into bed right now. The can's up next to the Day Room."

I chose bed. "Take it easy," Art said. "I go off at eleven. If you want another pill before then, just poke your head out."

He stepped outside, inserted a key in a slot, and an overhead light in my bedroom flashed on. It was still light outside and I said I didn't need the light. He turned the key again and the light went off.

This is a hell of a mess, I thought, undressing. Impetuous

is right. What am I doing here with a lot of crazy people? I'm not crazy. But I thought of the two attempts at suicide; I saw again the blood flowing from my wrists; I remembered coming to in Kent County Receiving Hospital in Grand Rapids, after taking the sleeping pills. I remembered, with horror, that my wrists and ankles were strapped to the bed and that I shouted protests until my throat was raw.

I walked to the window and looked out at the snowdrifts that rippled on a pine-studded hillside in the dying light. A woman was coming down the slope, stumbling through the snow. She wore a brilliant red scarf tied under her chin and a mannish gray coat. There were red mittens on her hands. As she reached the bottom of the hill, directly under my window, she looked up. She could not see me because of the screen, but I could see her. Even in the fading light I could see her eyes. They were dark and beautiful.

I did not know then that Suzy had passed my way.

the SECOND day

At 5:30 A.M. the overhead light went on and a baritone voice bellowed, "Time to get up! Daylight in the swamp!"

I blinked in the glare. A pink-cheeked attendant stood beside the bed, grinning down at me. He had relieved Art and would be going off duty in an hour. "Looked in on you a couple of times," he said cheerfully. "Man, were you ripping 'em off!"

"Guess the pills did it." I felt rested, more cheerful.

"Good old pills! You won't need 'em after today, though. Looking real chipper."

I dressed and went through the door marked "Toilet." It was crowded with men clearing their throats and spitting. There were two urinals, four toilet bowls without seats, and three lavatories. Three messy towels were draped over the swinging doors of the toilets; they were messy because most of the men merely sprinkled water on their hands and wiped off the dirt on the towels.

In a corner next to the urinals crouched a sandy-haired man with a gaunt and ashy face. He appeared to be praying:

he was oblivious to the others until he looked up and saw me staring.

"You're the inspector," he said, his face lighting up. "I'm glad you're here. Now you can give me some advice."

He got up quickly and led me into the hall. Seizing my arm, he whispered, "They're going to electrocute me for my sins, but I'm fooling them. I'm not eating and I'm not drinking. They won't electrocute me so long as I don't eat or drink."

I felt absurd standing there; I couldn't think of a thing to say. "You know me, of course," the man said impatiently.

I shook my head.

"Name's Franklin. Of course you know me. You're the inspector, aren't you?"

My voice came back. "No, I'm just another patient."

"You can't fool me; I know you're the inspector."

A tall bald man in his sixties pushed Franklin away. "Don't have anything to do with that bastard!" he shouted at Franklin. "He's nothing but a God-damned chicken thief from Hastings!" He glared at me, turned, and stalked into the Day Room.

The pink-cheeked attendant came to my rescue. "Don't pay any attention to those guys. They're harmless." He explained that Franklin, once a prosperous merchant, had been taking electro-shocks, was now terrified of them and believed that they were preliminary to his electrocution. "Thinks he's sinned," said the attendant. "Probably cheated once or twice on his wife and is all mixed up about it."

I asked about the old codger. "Oh, he's always accusing someone of being a God-damned chicken thief from Hastings. He's German. Reads the Bible all day and yells Heil

Hitler the rest of the time. Doesn't know the war's over, I guess."

I stood in line and washed. "When do we shave?" I asked the man next to me.

He laughed; that is he opened his mouth and a mirthless ha, ha came forth. "Tuesdays and Saturdays are shave days," he said. "The barber shaved us yesterday. You see," he explained patiently, "yesterday was Tuesday."

"We aren't permitted to shave ourselves?" But he was no longer interested; he wandered away and a youth with waves in his hair took his place.

"No one shaves on this floor," he said. "On D-1 you can shave yourself and the doors aren't locked, but up here the barber shaves you twice a week and that's all there is to it. Say, are you the new guy?"

"I guess I am."

"Got a big belly, ain't you? Why the hell do you eat so much?"

I am fatter than I should be, but I don't like to be told about it. "None of your damned business!" I said.

"Now is that nice?" He smiled ingratiatingly. "Got a cigarette?"

Baffled, I pulled out a pack. "I don't want you to run short," he said gently, and I said I had a carton in the Treatment Room. "Oh, in that case..." he said and, grabbing the pack, he scuttled out into the hall. The other men roared with laughter, and shortly I joined in. But then and there I named the youth The Brat, and he was well named.

The Day Room was icy, and the old men complained about it. They coughed and blew their noses and some expectorated on the floor after carefully looking around.

The old men, I soon learned, were forever crying that there was not enough heat. They slammed shut the screened windows whenever a patient, seeking a breath of fresh air, ventured to open them. It was a feud that ran on from 5:30 A.M. to 9 P.M. Art had tried to appease both sides by opening the windows at night, but only the fresh-air fiends, of which I was one, thanked him for it.

The Day Room was about forty by thirty-five feet with sixteen windows on three sides. Straight chairs and rocking chairs with leather seats lined the walls. There were two hard benches, two large tables, two small tables, and a ping-pong table. In one corner was an upright piano. Near the door leading into the long hall was a drinking fountain that belched warm water even in sub-zero temperatures. The flooring was asphalt tile on cement.

I sat at one of the tables and thumbed through an old magazine. Across from me was a chubby little fellow with a pink face and a fringe of white hair around his pink scalp. He regarded me suspiciously for a few moments, then said cheerfully, "Thought you were one of the gangsters for a moment. Guess not. Now, don't get the idea I'm crazy. Lots of crazy ones here, though. That old fellow in the corner is really nuts. Religious mania. And that little guy all crippled up. Had a stroke. Say, he'd be better off if they took him out and shot him!"

He paused, squinting his eyes at me. "Ever play the market? No? Simple, if you know the ropes. I cleaned up 25,000 bucks yesterday."

"You play the market here?"

"Oh no. Got a pal in Detroit who buys and sells for me. They call me The Financier up here; think it's funny, but that's what I really am. Cleaned up in Detroit, but that's a bad place. The gangsters got on to how much dough I was making and were after me. Came right into my hotel, can you beat that? But I fixed 'em. Went to the police. They were very considerate, suggested I come up here where I'd be safe."

He rolled a cigarette with tobacco issued by the state, leaned close and whispered, "Trouble is the gangsters got wind of it. They're all over the place now, trying to get at me. Even climbed a tree to look into my window at night."

The man who had explained to me about shaving rushed excitedly into the Day Room. He carried his shoes in his hands; his socks were coated with dust and floor polish. "Ten minutes more!" he exulted. "Better get in line, boys!"

"That's Boy Blue," said The Financier. "Always wears blue slacks and shirts. Silly bastard starts an hour before mealtime trying to get us up to the door. He's always the first to get into the dining room and fill his tray. And he's always the first to leave. He's a God-damned pest."

"Why is he carrying his shoes?"

"Says he has a bad corn, but he just wants to attract attention. You'd be surprised," The Financier said virtuously, "how many of these nuts like the limelight. Like that old fool over there." He pointed to the corner where the piano squatted.

In a rocker squeezed between the piano and a grille-shielded radiator sat a little man whose feet barely touched the floor. He wore two sweaters and had a thick muffler wrapped around his neck. On his gray hair, combed straight forward into long bangs, was a hunter's cap with ear muffs. Cradled in his arms was an old, weather-beaten guitar held together by strips of cloth. He rocked and rocked, whimpering to himself.

"That's Willie," said The Financier. "He's always cold, or says he is. Not much blood in his veins, I guess. You ought to hear him play. Drives you crazy, if you aren't that way already. He's deaf and almost blind, too."

As if sensing that he was under discussion, Willie stopped his rocking and whimpering and carefully adjusted the guitar so that he could strum it with his left hand. Plunk, plunk, he went, and the loose strings whined and growled. A look of peace spread over his bleak little face, but over his alone, for there was no music in his fingers and none in his guitar: one chord over and over, filling the Day Room with an unearthly din. Shudders went up and down my spine, but no one else appeared to mind. Some glanced at Willie and sighed; others seemed not to hear him, their eyes looking far away, as far away as were their minds.

The Financier's laugh bubbled to the surface. "Now he's going to sing. That *is* a treat."

More weird than the clamor of his guitar was the voice of Willie. One moment there was a soprano-like screech; the next, Willie, grimacing and bending almost double, was a basso, growling and grumbling far down in his chest. He sang the same song three times before I could catch the words. They told about a trial and someone—the judge perhaps—kept repeating, "No matter who your father is, you are your mother's son."

The Financier spoke with a faint trace of pride. "That's his favorite. You get used to it after awhile. Like apple butter instead of butter on bread."

Willie paused, and far down the hall came a new clamor. The breakfast bell. Boy Blue bobbed back into the Day Room, jumping up and down in his stocking feet. "There it is!" he exulted. "There's the bell!" Out into the hall he sped.

The others rose slowly and as slowly walked from the Day Room. Only one made haste, a fairly young man with a bald head who carried a huge roll of music under his arm. As he passed me I saw that the front of his jacket was streaked with food stains.

"That's Ralph, the piano player," The Financier said. "He can play anything, but he won't if you ask him. He never speaks to anyone but the doctor. Crazy as a loon."

Two of the patients held back: Franklin, still crouching in his corner by the urinals, and Johnny, a boy of sixteen, who sat on the ping-pong table swinging his legs and staring out at the snow. He had curly chestnut hair and down on his thin cheeks. "Come on, Johnny," called the day attendant, and at the same time he nudged Franklin. "You eating breakfast, Franklin? You better or you'll get a tube feeding. You know what the doctor said." But Franklin just looked at him through his fingers. The attendant shrugged, walked over to Johnny, and gently pried him from the table. "I'm Ken Bates," he said to me. "Getting along all right?"

"A little bewildered."

He nodded. "Gets you at first. Won't bother you long. Hustle up, Johnny." He paused to pull Franklin upright and guide him along the hall. "These two fellows don't want to eat. Make a lot of work for us."

Franklin moaned, "If I eat they'll electrocute me." His face brightened momentarily. "But the inspector's here; he'll fix things."

Ken Bates shook his head. "Not much hope for him. Have to feed him through the tube pretty soon, I guess."

He unlocked the door leading to the neutral space and the dining room. Boy Blue darted through and was sitting at the first table with his tray before the fifth man was served.

[*17*]

As if by agreement Franklin and Johnny trailed off to a corner, refusing to pick up trays. The Financier bowed gallantly to the women behind the steam tables, wishing them all good morning and slipping extra pats of butter to his tray as he did so. Other patients tried it, and some were caught and rebuked. Butter was served at breakfast only.

Breakfast was plain, but filling—all the toast one could eat, oatmeal with milk, canned apricots, and coffee. Most of the chairs were occupied by the time I was served, and I went to the last table where Ralph sat alone, spooning great mouthfuls of cereal into his mouth. As I pulled out a chair he rose abruptly, lifting his tray, and moved to another table.

"Likes to be a lone wolf," said Bates, coming up with Franklin and Johnny. "Don't let him get your goat." He fetched trays for the two hunger strikers and patiently fed them. Franklin gulped and swayed his head away from the spoon, but Johnny obediently swallowed the food, occasionally smiling to himself. I was hungry and left nothing on my plate. Boy Blue gulped his food in great chunks, as does a starving dog, then sat back, drumming his fingers on his tray.

Back in the Day Room, the more active patients moved the chairs and tables to one side, two sweepers quickly pushed their brushes over the cleared space, and were followed by two more men with mops. When the floor was dry a young alcoholic with a movie-star face guided an electric polisher over it. Then the furniture was moved back, and the same procedure was followed on the other side of the room.

Few of the older men helped to move the furniture, but they watched every move of the workers and shook their heads and clucked among themselves if a sweeper or a mopper missed a corner. Boy Blue was everywhere, getting in the way and walking on the polished floor in his stocking feet. Ralph and The Brat disdained all physical labor, even refusing to move the chairs in which they were lolling.

"Ought to castrate 'em," growled The Financier. He laughed softly. "Or maybe that's their trouble now!"

Shortly after seven o'clock Miss Brown, the registered nurse in charge of the floor, came on duty followed by half a dozen student nurses. Even the old men brightened up; they liked the little attentions the students gave them, and when toothbrush call was sounded by a sweet-voiced brunette, they obediently trooped to the lavatories. The toothbrushes, each with a taped name attached, were kept in a cupboard. Even that was locked to foil the kleptomaniacs. Only Heilhitler refused to answer the call. "What the hell," he spouted, "I only got six teeth!" But the little brunette coaxed, and finally he lumbered to the lavatory.

At ten there was a stir in the hall, and the ward doctor came in. Franklin's face went white and he tried to hide behind one of the swinging toilet doors.

"No treatments today, Franklin," Miss Brown said. "Tomorrow's Thanksgiving, you know. No treatments before a holiday."

He sighed and the blood came back into his face. But the doctor was made of sterner stuff. "I'll give you two days to get back to eating, Franklin. If you don't, we'll use the tube. And I mean that; it won't hurt me, you know."

He turned to me. "Maybe you can help this chap. Put some sense into him."

"I doubt it. He thinks I'm an inspector."

"Well, try it. Give you something to do. How are you feeling?"

"Quite chipper."

He took out a stenographer's notebook. "Sit down; let's hear about it."

So I told my story again. He said nothing until I was done, then asked casually, "Any idea why you do these things?"

I said I had an idea, for what it was worth. My first wife and the mother of my two daughters died ten years ago. I never quite got over it, I said, but I was doing pretty well until four years ago when my older daughter also died. Then I didn't seem to care about anything, I said, though I still had my younger daughter in California and had married again. "My second wife is a fine person," I said. "She's put up with a lot."

"Most wives do. Why do you think suicide will settle everything? Think about your second wife and other daughter when you tried it?"

"I guess not. Just thought of getting out of it."

"Out of what?"

"Life."

"Baloney!"

I sat up straight. "What's that?"

He grinned. "Got under your skin, eh? Let it ride; I'll tell you some day when you're ready to listen."

That was a new approach, quite different from those used by other psychiatrists I had seen. I was resentful, but curious. I thought: this man is going to treat me and I have a feeling that his medicine is going to be bitter, but I am going to swallow it.

He stopped taking notes, explained that the various tests I would have to undergo would not be given until after the holiday weekend "Because a large part of the staff is taking a rest. We work hard here; we work like hell. You just loaf over the weekend; I'll give you a book I want you to read. Save a lot of time that way."

"I'm beginning to feel better already. When I look at some of the other patients, I realize that I am not so badly off."

With a non-committal "We'll see," he moved on, chattering amiably with some of the patients; shooing others from him, including The Brat, which did me good; giving orders to Miss Brown. "No more pills for Lewis," he said. "He isn't constipated. Caught him in the can myself!"

Abruptly he sat on the piano bench, ran his hands over the keys, and launched into the best boogie-woogie I have heard outside of Harlem. Ralph, sitting a few feet away, pouted and rustled his papers; then he jumped and hurried from the Day Room. He almost swished.

The doctor chuckled. "I always forget that Ralph's jealous. See you tomorrow."

"God damn him!" said The Financier. "I wanted to draw five hundred dollars, and he wouldn't sign the order."

"Five hundred dollars! For what?"

"Shirts. My God, man, you don't think I'd wear state shirts? I pay fifty dollars for a shirt. Silk shirts, like this one."

He was wearing a filthy print shirt that cost no more than two-fifty…. I don't know, I thought, that I am going to like it here.

the
THIRD
day

Snow was falling on Thanksgiving Day, but the sun was peeping through. Outside my window a tractor snorted down the hillside pushing a plow as big as itself, clearing a path from Receiving to the Center, a massive, ancient building where the executive offices are located. Receiving is comparatively new and resembles a modern high school, but the Center and smaller buildings, called cottages, that sprawl over a vast acreage, are as old as some of the pine trees that dot the white landscape.

Thanksgiving never has meant much to me in my grown-up years, but it meant a lot when I was a boy and lived on a farm only eighteen miles from where I was now. My mother and grandmother spent days preparing for it; there seemed always to be visiting relatives from faraway places with presents and exciting stories. But there were no stories after Thanksgiving dinner; everyone sprawled in easy chairs and groaned or fell asleep. Even we children were strangely quiet until our abused stomachs had recovered from the shock.

On D-3 that morning there was little interest in Miss

Brown's announcement that we were to have turkey for dinner. "All you want," she said cheerfully. "White meat and dark meat." A few smiled expectantly, but most of the patients did not care. Some, in fact, were not aware, until many days later, that Thanksgiving had come and gone.

But Miss Brown and Bates, and, later, the student nurses, were determined that we exhibit a holiday spirit. Bates announced that there would be no showers nor baths because it was Thanksgiving. (Thursday is bath day.) This caused a mild stir, for many of those on D-3, especially the old men, loathed bath day and thought up the wildest excuses to escape soap and water and a change of clothes.

We had breakfast; the Day Room floor was swept, mopped, and polished as usual; and then we sat looking at each other. Willie, who had hidden his guitar behind the piano, rocked in his corner, his slender little body shaken by sobs. I was sitting next to him, and he suddenly turned to me and said in his piping voice, "They ain't got no right to keep me in this terrible place. I can do for myself. I want to go back to my home...."

Gradually his story, as he believes it, came out. For years and years he had been living in a little shack on state land, doing for himself and somehow getting along on forty dollars a month, his old-age pension.

"It wasn't no hardship," he said, and a little color came into his face as he talked. "I'm a vegetarian, you see, so I didn't have to buy no meat. I like beans and bread and syrup, and I like puddings. And I didn't have to pay no rest. It was pretty terrible, all right, to send me here, and the sheriff, he thought so, too."

Apparently Willie had been a hermit squatter, doing odd jobs in a little town a few miles from his shack and playing for a square dance now and then, Oh, yes, he said, he was in great demand for square dances. "I played better than I do now," he boasted. "And I had a mouth organ that I played right along with the guitar. Them people at the dances, they said I was better than any orchestra." He wet his hand and smoothed his gray bangs, preening himself. "Everything was all right and I was getting along fine when them Polish people moved in. Them foreigners! Why do they let them come into Michigan, do you know?"

I murmured something, but he could not hear me. His blue eyes that seemed so clear but were almost sightless came close to mine. "You wear glasses, I see. Now, I wouldn't need glasses if they would let me out of this terrible place so I could do it for myself."

It seemed from Willie's story that those Polish people had bought the land on which he squatted and finally had called upon the sheriff to evict him. And probate court had ruled that he no longer could care for himself and should spend the rest of his days at Traverse City. The doctor told me later that Willie, harmless, not even eccentric, lives in a world "no bigger than his head" and never will return to the little shack for which he longs.

When they brought him to Receiving, he could not—or would not—eat or drink, and he sobbed day and night. They finally ascertained that his guitar had been left behind in the shack; after much correspondence, during which Willie pined away, it was fetched to the hospital, and Willie began to live again.

"I play mighty fine for an old man," he confided. "I know all the old pieces and I made up one myself. I call it *On the Banks of the Old Tennessee*; would be mighty tickled to hear it, I betcha."

He agreed to play it for me. The tears ceased and a smile wrinkled his face as he strummed. The chord was the same, the whines and the growls were the same. Only the words were different.

"On the banks of the old Tennessee," sang Willie, and that was all I could make out. I doubt that there were other words, although Willie insisted that "there are lots of words, but you have to listen careful."

I thanked him when he was done and he jerked his head in surprise. "Why, that's nice of you! No one ever thanks me here, and I play a lot for them. You see," he said eagerly, "how I could do for myself if they would let me out of this terrible place." And he put the guitar behind the piano and went back to his rocking.

At mid-morning, when all the beds had been made and the Day Room carefully dusted, the student nurses relaxed. Two of them played ping-pong with youth from the insulin ward, which is part of D-3, and the others cajoled Ralph into going to the piano. For some reason, probably because it was Thanksgiving, he played only hymns. The student nurses, grouped around the piano, sang sweetly; Miss Brown stood at the entrance of the Day Room smiling her kindly smile, and Bates came in, smoking an old corncob pipe, and listened until the office telephone rang. The sun came through the windows and shone on the students' solemn, young faces, and suddenly I wanted to cry. Suddenly I realized I was getting along in years and I was more lonely than I had ever been before. But I knew what such thoughts might lead to, so I walked out to the hall, around to the insulin ward and back. I did this for half an hour until I was dripping with perspiration and Miss Brown finally stopped me.

"Working up an appetite for turkey, Jack?"

It was good just to hear my name spoken. I admitted that I was feeling hunger, and everything seemed better then. Miss Brown seemed to understand; in a business-like manner she explained some of the hospital rules. I would be permitted to draw two dollars a week from my money, which had been sent to the accounting office in the Center. That would buy one carton of cigarettes, and I smoke a carton a week. How could I buy anything else?

"What else?" Miss Brown asked gently. I had no answer. "In a few days," she said, "the doctor probably will give you ground parole. That means you can go outdoors from one to four P.M. and to the canteen. You'll want to buy some candy or a cup of coffee there, but you'll have to ask the doctor for an extra chit. Maybe for another dollar?"

Three dollars a week for mad money! It seemed unreasonable, considering the money I had in the accounting office. "Many patients do not have any money on which to draw," Miss Brown said, still gentle, and I was ashamed of my thoughts.

"Willie?"

"Nothing. There is no one to send him money, I guess, but at Christmastime a school teacher he knew long ago sends him a box of home-made candy."

The mood was entirely gone. I went back to the Day Room and watched the ping-pong game. Ralph had ceased playing and was scraping food stains from his coat lapels. Two student nurses were trying to interest Heilhitler in a picture puzzle and were getting nowhere. I wrote a letter to my wife; I wrote for the hundredth time that I regretted what I had put her through, but that I felt something could be accomplished here. I wrote cheerfully and with hope and, in my ignorance, predicted that I would be home in a few days.

The Financier came over to say that I should not seal the envelope. "The doctor has to read it, you see. Just leave it in the office and they'll put a stamp on it."

Thanksgiving dinner was even better than Miss Brown had predicted. There were generous slices of turkey, huge mounds of mashed potatoes with gravy, a tasty dressing, cranberry sauce, and pumpkin pie. We ate until we could eat no more, but so strong is habit that several of the men asked for second helpings, wrapped turkey legs or wings in paper napkins, and smuggled them out of the dining room to be eaten later.

Franklin, who had choked down some mashed potatoes, approached me in the Day Room where he rarely appeared, preferring his corner by the urinals.

"Please give me the straight dope," he pleaded. "When are they going to execute me?"

I said that no one was going to execute him, that the doctor had even indicated there might be no more electro-shocks if he improved, but he did not believe me.

"But you don't understand," he said impatiently. "They made me eat some dinner, and that means the time isn't far off. Every time I eat or drink they try to electrocute me."

"But you don't feel the treatments, do you?"

"Don't feel them?" His face paled and he licked his lips. "How would you like to be held in bed and have that electricity going right through you, singeing you?"

That was an exaggeration. Bates had told me that Franklin received fairly weak shocks, similar to those given out by machines in amusement parks. But each treatment meant to Franklin a rehearsal for his electrocution.

I asked how he connected his expected electrocution

[*27*]

with eating and drinking. He looked carefully around before answering. "I wouldn't tell anyone else, but I can tell you because you are an inspector. There's no connection; I just say that to fool them. And I'm going to fool them about electrocuting me by starving myself to death. It won't take long."

"But they'll tube-feed you."

He winked slyly. "Maybe once or twice. I overheard the doctor telling the nurse that he didn't like tube-feeding because sometimes the food gets into the lungs and pneumonia can carry you off like that."

I tried to talk to him about his store and his wife and children. "The store isn't mine anymore," he said. "My wife took it over when she sent me here; I had to sign a paper. I don't get any letters from her any more," he said. "I don't write, either." He was not emotional about it. He said, "I don't blame them. They know I have sinned. I am willing to pay for my sins, but I want to pay in my own way." He would not tell me what his sins were. "I have sinned all my life," he said.

I tried to change the subject. "Miss Brown tells me that you are a fine pianist."

For a moment a deep hurt glazed his eyes. "I used to play, but it's no good any more. It makes me think about other things too much, and I mustn't forget my sins,"

Morbid curiosity, perhaps, kept me listening to Franklin for more than an hour, but in the days to come I grew to dread his approach. He counted me as a friend, although insisting that I was an inspector (of what I never found out) and followed me whenever I walked down the hall. It was the same story each day—sins and electrocution. At times I would lose my patience and tell him to go to hell, that I was weary of his melodrama. Then I would be ashamed and would listen to it all over again.

Other patients approached me after dinner. All were curious, but none—not even The Brat—asked why I was in the hospital. There seemed to be an unwritten law that a patient was free to talk about himself but no one might try to induce him to talk. Some of the men spoke pleasantly enough and wished me well; others talked briefly of the snowstorm and went back to their chairs. I noticed that each man had his favorite chair—Willie in his rocker by the piano; Ralph across the room near a windowsill where he could pile his sheet music; Heilhitler in another corner with his Bible on his knees. Johnny always perched on the ping-pong table when no one was playing; he never spoke, spending the entire day either frowning or laughing softly. Only Boy Blue had no place to call his own; he rarely sat in a chair more than three minutes. All day long he paced, pounding his hands together when they were not carrying his shoes. His hawk-eyes watched the windows and, if one was opened, he knew it almost immediately and rushed to close it. He watched the clock, too, warning all of us far ahead of time when we could expect the dining room bell to ring.

Boy Blue was unpopular. Only one man seemed to be able to endure him at close quarters—Big Jim, once a famous miler at Michigan, now grown senile, a ridiculous figure in his state clothes, which he never could arrange correctly. Often his trousers were on backwards, and once he painstakingly tore off the trouser legs from cuffs to knees, announcing that he had finally found his knickerbockers and was now ready to go to school. He had a magnificent shock of white hair but never used a comb or brush; he preferred to lick his fingers and run them through his hair. Boy Blue always looked for Big Jim on his pauses in the Day Room. Sighing, he would sink into a chair next to Big Jim. "My, it sure is good to sit down," he would say, knowing full well that he would be up and gone in a few minutes.

If Ralph was at the piano Boy Blue never missed exclaiming, "God, that man sure can play that thing!" He had three stories that he told a hundred times a day. One began: "Yes, I've got forty-five acres fifteen miles south of Ovid. I've got sixty head of cattle and 2,500 dollars in government bonds in the bank...." Another began: Well, twenty-six of us bought this hunting camp near Rapid River," and then would follow a minute description of the first deer he shot.

The third story was about his elder son, killed in World War II: "I didn't want him to go, but he went. We got the telegram and that's all we heard. We wanted him shipped home, but they said they never found his body." It was shortly after the telegram came that Boy Blue was sent to the hospital. He was permitted once to go home, but was back in a few days. "I like it fine here," he said at the time, and this viewpoint remained unchanged. He did not feel a prisoner, as did some of the patients. To him the brick and mortar of Receiving meant safety and comfort.

Big Jim, who had heard Boy Blue's stories countless times, rarely failed to express interest. They were always new to him, but the others would not listen. They cursed Boy Blue or moved away from him; they shouted, "Shut up!" when he announced the dinner bell that all but Willie could plainly hear. And they taunted him when he removed his shoes. Thanksgiving Day was no exception, but Boy Blue did not appear to mind. He chuckled when scorned, and moved on. But I heard him talking to himself as he stood at a window peering at the gathering darkness. It seemed to me that he was whispering, "My boy, my boy!"

the
F O U R T H
day

The day after Thanksgiving I got into the swing of things. A sewer backed up somewhere and flooded the basement room where incoming patients' clothes are listed and taped with their names. My clothes, tied in a sheet, just escaped the flood and were promptly sent up to D-3. I suspect that the hardworking women who use sewing machines to affix the tapes welcomed that flood.

Bates said apologetically, "Guess you'll have to sew on your own tapes. Here, I'll show you how." He threaded a needle, took a piece of tape on which my name had been stenciled, and carefully sewed it on the inside of the collar of a sports jacket. Alongside it he sewed another tape bearing the words "Rec. Hosp." He used fine stitches but worked swiftly. I tried it on a shirt, but the thread became knotted, the shirt bunched at the collar, and the tape, instead of fitting snugly, waved in the breeze from the open window in the Clothes Room. (Bates liked fresh air, too.)

"There'll be peace in Korea before I finish this lot," I said in dismay, looking at the heap of clothes. But Bates said that in a day or two he would ask some of the student nurses to help me. So I settled down to the task and somehow attached enough tapes so that I had a complete outfit of my own clothes. Bates dropped in at intervals, and Miss Brown came in, too, smothering a smile as she observed my crude efforts but voicing praise. Why is it that women are such gallant liars when men try to invade their fields?

A little man with thinning hair stood in the doorway observing me for fifteen minutes. When I finally commented, "This is a hell of a thing for a man to be doing," he smiled and replied, "That's woman's work. But I'd rather do that than peel potatoes. They're always putting me in the kitchen to peel potatoes."

I had noticed him standing by the hour at the window near the lavatories. Now and then he would produce a pocket comb, wet his hair, and carefully arrange a curl in the middle of his forehead. It was no surprise to hear that he was called Curly. His only explanation for the curl was: "I like it that way."

"My wife did all the sewing on my clothes," he offered suddenly. "Say, I have a nice wife; she comes to the hospital every day, but they won't let her in. She stands outside, and I look out the window and see her. "Say, don't you think it's nice that she comes every day? But I wish they would let her in."

When Curly had gone back to his window, Bates said that Curly's wife came to see him last spring, a year after he was committed. "When she left, she told us she would be back next spring. Quite casual about it. But Curly thinks that he sees her outside and he's built up this story that we won't let her in. He has ground parole and he spends all his time outside looking for her. You'd be surprised how some wives change once their husbands are in here. Seem to be tickled to death to wash their hands of them. Women," Bates said gently, "are stinkers sometimes."

"They've always been too lenient with me," I said, to my surprise, for many times I had argued otherwise.

"Oh, I meant nothing personal!"

I remarked to Bates that a pair of gloves which I had been permitted to keep in my room had disappeared. He was annoyed. "That's Ted or The Brat. I'll find 'em for you." He searched for them later in the day and went through their rooms, but the gloves were never found.

Ted, a pimply-faced youth who was feeble-minded, spent his days wandering up and down the hall and around the Day Room. Always he carried a 1951 winter Montgomery Ward catalogue. Walking or sitting, he was forever thumbing through it; he preferred the section given over to women's lingerie. When his mind wandered more than usual, he left it on one of the tables in the Day Room, but always returned in a few minutes as does a dog that suddenly remembers where it has buried a bone. If another patient happened to be glancing through the catalogue, Ted was in misery, pacing up and down, his hands and eyes fretting until he could, with a pounce, recover his treasure. When he was exhausted by his walking, Ted lay on one of the three benches; at intervals he held his hands over his eyes and chuckled.

"That's when he's hearing voices," Bates explained. "He says they tell him jokes."

Ted went into the rooms when they were unlocked early in the morning and helped himself to whatever caught his fancy. Being young, he preferred candy, cookies, and gum. He took cigarettes, too, and once he appeared in the Day Room smoking a cigar, but he was violently ill, so ill that he left his precious catalogue on the ping-pong table for an hour.

Bates said that the kleptomaniacs were a bother. "We have three of them up here now and they never seem to rest. We have to shake them down ever so often. They don't seem to mind when they are found out; just shrug and go right back to it.

"We had a chap on D-3 who was a terror. He'd take anything that wasn't bolted down. He went so far as to pretend to examine another patient's tonsils, and all the time he was trying to remove the patient's false teeth!"

Dressed in my own clothes and feeling more comfortable, I went back to the Day Room, promising to resume the sewing task in the afternoon. But Miss Brown said that permission had come through for me to have ground parole and I could go to the canteen at one o'clock if I wished.

"But I have no money!"

Miss Brown said that she had made out a special order for me. For two dollars. "We make out the orders on Sundays," she said, "and the money is delivered on Fridays. Since you came in on Tuesday, we had to have a special order for you."

I was in a dither to spend the two dollars, but I knew that I would be out of cigarettes before next Friday—and a carton cost two dollars at the canteen. Perhaps I could buy a few packs of cigarettes to tide me over the week-end and trust that the doctor would give me an extra chit for mad money. I sought out The Financier for advice and he said that I had the right idea.

"Get all you can," he said, "After all, it's your money."

At one o'clock six of us lined up in front of the door leading to the stairway. The snow had stopped falling and the sun was pushing through. I scorned an overcoat and I never wear a hat, but Miss Brown chided me and sent me back into the Clothes Room for the coat. "And put on your rubbers," she said. I felt that I was back in the first grade.

Finally we were outfitted to Miss Brown's taste, the door was unlocked, and we trooped down stairs. The sun was brilliant on the snow, the fresh air cleared one's head, but privately I thanked Miss Brown for sending me back for a coat There was a strong wind shaking the pine trees free of snow and driving it into our faces with needle-spray force.

The canteen was in the basement at the rear of the Center. A sign on the door announced that the canteen was open from 8:30 A.M. to 4 P.M. Only until noon on Saturday; closed on Sunday. It was jammed; men and women were standing at the L-shaped counter munching sandwiches and drinking coffee or ordering candy bars, cigarettes, cookies, crackers. Behind the counters were shelves filled with these and canned goods, ball-point pens, pencils, stationery, handkerchiefs, and cigarette lighters. No matches, and one had to have an official OK to buy a cigarette lighter or lighter fluid.

There was one table in the canteen. Two chairs went with it, but there were five persons grouped around the table; the three chairless ones were sitting on up-ended Coca-Cola crates. Near the Coke machine were other crates serving as chairs. There were a babble of voices and the delicious odor of coffee.

I scanned the menu posted on a wall:

Hamburgs	20 Cts.
Hot Dog	15 Cts.
Coffee	5 Cts.
Hot Chocolate	10 Cts.
With Milk	19 Cts.

Recklessly I ordered a hamburger "with everything" and coffee. Then I bought four packs of cigarettes. I wanted a candy bar, and while I was debating the wisdom of continuing my spree, someone back of me said, "Have you got a penny?"

I turned. She was looking up at me as she had outside my window the first night. She wore the same mannish gray coat, red mittens, and a scarf from under which peeked black bangs. Her eyes were brown, as I now saw, and as beautiful as I had imagined when I first glimpsed them in the twilight.

"Oh!" she said. "I thought you were another man!"

A red-headed girl at the table laughed. "Come off it, Suzy; you know you always tackle the new ones." She looked me up and down. "You're the new guy on D-3, aren't you?"

"How did you know?"

"Word gets around in this joint. You've got a new car, too. How about taking off?"

"They won't let me drive it."

"Hell," the red-head said, "they won't let us do a lot of things, but we do 'em anyway! Wait until you've been here a few years." She tilted a Coke bottle and drank deeply. "But watch out for Suzy. She's the prize beggar around here."

Suzy spun around; she choked and stammered, and when the words finally came they sounded almost like baby-talk. "Shut up, Dod-dam 'oo!" she shouted, shaking a mittened fist at the red-head. "I am not no beddar, dod-damn 'oo!"

A woman clerk behind the counter sighed. "That's enough from both of you. Quiet, or out you go. You want to lose ground parole?"

They glared at each other. I turned to Suzy. "You're welcome to the penny." I noticed that she had a turned-up nose and that the brown eyes were more beautiful when she was angry. But the anger left them; the baby-talk also ceased.

"Thank you. You see, I have nine cents and with another penny I'll have a dime...."

"And with a dime?"

"Two candy bars. Chocolate and marshmallow. I like them at night."

"May I treat you?"

The eyes flashed. "No! I'm not a beggar, no matter what she says. But a penny... well a penny is different. And I *did* think you were someone else."

"Nuts!" The red-head stamped out. Suzy ignored her. I got out the penny; Suzy thanked me for it and bought her two candy bars. "You will be here tomorrow?" she asked. "I have to go now."

"By all means," I said. "And with a pocketful of pennies."

She turned away. "That wasn't funny."

"You're right," I said. "It wasn't funny. I'm sorry."

She smiled. "I'm sorry, too, for acting that way. I get so mad sometimes. Well, goodbye."

"Goodbye."

The patients watched her go; as the door closed behind her they turned, as one, and regarded me solemnly. Now what? Am I a defendant facing a jury? But the clerk broke the embarrassing silence.

"You've made a hit," she said. "And with our Suzy, of all people!"

I felt as I had felt many years before when my sisters teased me about the new girl next door.

the
FIFTH
day

Bates was frank about it. "If you feel like doing a bit of work we could use you," he said. "Most of these chaps won't do a damned thing, and we can't force them to."

I said that I would welcome a chance to do something, but warned him that I had never been able to master the art of bed-making.

"We'll put you on the sweeping detail. How's that?"

He introduced me to Jacob, and Jacob took me to the Utility Room and opened a locker in which were two floor brushes. "I'm sorry," he said, "but you'll have to use this one. It's broken and patched up, but the new one I use." He smiled. "Seniority rights, you know."

We brushed one side of the Day Room, then moved into the hall. Jacob showed me how to brush out the private rooms; he emphasized that I should sweep carefully under the beds "because some of these fellows chew on their pillows and the feathers go every which way."

Jacob was tall and gaunt with a fringe of white hair. He confided in me, as we moved slowly down the hall, that a sister had committed him, the food was terrible, and he entered the Day Room only to write letters because "I can't stand that fiendish cigarette smoke."

I apologized and put out my cigarette. "Oh, you don't have to do that," he said. "One doesn't bother me. But smoking is no good for you, you know."

By the time we had reached the insulin ward he was advising me about food. "You really shouldn't eat everything here. I've watched you, and you take anything they offer. If you keep on, your bowels will be all tied up."

I said that my bowels were getting along fine and I thought the food was remarkably good considering the state's maintenance figure.

"Oh my," he said, "you don't understand. It's terrible the things they do with the food. Why, they bring the bread over here in dirty boxes!"

The bread was home-made and delicious, and I said so. Jacob shook his head. "You'll learn. You'll be like me if you stay here long enough." He leaned on the brush handle and regarded me accusingly. "I've noticed that you like meat. Of course, it's every man for himself, but I don't understand how people can eat meat. I," he said, drawing himself up, "am a vegetarian."

"Every man for himself," I murmured, but Jacob was not to be put off. "I can't eat a tenth of the stuff they serve," he said. "I like simple things, so in the afternoon I go down town to a super market and buy a loaf of whole-wheat bread and a small bottle of cane syrup. I wouldn't think of eating it up here, so I just walk around the grounds and kind of nibble when no one is near."

I said, "What I'd like right now is a juicy hamburger with mustard, mayonnaise, chopped onions, and tomato."

"Oh, good Lord!" said Jacob, gagging.

[*40*]

But he was a good sweeper and took pride in his work. He said that he thought I would make a good sweeper because I was thorough, although a bit slow. "The last fellow who worked with me was fast, but it was a shame the way he left the rooms. I said I wouldn't work with him any more. You have to stand up for your rights here."

Jacob had been committed twice to the hospital. On D-3 he was the most gentle of men, speaking always in a hushed voice and keeping to himself. But at home with his sister, with whom he had lived most of his adult life, he became the domineering male, roaring his orders about food and smashing plates and windows if the orders were not followed. He boasted of this to me, saying, "It's the only way to get along with women. Thirty years ago, when I was twenty-five, I learned that. My wife wanted to wear the pants and I let her for five years. Then one day she refused to sew a button on my pants and I hit her on the head with a frying pan. Do you know what she did? She divorced me!"

When we returned to the Day Room the doctor had arrived. He beckoned to me and introduced me to a man who had come in an hour before and was now loudly protesting that "It's a God-damned shame I can't get some God-damned state clothes that fit!" His indignation probably was justified, for he wore skimpy trousers that stopped six inches above his shoes and a shirt that had burst under the arms and down the back.

"This is Len," said the doctor. "He's the damnedest alcoholic you ever saw and we can't get anything into his thick skull, but you'll like him because he has a sense of humor and acts grown up, except when he's drinking."

Len shook hands, shifted his cud of chewing tobacco, and said, "I came here to dry out, but all I get is hot air."

The doctor beamed. "You've been getting something else judging from your belly. Better put on a diet again. What happened this time, Len?... Len," he said in an aside, "has been here before, and probably will be back next summer."

"If you didn't have some God-damned alcoholics on D-3 you wouldn't get any God-damned work done," said Len. "These nuts won't work, you know that. And this time I just got fed up with my wife nagging me."

About drinking?"

"What else?"

The doctor slapped him on the back. It was obvious that he knew he could not reach Len, could never get Len to admit why he drank. It also was obvious that he liked the man.

"Well, Len," he said, "You tell Jack all about your troubles. He's got troubles, too, he says. You two can weep on each other's shoulder."

"He gets me all riled up," said Len when the doctor had gone. "He likes to stick the barbs into you, but I go for the guy. Had him up to the cottage a couple of times. What's the matter with you? Wife trouble?"

"Oh, no!"

"That's what they all say, but it's usually wife trouble." He laughed deep down in his belly. "Don't mind the things I say. I've always got a chip on my shoulder. Right now I'm off my wife and daughters and I'm apt to say anything. God damn it, why can't a man get drunk without his womenfolks raising hell about it?"

"Don't all womenfolks?"

"Guess so, but I'll match mine against all comers. Jesus, I could do with a drink now, but I'll be damned if I'll ask the doc. I'll suffer," he said, grinning, "but not in silence."

[42]

Len, whose ways were well known to the doctor, was given ground parole immediately and we went to the canteen together before the early Saturday closing. Len appeared to have recovered from his drinking bout, although he said "my guts are all tied up." He knew several of the patients in the canteen and greeted them lustily. He got two nickels for a dime and bought Cokes for us. "Now," he said cheerfully, "I'm dead broke. Forgot to bring any dough when I stalked out. Truth is, my wife was going to divorce me a few years ago, and she got a court order tying up all my dough. She gave up the divorce idea, but that God-damned order still holds, and when I want any dough I have to ask her to write a check. Burns me!"

Suddenly I found myself telling Len my story. In the days to come we were to disagree about many matters, but always he listened to what I had to say, perhaps shook his head over it, yet gave the impression that what I had to say was of supreme importance at the moment. He shook his head when I was done. "Jesus!" he said, "I never got to feeling that low. You play along with the doc; he'll fix you up. He can't do anything for me because I just like to drink, and I'm going to drink until I die."

I said that the modern viewpoint is that alcoholism is not necessarily a disease but a symptom of a disease. It is a warning signal that something is wrong deep back in one's mind and if that something is dug out, then alcohol is no longer a problem. I said that so many persons had told me I was an alcoholic that I believed it. I said I had joined Alcoholics Anonymous, but it didn't work for me.

"Oh, that outfit!" he said.

"It's a fine outfit. It works for some; it doesn't work for

others. When I joined AA I wanted to find out why I drank when I was sunk, and I didn't find out. That's why I'm here."

"I can see," said Len, "that the psychiatrists have got you. Sometimes I think maybe they're on the right track, but I'm too old to change. When the doc talks to me I just freeze up; it makes him sore as hell, but I can't give. Maybe we're all afraid. That's why this joint is filled. God damn it, why did you have to bring this up?"

"I don't know, except that in the few days I've been here I've felt hopeful. Perhaps I'm getting to know myself. Or perhaps I'm beginning to realize that there's another self that takes over. I can't put it well; I don't know about these things."

"Have another Coke," said Len. "Hell, I forgot; I'm broke." I bought the Cokes and we sat on Coke boxes and watched the other patients. Len gave me the case histories of those whom he knew; he spoke affectionately of some, derisively of others, and the thought came to me: This man is at home here; it is like a club to him.

He grinned at me. "Old home week, eh?"

"You're a mind reader, too?"

"You were as obvious as a bitch in heat. Okay, what's wrong with holing up here now and then? You get away from the women, and that's something."

"There are five men in here and about twelve women."

Again the belly laugh. "But we aren't married to any of 'em! That's the beauty of it!"

Len was greeted by a fat girl who burst through the door shouting, "I'm going home! I'm going home!"

The others regarded her enviously. "That's swell, Lil," said Len, "but what the hell's the idea of leaving just when I come back?"

"Oh, I'm not going until just before Christmas. They've got to get the okay from my old man first" She wiggled her rear at Len. "Well, you old bastard, tied one on again, eh?"

"And how! Thought I'd take the rest cure. Lil here," he said, turning to me, "goes home about once a year. She never lasts more than a month, then she's back. Ties one on and gets in trouble, as grandma used to say."

"Gets knocked up, he means!" Lil laughed, shaking her big breasts, showing three teeth the state dentist had left her. "Probably'll do the same thing this time." She plunged over to the counter to order a hamburger.

"Heart of gold," murmured Len. "Lil can't say no. Lot of 'em around here are that way. Say, you been to one of the dances yet? No, haven't been here long enough. They have 'em on Thursday nights. You got to see one of 'em; regular circus. The student nurses go, too, and they're damned cute. I'll fix you up with some of the women patients. You'll laugh until your belly hurts."

Len said that only the "good' patients were permitted to attend the dances. Those inclined to run away or to become too excited remained in their wards. "Even so," said Len, "someone is apt to take off after a dance while marching back to his ward. But a guy wouldn't get far in this weather. He'd come back, begging to be let in where it's warm."

He was telling about one woman whose boy friend engineered her escape, when Suzy came in, she smiled at me and continued on to the counter where she began ordering from a long list given her by women on her ward who did not have ground parole.

"Well!" said Len, "got one picked out already, huh?"

"That's Suzy. I met her yesterday. She borrowed a penny."

[45]

"They all do, and not just pennies. You'll learn to say you're broke; otherwise you will be."

When Suzy had given all her orders she came over and sat on a nearby Coke crate. She removed her mittens, searched through the two pockets of her coat, and finally brought out a penny. "Thank you," she said, handing it to me.

Len's eyes popped. "I never thought I'd live to see it! Who's this wonder girl?"

"Suzy, this is Len. He's on D-3 with me. He's kind of breaking me in because he's been here before."

"Suzy," said Len, "You have just made a liar out of me by returning that penny."

She smiled complacently and turned to me. "Do you like it on D-3, Yack?" She had heard Len use my name.

"Jack," I corrected.

"Yes, Yack," she said, and so it was from then on. I offered to treat her to a hamburger and she accepted. Len shook his head over me and went to the table to join a group around Lil. I got the hamburgers and we munched in silence until Suzy said, "Why are you good to me?"

"Good? One penny and one hamburger!"

"I don't mean that. You're kind; you don't laugh at me. Sometimes I—well, I act funny, I guess. I have a bad spell and then the others laugh at me."

"I'll never laugh at you, Suzy. What are these bad spells?"

That was a mistake, of course; I had violated Rule One. Suzy said only, "I don't like to talk about myself," and I apologized.

"I think you are beautiful," I said.

Her eyes opened wide. "Why, no one ever called me beautiful before! Thank you, Yack!"

The clerk called her. "I have to hurry back with the orders," she said. "Anyway, the canteen closes at noon today, you know."

She was smiling a pleased little smile as she left. Len came back ready for more chaff. "Who gave you that dreamy-eyed look?" he asked. "Suzy?"

I said, "I was just thinking how many times I've called women beautiful and how few times I've meant it."

"Oh, God!" said Len. "A philosopher!"

the
SIXTH
day

Sunday morning the doctor came early. He said I would attend staff the following Tuesday. I looked blank.

"It's routine," he explained. "Members of the staff will be there and the social workers and so on. I'll tell them about you and then they'll ask you a few questions. After that we'll talk you over."

"Nicely, I trust."

"Not always. We have to be pretty blunt around here. Not enough help, not enough time. By the way, I've written your wife asking her to come up for a day. Like to get both sides of the picture."

"That's fine. I'm sure she'll come."

"Are you?"

"Why do you say that?"

"Never know what a woman's going to do. Don't have to be a psychiatrist to appreciate that."

After the doctor left, Miss Brown made a list of the patients who wanted to attend church services in the auditorium. Only six evinced any interest.

"Sissies!" shouted The Brat as the six filed out to the Clothes Room.

"That kid gets my goat," said Len. "Nearly took a sock at him last time I was here. They had him on insulin for awhile and he was sweetness and light and they sent him home. He was back in three months.

"What's his trouble?" There I went again! But it seemed that it was all right to talk about others. Len said that the doctor had told him The Brat had mother trouble, but Len said he figured The Brat was a homosexual. "You can smell those guys a mile away. Guess that's why I can't put up with him."

The Brat had been through the Battle of the Bulge, had come home finally to weep on his mother's shoulder and tell her how terrible it had been. The next day he said that he had married a German girl and she was following him across the ocean. Months later he insisted that she was living in Springfield, Massachusetts, and he was afraid she would catch up with him. That was when he was committed to the state hospital.

There was no German girl. There was only his mother and, because of their deep-rooted fascination for each other, which neither understood, they wept together or they quarreled. That was the doctor's theory, at which Len scoffed.

"Look at him now!" Len said. The Brat had joined the student nurses in a game of casino and was feeling the leg of one under the table. She spoke sharply to him, and he grinned.

I said, "He doesn't act like a homosexual at the moment!"

Len grunted. "She ought to report him to Miss Brown. But those students hate to make a fuss. Those kids put up with a lot."

The Brat, deserting the card game, sidled up to me. "Got a cigarette?"

Before I could answer, he plucked a cigarette from the pack in my shirt pocket.

"Put it back," I said.

"Huh?"

"Put it back—and fast!"

He did, grinning at me and waiting.

"Now," I said, taking out the pack, "have one."

"Cripes!" he said. "We got an Emily Post with us!"

Len said furiously, "Get out of here, you little bastard, before I make hamburger out of you!"

The Brat strolled away, laughing softly to himself. As he passed the ping-pong table, his hand shot out and pulled down the zipper on Johnny's pants. Johnny looked down in bewilderment, then his face puckered and he wept, holding his hands over his fly until Curly came by and zipped it up for him.

The Brat slithered to the piano bench and pounded on the keys. Little Willis leaned forward eagerly, hastened behind the piano, and emerged with his guitar. Shortly he and The Brat were engaged in a weird duet. "Those guys sure can play!" Boy Blue said happily.

The Financier bowed stiffly before Len. "Can you spare a hundred until tomorrow? Doc'll sign an order for me then."

"Oh, God!" said Len. "Another quiet Sabbath! No, I can't spare a hundred. I can't spare a penny."

The Financier nodded understandingly. "Quite all right. I just wanted to pay off the gangsters. They're pressing me pretty hard right now." He bowed and withdrew.

"Let's take a walk," suggested Len. "This Day Room is getting me down."

We walked down the hall, down to the door that led to the neutral space and the elevators and back. We did it ten times. On the tenth trip the door was suddenly unlocked and Bates entered with a tall, flat-nosed, red-haired and red-bearded youth.

"My God!" exclaimed Len. "Look what the storm blew in! Red!"

The red-head grinned. "They told me you was here, Len. Like old times, eh?"

They shook hands; then Red was hustled away to Bath. "What a guy!" said Len. "That Red's been here before. Took off one night and I guess they just caught up with him. Bet he's got a story to tell."

We heard the story an hour later in the Day Room. Red borrowed a cigarette. "Pay you back tomorrow…. Boy, did I have a time while I was out!"

He had scrubbed and changed into state clothes, but he would have to wait until Tuesday for a shave. "Two weeks' growth," he said. "Prickles like hell.

"Remember the night I took off, Len? I was headin' for home, but two miles out of town I picked up a ride. Guy and a doll, and would you believe it they had half a case of beer and two fifths of whiskey in the back seat. They was drunk as hell."

"You, of course, refused a drop?" said Len.

"They forced it on me! A swig of whiskey, then a beer chaser; an unmixed boilermaker, kinda. We was all polluted by the time we got to Ludington. The guy pulled in at one of those roadside picnic tables and told me to get in the front seat. Then he and the doll, they got in the back seat and knocked off one. I was feelin' kinda hot myself, cooped up in this joint three months without any tail, and all that going

[*51*]

on in the back seat...." Red paused to borrow another cigarette. "Pay you back tomorrow.... Well, the guy finally got it over with, and we kept on goin' south. Around Holland somewheres we put up at a motel, all three of us. The guy was a good guy and paid for me. And then what? He has a few more drinks and passes out cold."

The next day, said Red, he got out at Watervliet, planning to hitch-hike inland to his home. But he met some winos and he got drunk again. Two days later he got a job as bricklayer, his trade, and stayed on in Watervliet for two months, saving his money and getting drunk only once a week. On his last drunk he got into a fight, the police picked him up, and he was shipped back to the state hospital.

"I never did get home to see the wife and kids," he said in a wondering voice.

Art Ammidon called Red away. I asked, "Is that on the up and up?"

"Sure," said Len. "The guy's punch drunk. Been that way ever since he was in the Marines. Seems all right until he goes on a bust. Then he's a madman."

"But if he took off to go home...."

"Something funny there. His brother died, and Red married the widow. Married by a justice of the peace. Red's a Catholic, but after that he quit the church. Used to leave his wife for weeks at a time on a bust. But, Jesus, he's lived— the war and all."

You could tell that Len liked Red, even envied him, perhaps. And when Red came back he regarded Len fondly. "Art says Doc won't keep me here long. Probably put me back on Six."

"Ward Six is a tough one," Len explained. "Don't envy you, kid."

Red grinned. "They won't keep me here long. Just take off again when I get the chance. Hey, look what's comin' in!"

Two more patients had arrived. One was short and emaciated; he had boils on his neck; his hair was close-clipped and he wore an old-fashioned shirt without a collar—only the neckband and a collar button. He headed directly for our corner and sputtered at us in a language none of us could understand, but he would not stop. The words flowed from him and he held up his hands beseechingly. Art came finally and took him away.

The other man was tall and slender, slightly bald, and he had no teeth. He sat quietly for several minutes, then he ran to the corner where little Willie sat and banged his head against the wall. He crossed himself, muttered something, and went back to his chair.

"Christ!" said Len. "One of those!"

I was mystified. "Religious bug's got him," Len said. "I've seen 'em before. When he butts his head that's doing penance or whatever they call it. Then he says a bit of the Rosary or something and is all right for a spell."

Red said this bitterly, but there was a hurt in his eyes, "Religion's got a lot to answer for in this joint."

Three times in the next half-hour, while we sat in our corner smoking and talking, the tall, thin man raced across the Day Room and banged his head against the wall, not hard, but hard enough that we could hear it. I felt a little sick inside, but Len and Red were amused. "We'll call him The Flash," said Len. "He sure can cover ground."

Art came in with another attendant from the floor above, and The Flash also was led away. Len and Red rambled on, damning the doctor, damning their wives, damning the world in general, yet always finding time to chuckle or laugh at the other patients. I did not join in; the mood of depression was setting in again. Was it The Flash or Collar Button? I didn't feel too sorry for The Flash, just sickish; it must be Collar Button with those begging hands. But why did I become so upset over others? Why had I wept the night Sacco and Vanzetti were executed?... Tom Mooney.... The Bonus Army marchers.... Why, at this late date, did the thought of them unnerve me?

Well, let it come, I thought, for I had been through it many times before. Always the same routine. Sacco and Vanzetti— who walked with me that night when they were executed? Who wept with me?... Eleanor.

Do you remember, Eleanor, how dark the night was and how we stumbled out to the end of the rocky breakwater and listened to the waves? Do you remember Rockport, Massachusetts, that night, and how you said, when the weeping was over, "I could never love you if you felt differently?"

Eleanor does not remember.... Eleanor is dead.... Our daughter is dead....

"Hey," Len whispered, "something wrong?"

I rushed blindly from the Day Room and into the Utility Room where I thought I would be alone. But Curly was there, staring out the window. He turned, and his curl bobbed ridiculously. He took me by the arm.

"Say," he murmured, "you're all upset. Come look at the snow; it's real pretty. Say, it's all right; I get lonesome, too."

the
S E V E N T H
day

At breakfast on Monday there was much talk of the labor that lay ahead. Monday, Bates said, was cleanup day. All the rooms had to be scrubbed with brooms and suds, then mopped. The furniture had to be pushed out into the hall and polished; the sheets had to be changed.

Jacob and I did a thorough job of sweeping. "You don't want to leave a speck on Monday," he said. "If you do, someone's sure to squawk." When the sweeping was done I helped to move out the furniture, but Jacob refused. He said, "If you do more than your regular job they'll load everything on you. You'll see."

But I wanted work, and when Bates asked me if I would help him sort clothes I welcomed the extra chore. In the Clothes Room was a huge pile of fresh laundry—state clothes and the patients' own clothes jumbled together. We had to go over each garment, looking for the tags; the state clothes went into three pigeon holes, the patients' clothes into other pigeon holes, each bearing the patient's name.

Bates opened the one window in the Clothes Room and we went to work. It was peaceful in there, and Bates must have guessed that I had been upset the day before, for he chatted about the patients and about his job until my thoughts were no longer dreary.

"Now, you take me," said Bates. "I've worked in factories and such; earned good money, too. But I wasn't happy doing that work. I grumbled every night when I came home. I liked the pay check, but that was all. So one day I just up and quit and got a job here. The pay isn't much, but I like being here; I like taking care of these guys and seeing some of 'em come out all right. My wife is an attendant here, too, and she feels the same way. You know, we talked last night about my taking a course in nursing. I'd like to be a nurse. My wife says she'll support us while I take the course. Now, that's something, isn't it?"

"That's splendid."

"Now, you take these patients," said Bates. "Most of 'em, when they come in here, are way down in the depths. Most of 'em talk suicide. You'd think this place would make 'em feel worse, but it doesn't. It's hard to explain, but they get the idea here that someone cares about what happens to 'em, and that perks 'em up. Of course there're quite a few who get to like this place too much; it's a refuge for them, and although they may beg to be sent home, what they really want is to be told that they never will have to go home.... You want to go home, don't you?"

"Not until I'm fixed up. I promised I'd stay until that time comes, if it does."

"It'll come all right. You've got the right attitude. The doctor may get your goat at times, but if you keep an open mind he'll fix you up."

"My mind's open. I think it is, anyway."

"Now you take this new guy," said Bates. "He hasn't got

an open mind. He isn't crazy, as they say, but he won't see or won't admit what's wrong with him."

"You mean the one who batted his head against the wall?"

"That's the one. He's been in here I don't know how many times. He's had seventeen or eighteen electros. They fix him up for awhile, he's sent home, and then off he goes again. Well, it's plain that there's something at home that he wants to escape, probably his wife, and so all of a sudden he gets the religious bug and acts up and back he comes here…. You got anything wrong at home?"

"Why, no. Anything wrong I caused myself."

"Now you take your case," said Bates. "It's none of my business, but around here we can't help but think about individual cases. Now, you've been a newspaperman and you've seen lots and to me that seems a pretty exciting job."

"It was, but I've lost interest."

"Well, maybe you actually haven't. Maybe you just said to hell with everything—after your wife died, I mean."

"Yes."

"Saying to hell with everything is kind of giving up. There's always something that's left. We had a man in here once who gave up because his baby was run over and killed. He said there was nothing left for him, but he had a nice wife and two other kids, and he made good money as an insurance salesman…. A seagull straightened him out."

"A seagull?"

"That's what. You've seen 'em flying around here looking for food; they come in from the bay. Well, there was one seagull that seemed always to flop down outside this man's window. Every day that seagull came around, and pretty soon the man got interested. When he was given ground parole, he used to go outside his window and wait for the seagull.

[*57*]

They got quite friendly and the man fed him every day. He could hardly wait for one o'clock to come so he could go out and feed the seagull.

"One day the seagull didn't appear. The man waited until four o'clock, and then he came back and said that he figured he was ready to go home. They asked him why, and he said that he'd been so wrapped up in the seagull that he'd forgotten to think about himself. He said that probably the seagull had been hurt or killed, but there was nothing he could do about it. He said that he would miss the seagull, but that he had a wife and two kids and he thought they deserved as much attention as the seagull.

"Of course they let him go. We hear from him now and then, and he always writes the same postscript: "Thanks for the seagull."

"That's a fine story! A magazine would like that story. And the title is a natural: 'Thanks for the Seagull.' You ought to write some of these stories, Bates."

"Why don't you? Or have you lost interest?" He grinned at my sheepish look. "All right, that ends today's lecture. Let's take these leftover clothes to the right floors; that laundry sure can ball things up at times."

We took a bundle of the clothes up to D-4, the floor where the tougher new patients are put. Bates pointed out two strong rooms used for the violent patients; both were unoccupied. The Day Room appeared the same as the Day Room on D-3, but there was a different atmosphere; sullenness and hatred filled the air.

"You notice it right away?" asked Bates. "But these aren't hopeless cases by any means. Some of 'em will snap out of it, and then they'll be moved down to D-3. They have a lot of fights up here; you can't drink Cokes up here. Bottles make good clubs, you know."

I saw Collar Button in a corner, and he saw me. He hurried over, and again there was the flow of words. "We can't figure him out," one of the D-4 attendants told Bates. "Had an interpreter in and all he could get was that the guy was a DP. Been in Michigan only a few months."

Collar Button suddenly stopped talking. His shoulders sagging in despair, he went back to his corner. I was glad to leave D-4.

We went down to the basement and left clothes for the outlying wards. We picked up clothes from patients on D-3— their own clothes with the tags attached. "That reminds me," I told Bates, "that I still have some sewing to do."

"Your sewing isn't so hot. When we get back I'll see if some of the students can help. There weren't any tailors in your family, that's for sure."

The student nurses were dancing with the boys from the insulin ward, but the students obviously weren't too happy about it; without a murmur they followed Bates into the Clothes Room and we began sewing on tags. To everyone's surprise, Ralph suddenly appeared and offered to help. "He likes to be near the students," Bates whispered.

One wondered why. When they spoke to him he never answered. At times he would permit himself a fleeting smile. But he listened eagerly to their chatter. He sewed swiftly and neatly, glanced contemptuously at my efforts. Red came in, took needle and thread, and also set to work. His big blunt fingers moved as swiftly as Ralph's; the two men were better at this tape business than the nurses, and I heaped praise upon them with the ulterior motive of a Tom Sawyer.

"I learned the trick in the Marines," Red said. His face clouded. "Learned a lot of others things, too."

One of the students urged, "Such as?"

Red grinned. "Wouldn't you like to know? Or would you?"

"Oh, I didn't mean *those* things!"

"What things?"

She blushed, but stood her ground. "Nurses, even student nurses, get around, Red. Tell us some of the—well, some of the nice things."

"My God," he said, "she wants to hear nice things about the Marines!" A savage look came over his face. "By God, I'll tell you some nice things!"

"Now, Red!"

"You asked for it!" He rushed on, his fingers still moving nimbly. "Remember all that horse—all that baloney during the war about how terrible the Japs were for killing their prisoners? Remember how you folks at home said that wasn't cricket or something? Well, by God, the Japs weren't any worse than the Marines. We took prisoners, yeah, but we didn't keep 'em.

"We took 125 one day. Know what we did? We marched 'em down to the beach and said, 'Now, you bastards, start swimmin' for home.' And when they got out a bit and was swimmin' for dear life we let go at 'em. It was like shootin' floatin' ducks.

"Oh, Red, you didn't!"

"The hell I didn't! Do it again, too. All this stuff about rules of war—that's crap! I never hated anything or anyone like I hated them Japs."

The student who had started it said quietly, "Except, perhaps, yourself."

He stared at her, and his face behind the red beard went limp. "Jesus!" he said. He got up, dropping a pair of my socks on the floor "Below the belt!" he said, and walked out.

Ralph's eyes shone; he licked his lips, and his fingers shook slightly. He liked that, he enjoyed every minute of it. The student nurses felt it, too, and became uneasy—all but the one who had spoken to Red. One by one they made excuses and left. Ralph made no excuses; he walked out, still licking his lips.

"Was I wrong?" asked the student nurse. "Did I hit below the belt?"

"You forget," I said, "that I am a patient here and I'm not supposed to have opinions."

She said, "That's silly! They want patients to have opinions. They want them to think for themselves. If they don't, how are they going to get well again?"

"Does that make sense?"

"Of course it does! You weren't thinking yesterday, were you?"

"Maybe not. Say, what is this? First Bates, then you."

"Everyone here wants to help you, Jack. I guess they think you're worth saving."

"I don't know why."

"Little boy, aren't you?" said this twenty-one year old.

the
EIGHTH
day

A thaw set in on Tuesday; ice melted on the little brook that ran by the Day Room windows and water dripped from the pine trees. But I had little time to appreciate the touch of spring; staff day was here.

It was too early for the barber, so I was permitted to shave myself in the attendants' bathroom, with Goodman, an attendant I had not met before, standing nearby. The safety razor they lent me was dull and my beard was thick, but I managed to hack it off and felt ten years younger.

Goodman took me downstairs to be photographed and fingerprinted. The man in charge had gone to high school with one of my sisters, and I told him the news of her and the rest of my family. At first I felt embarrassed, but he soon put me at ease by his friendly attitude. From the fingerprint room we went to EEG, where an electroencephalograph was made to determine if there were any brain injuries. Psychometric tests followed; I scored 100 in one and 85 in another, and preened myself.

A quick visit to the hospital dentist and then it was ten

o'clock and time for staff. Three of us waited for half an hour in an office adjoining the staff room; then I was ushered in by the ward doctor and seated at a long table next to the superintendent, Dr. R. Phillip Sheets. Around the table were other staff doctors and social workers. At one end of the room was a group of student nurses; at the other end sat a Catholic priest and the hospital chaplain.

They had me tell my story, which they already had heard from the ward doctor; then Dr. Sheets asked, "And how do you feel now about this suicide business?"

"At the moment it seems very foolish to me. With a few exceptions I have felt much better since entering the hospital. I think it is because I have seen so many patients who are much worse off."

Dr. Sheets and the ward doctor smiled. They questioned me about my home life, and I insisted that any fault there lay with me. They had me describe some of my experiences as a New York newspaperman and expressed interest in two books I had written, one about the Dreyfus case in France, and the other a biography of Aaron Burr.

"Ah, yes, the Dreyfus case," said Dr. Sheets. "A tragic case. You seem to be interested in the underdogs."

"Always have been."

A young doctor commented, "To the psychiatrist that might indicate that you felt at times you were the underdog."

"I can't recall ever feeling that way."

"How were your books received?"

"Good reviews, but I regret to say that I was unable to retire on the proceeds."

They laughed politely. "How often," asked the young doctor, "do you have these periods of depression?"

[63]

"That is difficult to say. Usually some incident sets them off. They always are based on the same thoughts—about my first wife and our daughter."

"Your present wife is aware of this?"

"Yes, and she has been supremely tolerant. I know that I could not be so tolerant if the situation were reversed."

"How does your wife feel about your coming here?"

"She urged such a step some time ago."

Dr Sheets asked how I found the hospital food. I said that I was amazed how good it was, but added that I was afraid I never would become a whole-hearted addict to powdered eggs, served from time to time. Again a laugh went around the table and I was excused. I felt pleased with myself and strutted a little, I'm afraid, when I was returned to D-3.

"How was it?" demanded Len. "Tough?"

"No, they made me feel right at home."

I went over the questions and answers with him, but he was not impressed. "They've got some idea about you that they didn't tell you. Doc probably will one of these days."

"They seemed to feel that I was coming along all right," I said confidently.

The doctor ignored me when he visited D-3 in the afternoon, and I became even more confident that I had conducted myself well at staff. Miss Bell, a nurse, came to D-3, and the new patients, including me, were given smallpox inoculations and typhoid injections. Miss Bell said that she had known my mother well, and we talked of neighbors we had known when I was a schoolboy living on Washington Street.

The chaplain, the Rev. Lorenz C. C. Grueber, introduced himself and talked of my appearance at staff. "I find it hard to believe," he said, "that you feel there is nothing left for you because your wife and daughter are dead."

[*64*]

"I know. I know how it must appear to others."

"You, of course, believe in a hereafter?"

"I've tried hard to believe but haven't been successful. I truly envy those who do believe."

"Perhaps if you tried a little harder," he said patiently.

"I shall try," I promised. I liked The Reverend, as all the patients addressed him. He never preached to nor scolded them on his rounds of the wards. He was tolerant of the alcoholics, obviously enjoyed their company, and did not hesitate to say that he liked a glass of beer now and then. "But only now and then." He would smile, and they would accept his mild rebuke. With the mental cases he talked as he would with normal persons. He had a fund of homey stories which they enjoyed, and always there was an air of relaxation when he was in the Day Room.

"There's a young woman in the business office who asked me about you," he said. "She is coming up to see you some time."

Her name was Eloise, and I recalled her as a three-year-old who played with my younger sister. "This is getting to be old home week," I said, telling of the fingerprint man and Miss Bell.

"Do you good to have them here," said The Reverend. "They won't say a word outside and, anyway, you have nothing to be ashamed of." He smiled his kindly smile and moved on.

Franklin darted from his corner by the urinals and seized his arm. "Are my sins forgiven? Are you sure?"

"Franklin, your sins were forgiven a long time ago."

"But they still want to electrocute me. Couldn't I get life imprisonment instead of electrocution?"

"Franklin, as a man of God, I promise you that no one

here is going to harm you. You will take my word, won't you?"

"I don't know," Franklin moaned. "I don't know."

The doctor made a second visit in the afternoon and beckoned me to the corner where Ralph usually sat. Ralph had been taken to C-3, the Women's ward, to play the piano for them.

"Jack," the doctor said, "I'm going to give it to you in one jolt, and it's up to you whether you take it. Now, at staff you said you were forgetting your troubles somewhat because some of the other patients were worse off. You probably saw Dr. Sheets and me exchange smiles. We're old hands at this business, and we aren't fooled very often."

"Fooled?"

"Oh, I don't mean that you were trying to put anything over on us. You actually thought the other patients were making you forget your woes. Now we aren't going to go back and look into your infancy, with its mother complexes and all that. We don't think we have to in your case. But I do want you to recall when you were a kid of five, say, and some of the things you did to get attention.

I said, "That's easy. I had a slight touch of polio when I was an infant, and it marked one foot a little. I remember very well, when I was older and we were receiving our presents on Christmas, that I complained of my foot hurting. It wasn't, but I was so excited about Christmas that I wanted more and more attention. Is that what you mean?"

"Exactly. This last year you've gone back to being a child of five again. You've found something to take the place of that foot."

"I don't follow that."

"Your attempts at suicide. While your first wife and

daughter lived, you were the center of the family, weren't you? They adored you and showed it, didn't they?"

"Yes, I think that's true."

"All right. You lost your wife. Then you lost your daughter. Your other daughter married and moved away. You married again, but there was something missing. I don't say for one minute that your grief was dishonest; it is not easy to lose a wife and daughter, but you have permitted these losses to magnify themselves. You have craved to be the center of the family again; you have wanted the attention you used to have and you have reached the point where you will do anything to get that attention."

"You mean I cut my wrists and took sleeping pills just to get attention? Why that's absurd!"

He sighed. "It's not absurd! I mean exactly that!"

"But I really wanted out!"

"You thought you did. On the surface you did, but you were letting your subconscious run you. And your subconscious was saying: 'Even at the risk of dying, these acts will get me the attention I want.'"

The doctor went on, "Now, people rarely kill themselves when they cut their wrists or take too many sleeping pills. Someone usually comes along and saves them."

I found my voice. "That's a tough one to swallow."

"I know it is, but you'll have to swallow it if we are to fix you up. Once you recognize the motivation behind these acts, once you are able to be the real you and not a kid of five, you will be all right. Don't hurry; it'll take some time."

I could not say goodbye when he left. Len and Red came over. "Gave you the works?" said Len, and I nodded.

"Want to talk about it?"

"Not right now."

[67]

They went away. Miss Brown came in with a letter that had arrived in the late mail. It was from my wife. I opened it eagerly.

My wife wrote that she was through. She wrote that she did not want to see me again.

the NINTH day

When the doctor let himself into D-3 from the neutral space, I was standing near the door. I had been waiting there for an hour.

I asked, "Did you get a letter from my wife?"

"Yes," he said. "Come along and we'll weep on each other's shoulders!"

We went into the Day Room. "Your wife is not coming up to see me. She doesn't think it will do any good. I suppose she wrote you that she doesn't want you back?"

"Yes."

"You won't believe me, but I think both of you are getting a break. You should not have married again; it wasn't fair to either of you. You wanted the life you once had and you didn't get it. I don't know what your wife wanted, but surely she didn't want a man who was trying to kill himself."

"I thought I was trying to attract attention!"

"I'll not go over that again. Been thinking about it?"

"Yes. But getting nowhere."

"I said it would take time. I wish you didn't have this other thing to fuss about at the same time, but there it is. Forget it for awhile. I'm going up to D-4; want to come along?"

We went upstairs. The Reverend was there trying to talk to Collar Button. "He is afraid of something," The Reverend said, "but I can't make it out."

An idea struck me. "Perhaps he's been in a concentration camp and thinks the hospital is one, too."

The doctor nodded. "Could be. He certainly has had a tough time some place."

Collar Button knelt in an attitude of prayer. He seemed to sense that the doctor was interested in him, and it was to the doctor he appealed. The doctor patted him on the shoulder, but he shrank away, fear flickering across his face. Well, they'd find out his trouble in a few days. I thought with a trace of bitterness: Perhaps he's trying to attract attention, too. But I didn't believe that; something real was tormenting Collar Button.

When the doctor completed his rounds, I went back to D-3. The Flash was butting his head against the wall again. "He's going to get an electro tomorrow and is scared stiff," Len reported. "Say, there's a new guy just come in; oughta hear him. Maybe he'll cheer you up, or don't you need cheering up?"

I told Len and Red what the doctor had said to me. Neither was impressed, but Len said frankly, "Maybe the guy's right; I don't know. Won't hurt to give it a chance. Too bad about your wife; mine is giving me the silent treatment, I guess."

Red said, "I got a real hot love letter from my wife. She takes a lot from me and comes back for more. That's the way to 'em."

The new man strolled up. Lloyd was his name; he was a farmer and more than willing to talk about himself.

"Lloyd here says he doesn't know what's wrong with him," Len explained. "He gets pains in his head and stomach cramps. He says when he was a kid his pa hit him on the head with a plank, and when he was a bit older another kid hit him on the head with a baseball bat."

"But that wouldn't give me stomach cramps, would it?" asked Lloyd.

"That depends," Len said soberly, "on how hard you were hit. No, old man, I think your trouble is that other thing."

"What other thing?"

"Wife trouble you told me about."

"Reckon so," said Lloyd. He turned to me. "I'm outdoors working all day and when night comes all I wanta do is eat supper and fall in bed and sleep. But my wife, she's full of passion; she's always after me in bed. She wears me out."

"And she won't let him drink," Len interjected. "Can you imagine a woman not letting her husband drink? I mean, can you imagine a man letting his wife stop him from drinking?"

Lloyd said boastfully, "Oh, I get some drinks now and then. I got a neighbor; he's another farmer. He's got bottles of the stuff hidden in his barn and whenever I want a drink I go over and see him. He's always in the barn sampling the stuff."

"Tomorrow you ask the doc for a pint," said Len. "Doc's a good guy; he'll keep you supplied."

"Well now, I'll do that. I brought a little bottle of rye along with me, but they took it away from me."

Red said, "You oughta raise hell about that. They ain't got any right to do that. You tell 'em."

"Well now, I'll do that." Lloyd looked pleased and wandered away.

"Dumb ass!" said Len. "Bet he does call for a pint. Doc'll

probably kid him along. He's a great kidder. Once at staff a patient who was being questioned suddenly turned to Doc and said, 'Say, I know you. I knew you when you played the piano in a Bay City whore house.' Everyone around the table looked shocked, but all Doc said was, 'Which one?'"

Red chimed in, "See Old Tom over there; must be eighty. He came from a county farm up near Petoskey. He was just tellin' one of the student nurses that the county farm used to be a whore house.

"' Oh, you musn't say that, Tom!' she said.

"'Hell,' he said, 'I can still go to 'em and do a good job!' She scrammed out of here. Quite a guy, Old Tom; likes his whiskey and beer. Says candy ruins a man's insides."

Lloyd returning, overheard the story. "That's a funny story," he said. "I never been in a whore house myself."

"No?" Len pretended to be astonished. "Say, that's probably your trouble. You need a change of diet."

"I was a virgin when I got married."

"What's a virgin?" asked Red.

The two of them were prepared to take Lloyd for a long ride. I couldn't feel sorry for him; he was so obviously enjoying it.

The day dragged on; no one went to the canteen, for the grounds were drenched and tiny rivers ran along the paths. I got off by myself and read *The Glass Crutch*, which the doctor had given me. I could see why; it was the story of an alcoholic who used alcohol as a crutch when he felt that he could not face life and the crutch always gave way under him.

But then I thought: Why, after all, has the doctor given me this book? He's not worried about my being an alcoholic; he told Len that if I got my life straightened out I'd be able to drink as I used to drink. Yes, but your drinking was all wrong the last ten years. You went along for days, weeks, just having one now and then, having a few more when there was reason for a little celebration like the day you came home from the hospital after an operation. And then one day something would make you blue; you'd sit by the hour dreaming of it, wanting it. And finally you'd go out for a fifth; the drinks would make the dreams come closer and soon you were weeping and thinking: There's only one way to settle this. But if someone came in and had a few with you and sympathized, you cheered up right away. Sympathy, that's what you wanted.... Attention.

My God! I said to myself, I've gone and done it! I've admitted it!

Take it easy now. These things aren't cleared up so simply. Takes time, the doctor said. Let's look at the facts. When you cut your wrists what did you do next? You lay down for awhile and you thought: A lot of people are going to feel sorry about this; they're going to wish they'd been a little nicer. And they're going to miss you on the paper because you did give it all you had, and if Fred gets your job they're going to notice the difference.

Then what did you do?

You remembered you had locked the puppy outside and she was so little and might tumble into the river. So you called your best friend and told him about the puppy and what you'd done. You said to yourself: It's all right; I'll be dead before they get here. But you weren't dead. They had to drive fifteen miles, but they got there awfully fast—first, the deputy sheriff, then the kid police reporter you'd always liked, then the ambulance. Attention? Yes, you had it that time. In the hospital, too, with your own doctor waiting,

[*73*]

stitching you up, scolding you. Attention all over the place, even when you got home and were contrite and were forgiven.

All right, you've admitted that one. Now for the second time. Calling the doctor. I can't sleep, Doctor. No, not worried about anything; just toss all night. Oh, thank you, Doctor. Yes, I'll follow directions.

Follow directions, hell! When the pretty blonde from the drug store delivered the pills you thanked her, but you were thinking all the time: She's going to be shocked tomorrow.... Sitting there for an hour or so trying to get up your courage, probably, then swallowing all the pills at once. How hard they went down, as though they didn't want to, as though you, your real self, didn't want them to.

Your wife came home and found you out cold. You didn't know it at the time; today you have no memory of being rushed off to the hospital, of having your stomach pumped out. But didn't you know all the time that your wife would be coming home? Even so, you were taking a risk, but weren't you willing to take that risk? For what? For attention?

My God, was I that bad? Bad isn't exactly the word; the doctor says it's that other self that does the dirty work. Well, don't try to make excuses. You've got it out of yourself and you've held it up to the light and you've recognized it. That's enough for one day.

But I couldn't stop thinking about it. I thought of my wife's letter and how bitter I had been during the night. Now it didn't bother me so much. What had I expected? That I could go on and on, being forgiven each time? There was a fleeting thought: Maybe now that I've got this thing I can be forgiven just once more. It will be hard going it alone after I am out of here. But something whispered that there was no

[*74*]

solution there; I had to go it alone. I had to get rid of all the crutches.

But Christmas is coming on; that's a hell of a time to be alone—or in a state institution. Come now, better throw away that crutch, too. Don't let that foot start hurting again....

It was not an entirely different person who walked from the Day Room when Bates called, but it wasn't the five-year-old who had come in nine days before.

Bates asked me to help him transfer two of the patients to other wards outside the hospital. "And put on your rubbers," Miss Brown cautioned.

The patients were waiting in the Clothes Room, their few clothes wrapped in sheets. I was surprised to find that one of the patients was Heilhitler, and expected a scene. But he regarded me woefully, saying not a word. The other patient was Old John, half-blind, dirty, who spent his days picking cigarette butts from the trays and winnowing the tobacco from them. He leaned against the wall, unaware that he was being shifted.

Heilhitler knew, though, and there were tears in his eyes. He who thought everyone on D-3 was a God-damned chicken thief from Hastings was reluctant to leave his old chair. At heart he probably was reluctant to leave the chicken thieves. But the doctor said he and Old John must go, over to Thirty-four, where there were other old men sitting out their last days.

Neither man said goodbye to anyone. Bates guided them to the elevator, and I carried their bundles. We got into Bate's car and wallowed through the slush to Thirty-four, one of the old buildings with massive furniture, high ceilings, and wooden floors. The old men in Thirty-four stared at us but not curiously. Other old men were coming in every day; it was always the same, and no one cared so long as there were three meals a day and a bed at night.

Heilhitler wept as we stood before Thirty-four's attendant. Old John leaned against the wall again, complacent, resigned. Bates said goodbye to Heilhitler, and so did I; the tears rolled down his cheeks and he did not reply. Old John smiled and shook hands with us. "Glad to meetcha," he said.

Despite the slush, Bates drove around the grounds. "You need a little air," he said. "Another two days and the snow'll be gone. Then we'll probably all come down with the flu. Then we'll have another snow storm, you watch."

"Let it come!"

"Flu or snow?"

"Either one."

He looked curiously at me. "Say, the air's fixing you up all right. Or is something else doing it?"

"Something else."

He wasn't curious any more.

"If you're feeling so good," said Bates, "you can help me with Bath Day tomorrow. Is *that* a job!"

We smiled at each other.

the
TENTH
day

Bath Day started off slowly. Boy Blue said that he didn't want a bath. Bates said he had to have one. Boy Blue said he'd be damned if he'd take a bath. So Bates shoved him gently along the hall, helped him undress, and got him into one of the two showers. There he patted a few drops of water on his chest and stepped out. "Get back in there," ordered Bates, "and wash your feet! Look at those feet!"

Boy Blue obeyed, but he used up nearly half an hour of Bates's time. I stood in the Clothes Room and passed changes of clothes to Bates when he called the name of the bathers. Boy Blue had several changes; he also had a dozen handkerchiefs, but refused to use them, demanding instead that the state supply him with squares of sheeting.

Little Willie enjoyed the shower, probably because the water was hot. He rubbed on a little soap, then stood in the spray with a smile on his face, his hands folded contentedly in front of him. Willie had no changes of his own; he wore state clothes except for his sweaters, ear-muff cap, and scarf, which he wrapped carefully around his neck before he stepped into clean underwear. Willie took only ten minutes; he was Bates's prize bather.

The old men loitered; they got their clothes mixed up; lost their belts or suspenders. And, without exception, they demanded the best of the state clothes, some of which had been worn to rags. I was hard put to please them, and I lost my patience several times, but Bates was unruffled. He coaxed them into putting on blue shirts when they wanted white shirts; he undid their shoe laces for them, matched their socks, got soap and towels for them. Even the patients able to do for themselves made their demands upon him. Wasn't that yellow shirt back from the laundry yet? Where in the hell were those new overalls? Hey, close that door; we don't want them student nurses lookin' at us! Why not? Give 'em a treat! Chuckles, then, from the old men and bawdy shouts from the young ones.

Steam filled Bath and seeped into the Clothes Room. I was dripping when my turn came to shower. Thirty-nine men had passed through Bath by then, and it was nearly dinner-time. The doctor had come and gone, and I had not even glimpsed him. Len and Red stood at the entrance to Bath manicuring their nails and goading me while I showered.

"That's a tough job," said Red. "Jesus, looking at all those dinkuses!"

Len said, "I want to make a complaint. I had some falsies when I came in and now they're gone."

"You don't need falsies," Red said. "You need a breast pump!"

Miss Brown called to him.

"We're going to have trouble now," said Len. "Doc told me he's sending Red back to Six."

Red came back, his face a thundercloud. "By Christ, I'm

not going to take that! You know what? Doc's sendin' me over to Six!" He clenched his big fist and swung it against the door. The door shook. "Hell! I wanta break that hand; then I'll go to D-2."

"You keep pounding like that and you'll wind up in one of those rooms on D-4," Len warned, but he was able to calm Red and they walked up and down the hall until the dinner bell rang.

After dinner two big attendants came over from Six. Red took one look at them and said, "Okay, but I'm warnin' you; I'm going to take off first chance I get."

"Come on, Red," one of them said. "Welcome home!"

He borrowed a last cigarette and walked out defiantly.

"That's three gone today," Len said. "Means three more will be coming in soon. Poor Red, he'll miss the dance tonight. They won't let him out of Six for awhile."

The doctor did not come in during the afternoon. I dozed for several hours in a chair, felt fluish when I woke, and said I thought I'd skip the dance. But Len was insistent that I go. "You don't have to dance," he coaxed. "Just sit and watch."

"You've been loafing all day; I've been working."

"My loafing is over. I got to run the polisher, starting tomorrow. Bates said so."

"Good for Bates!"

I felt better after supper, and Jacob and I got through the sweeping in no time. "Going to the dance, Jacob?"

"Oh, my no! It gets awful close in the auditorium, I wouldn't think of going. Anyway," he said seriously, "I want nothing to do with women."

At six o'clock Art Ammidon took down the names of those who wanted to go to the dance. There were eight of us. We washed, put on ties (rarely worn on D-3), and lined up near the side exit. Ralph was there, his arms full of sheets of music. He played the piano at the dances. There were three youths from the insulin ward, and one of them carried a bottle of "juice" to be taken if the insulin began to work unexpectedly on them. They joked about their "juice" and offered some to Lloyd. He would have taken it, but they jerked it back.

Lewis, the constipated one, also was ready, complaining about his bowels but eager to be on his way, eager to do anything to relieve the monotony of the Day Room. Len, who had known him before, said that he had had a stroke and was getting worse each day. He cried when he received a letter from his wife, and he cried when he had one of the student nurses write an answer for him. He had high blood pressure and was on a diet, but he stole salt at table and laced his hamburgers with it at the canteen.

The Brat wanted to go, but it was against the doctor's orders. He stood nearby making remarks about our clothes. "One of these days I'm going to sock him," Len said. "I'm going to sock him good."

Shortly before seven an attendant came down from D-4. He got the list from Art and we filed down the stairs as our names were called. On the ground floor six men from D-4 were waiting; there were only two from D-2, but six more from D-1. A second attendant joined us and led the way through the slush to the auditorium two blocks away. Along other paths more male patients were splashing. There was little conversation; everyone was intent on getting there.

We trooped up to the second floor of the auditorium past more attendants and on to the dance floor itself. Ralph left us, bustling importantly up to the stage where the orchestra was waiting. There were several hundred patients already there. Three rows of theater seats were placed against the two side walls and the rear wall. On one side sat the women; the men on the other. The women also had the seats against the rear wall, but most of those were taken by attendants and student nurses.

Len gave me instructions: "You can cross the room to ask a woman to dance, but you can't stay over on their side. Oh, and you can take her back when the dance's over, but no one does. And you got to be a gentleman on the floor. No cheek-to-cheek business, no pinching, no feeling. Some women get away with a little rubbing now and then, but if the attendants catch 'em, back they go."

I saw Suzy sitting between two women attendants. She waved, and Len said, "Now you're caught; you got to dance with your girl friend."

"I'll sit out a few." I hadn't been to a dance in many years and I felt timid.

Promptly at seven the orchestra began playing. "Now the fun starts," said Len, his eyes sparkling. Half of the men jumped to their feet as if at a command and raced across the slippery floor to the women. Shortly the floor was filled. I sat back enjoying the spectacle—for that was what it seemed to be at first—while Len kept up a running commentary.

"Look at this old guy coming. One with the long neck and that fringe of hair. See, he's not looking at his partner or watching where he's going. All the time beaming at the spectators. And there's the Professor; used to be one, too. He likes to hold 'em close. Oh, my God, look what Lloyd's got!'

Lloyd had picked out a woman as tall as he and twice as big around. Her hair was done up in curlers made of strips of rags; her dress reached only to her knees, and she wore bobby socks and white tennis shoes. She had a dreamy expression on her face; when she smiled occasionally at Lloyd, a gap showed. Neither could dance; they simply walked around the room and did not seem to mind when they walked on each other.

Her face heavily rouged, a little white-haired woman in a red velvet dress and high-heel pumps danced with mincing steps, nodding to herself. She had been a school teacher, an attendant said, and had been in the hospital for many years. "She always wears the same dress to the dances. Don't know why it hasn't fallen apart."

There was a boy—he couldn't have been more than seventeen—with a shock of blond hair and a babyish face who carefully piloted a huge woman up and down one side of he room. Now and then he rested his head on her big breasts. She had a motherly face and used one arm to half-cradle him. Len kept track of them and said later that they danced every dance together, although that was against the rules—no more than three dances with the same person.

I laughed at some of them—at the short couple who tried fancy steps and fell headlong; at Lil, rubbing against her partner like any taxi dancer in a cheap New York hall; at the two fat women who stood in the middle of the floor and jumped up and down. One could not help laughing at times, and everyone laughed back. Everyone was having a good time; you saw no long faces, no blank stares. For two hours, once a week, they got away from themselves; they forgot, or submerged, whatever was troubling them.

I had come to see a show, and I had seen one in a way. But I found myself wanting to join in, and if anyone wanted to laugh at me that was all right, too.

The next dance I crossed the room to Suzy. One of the attendants looked sharply at me, then smiled. "Suzy's been telling us about you. It's nice that Suzy has a new friend. Sometimes she doesn't get along too well at the dances, do you, Suzy?

"Why did she say that?" I asked, after we had circled the hall once. I am not much of a dancer, belonging to the 1920 school, but it was easy to dance with Suzy.

A frown crossed her face. "I really don't know. Oh, you mean about not getting along well at the dances? I don't know that either. Sometimes no one asks me to dance."

"I'll ask you to dance. The next and the next?"

"Oh, no, then it would be over. Only three dances with the same person, Yack."

"Jack."

"I can't say it that way. You don't mind, do you? Sometimes a lot of words get mixed up and I can't say them the right way. Do you ever get mixed up, Yack?"

"Plenty of times. Why do you suppose I'm here?"

She said seriously, "Let's not talk about those things at the dance. Some other time. Sometime I'll take you up on my hill when the snow comes again and everything is white and quiet. I go up on the hill when things are mixed up."

"I saw you the night I came in. You stopped right under my window."

"Oh, you're on that side of D-3? Do you like D-3?"

"Yes—well, in some ways."

"I'm on Ward 11. That's near Receiving. From my room I can look over and see the Day Room on D-3. I saw the student nurses dancing with some of the men yesterday. Do you dance with the student nurses?"

"Not yet. I've been kept pretty busy with one thing or another."

"You dance with them if you want to. They're nice. They're nice to me."

"Thank you."

"Thank me? For what?"

"For saying I might dance with the student nurses."

She blushed. "I did sound as though I owned you, didn't I?"

"I like it."

Going back to Len after the dance I thought: And that's the truth! What's going on here? Building another crutch?

"Nice going," said Len. "Thought you were all tuckered out."

"Got my second wind, I guess."

"Crispy stopped by. She wants you to ask her to dance. Thinks you need cheering up."

Crispy was one of the student nurses. "Hell, I don't need cheering up!" But I danced with Crispy, and she was flirtatious in a little-girl manner and I could have hugged her for it. She talked about her boy friend in Korea and told mild jokes about the other students. Crispy was gay and wholesome; she reminded me of the daughter who died, and I was relieved that I could tell her so and not have that lurching sensation away down somewhere.

I wanted to have the next dance with Suzy, but Len approached with a plump, middle-aged woman with crossed eyes and pigtails. "This is Jack," he said, "Jack, this is Lena. She knows you're shy, so she's willing to dance with you!" He was horribly pleased with himself.

Lena and I danced. She kept chomping on chewing gum, and I would not have been surprised if it had been bubble gum. I was plotting various means of getting even with Len when she said, "No one ever asks me to dance." It was the way she said it—not complaining, not being arch, but stating a simple fact, that made me forget the crossed eyes, the gum, and the ridiculous pigtails. Always for the underdog, they had said rather accusingly. Well, the hell with them and their theory, anyway.

Len was chuckling when I returned to my seat. "Said I'd fix you up, didn't I?" His fat belly shook.

"She was lovely," I said. "Really lovely."

He gave me a startled glance. I added, "And I feel sorry for her."

"You're always feeling sorry for someone. Ought to cut it out. That's what comes from being a New Dealer."

Len had been a Republican from birth, and even at this late date spent hours growling about That Man. When Crispy floated by in the arms of a Negro patient and Len muttered, "By God, if my daughter danced with a nigger, I'd horse-whip her!" I let it go. Just as he let it go when I tried to argue why we were and should be in Korea. Friendships were too rare on D-3 to jeopardize them by shouting one's political views.

I had another dance with Suzy. We didn't talk much but agreed to meet at the canteen at one the next day. Suzy said she rarely missed a day at the canteen. "I've been here eight years, you know."

"That's a long time," I said for lack of anything better. "Eight years!"

"A very long time." She was silent during the rest of the dance. But when the orchestra leader announced that it was women's choice, a device to cheer the wallflowers, she hurried, smiling, across the floor. Lena was there before her, however. So Suzy and I had the last dance.

"Did you have fun, Yack?"

"More fun than I've had in years. To think I didn't want to come!"

"I'm glad you did!"

I pressed her hand. She had little hands—little hands that belonged in red mittens.

the
ELEVENTH
day

The doctor knew that I had something to tell him, but how he knew I did not understand. I told him the conclusions I had come to, and he said. "That's a fine start. Best of all is that you're not letting this domestic upset trouble you too much. You've got a long road to travel, so don't be impatient. I'll get some more reading for you and we'll talk now and then."

I asked if I could draw some extra money, and he asked why I needed it. "Well," I said, "I've been doing a bit of treating and...."

"Women?"

"Well, yes."

"Good! But don't get any ideas of marriage; you're through with marriage. You'd get mixed up again, sure as hell. More dough? Yes, we can fix you up with an extra chit once in awhile." He considered for a moment. "Like to go down town? Have a snort or two?" I stared, and he chuckled. "Surprised you, eh? I'm not worried; why should you be? I'll fix you up with a town parole right away. And here's an order for three bucks; you get your weekly two bucks today, so that gives you five. Paint the town, son!"

Crispy went with me to Center where I cashed the extra chit at the accounting office. Rather, Crispy cashed it, signed a receipt for the money, then handed the three dollars to me. Hospital rules do not permit a patient to draw from his account or sign a receipt

I treated Crispy at the canteen to a Coke and a chocolate bar. She said that was against the rules, too, but the student nurses didn't pay much attention to that particular rule. She said, her head cocked on one side, "If you're going down town today why don't you get a haircut? You really are getting shaggy."

"I feel at home now," I said. "All my life people have pestered me to get haircuts. But they cost a dollar now."

"I could lend you some money," said Crispy.

"You're sweet, but I wouldn't think of it."

"Not even to treat your girlfriend?"

"What girl friend?"

"I think her name is Suzy. You danced three times with her last night, remember? And they teased her when she got back to the ward. One of the nurses told me about it."

"They shouldn't have done that! Suzy has—well, spells, I guess you'd call them."

"You seem to know a lot about her!" Crispy munched her chocolate bar, smiling to herself.

"I don't know anything about her except that she is nice. Did you notice her eyes?"

"So you know nothing about her! All right, I'm only teasing! Come along, we've been out too long, and I'm supposed to be your guardian."

Back on D-3 Miss Brown said that my town parole had been approved and did I want to go right away? "You could have lunch down town," she said. "That would be a nice change. But—oh, I see you have on your rubbers."

The walk down town was invigorating. The snow was almost gone; there were puddles on the sidewalk and water gushed along the gutters, but the sun was warm. Before reaching the main business section I passed a small barber shop and recalled Crispy's suggestion. So I retraced my steps.

"Well," began the barber, "how are things at the hospital?"

I was startled. "How did you know?"

He grinned, pointing at my feet. The trouser legs had pulled up, exposing the tops of my socks and the hospital tags. "We get a lot of the people from there. Always glad to see 'em. We can tell 'em without the tags, usually. Most of 'em wear state clothes, you know."

As Keeper of the Bath, I did know. And apparently everyone else in town knew. Continuing on down town, I found myself glancing at passersby and wondering if they were from the hospital. But I saw no state clothes; it was too early, apparently, for other town parolees to be out.

I passed the new building of the *Record-Eagle*, and my thoughts went back many years to the day when I was taken on as a cub reporter. The *Record-Eagle* was in a dingy building then, and the editorial offices were on the second floor. I never forgot the *Record-Eagle* and the men who put it out six days a week. I wanted to go in; there must be some of the old-timers still there, and I had gone to high school with the present society editor. But, thinking of the barber, I went on.

I walked the full length of Front Street, which is the main street, getting a glimpse at the intersections of Grand Traverse Bay, which I had known and loved in my boyhood. Many times my grandfather and I had brought his launch around from Old Mission, in the heart of the cherry country, for repairs in Traverse City. And in the days when winters were winters, long before I was born, my grandfather had driven to town over the frozen bay. But never after his favorite team plunged through the ice.

My grandfather told us the story many times, and always the tears came into his eyes: "There they were, swimming 'round and 'round in this hole in the ice, following me and begging me with their eyes to save them. But I couldn't do a thing. I couldn't even cut the traces and let the sled sink. Finally it dragged them down.... I never crossed the ice again."

I recalled, too, that when I was fourteen, my grandfather, a young mechanic, and I brought the launch up from Muskegon, and off the mouth of the bay a storm blew up and the engine died. We wallowed in the trough trying to start the engine again, but it was old and tired. Finally my grandfather rigged a sea anchor of planks and said I, being the lightest, would have to go out on the forward deck and put over the anchor.

He tied a rope around my waist and held on to the other end while I did the job, teeth chattering, my whole body shaking with fear. When the task was done and I was safely back in the cabin, racked by seasickness, my grandfather said, "I'm proud of you, boy!" When we finally reached port the next day (the engine came to life at dawn), I staggered all over the dock from the motion of the night in the storm. But I walked on air, too, because of the words my grandfather had spoken.

My grandfather died on the farm at Old Mission, which

my parents had bought as a summer home, but all of us loved it so much that we spent five winters there. It was to The Farm—we never called it anything else—that I brought my first wife on our brief honeymoon. It was on The Farm a year and a half later that she announced she was pregnant. We came back once more, with our first daughter, the one who died, and after that The Farm knew us no more. Detroit, then New York; new work, new friends. But I never forgot The Farm.

Years later I returned with my second wife.... Conrad in search of his youth—I could see that now. My parents were dead; my sisters had moved away. Even my grandfather's coffin had been taken from the grove and shipped to another town. The Farm was... we moved on.

But who let it be haunted? Who, wandering through the grove and over the sand of the beach, let himself cry out that there was nothing left... only ghosts? Who missed the praise of his grandfather, the adoring tolerance of his mother; yes, even the blind faith of the Airedale that slept under the covers with him? Why, a little boy, of course—a little boy who never grew up.

Never before had I thought that way. More progress, I said to myself, but I was not cocky. I felt too humble, too grateful for that. And I wondered, as I sloshed back to the hospital never thinking of a downtown lunch, if the doctor had a reason for giving me town parole so soon.

I was too late for dinner on D-3, but Len had a chocolate bar, which he gave to me. "That'll hold you until you can get to the canteen. So you've got town parole? And forgot to eat! And forgot to stop at a tavern, too, I suppose?" He sniffed. "By God, you didn't take even one?"

"Never thought about it," I said truthfully.

He shook his head. "I'd think about it if I got town parole. But Doc'll never give it to me. Say, you missed it. A new nurse was up here for an hour—she's going to be on with Miss Brown—and she was walking around and chatting with the fellows. She came up to Ralph and said, 'Why Ralph, what have you got all over your coat?' It was last year's food, of course, the dirty bum, but Ralph got sore as hell and ran all over the place. He went to the piano and pounded on it, and along came Boy Blue and made his usual remark about how good that guy can play. Ralph screamed at him, 'Why don't you shut up?' That's pretty good for Ralph, the God-damned sissy!"

I was duly appreciative. Len said I had missed more. "The Flash got an electro. Jesus, was he scared! He pounded his head against the wall and prayed and prayed. Goodman and a guy from D-4 had to lug him in for the treatment. He yelled bloody murder then. Funny thing is he's perked up since."

The Flash was siting quietly, talking to the Financier. His face had a red mark on it near the forehead. He seemed to be relaxed and enjoying his surroundings for the first time.

But little Willie was rocking and weeping again. "I got some kinda misery," he said. "I couldn't eat nothing." His face felt hot.

Miss Brown brought two pills to him, and he had difficulty getting them down. "You'd better lie down until the doctor comes," she said.

Bates asked me to help him carry clothes to D-4. On the way up he told me that Collar Button had committed suicide the night before. "Got the straps off the mattress somehow and hung himself from those gadgets on the window."

I was shocked. "They didn't find out, then, what he was worrying about?"

"Guess not. Must've been something pretty bad."

"The poor guy!" Collar Button really had wanted out; no desire for attention there.

On D-4, usually a noisy ward, there was a strange silence. The men stood around in knots, some with envy in their eyes, some showing the simple fear of death. "What a way to do it!" said one of the attendants. "Slowly strangling! Never kicking or anything; otherwise we'd have heard him."

I told Len about it. "Jesus!" he said. "And I was kind of ugly to him that first day!"

I said, "This is one hell of a day! It started out fine; now look at it!"

"The old bastards are acting up, too, but that's natural. They tell me that whenever the weather changes these mental cases get all stirred up. Make good barometers."

Only Len and I reported to go to the canteen at one. Even Lewis was uninterested. "God-damned bowels got me all tied up again!"

When we reached the canteen, Lil rushed out to meet us. "Hey!" she said, "your girl friend wants me to tell you she won't be over. Got the flu or something. And when Suzy gets anything, she gets it good!"

"This *is* one hell of a day!"

Len said, "Hell, let's go back. I couldn't eat anything anyway. Wish I could stop thinking about Collar Button."

"Always feeling sorry for someone!" I mimicked him.

We turned and walked out. "Cheap bastards!" Lil yelled after us. "Don't I rate a hamburger?"

the
T W E L F T H
day

Breakfast, which I usually enjoyed, had no appeal. I drank some black coffee and sat waiting for the others to finish. Len asked what was wrong, and I said I thought the flu bug had taken over. But I helped Jacob with the sweeping, then found an easy chair and watched Len polish the Day Room floor. He had caught on quickly, and took a certain pride in his work. It enraged him when Boy Blue and some of the old men, suddenly deciding to be of help, pushed the furniture across the glistening floor.

"Damn it to hell," he shouted, "look at all the scratches you're making! Sit down, you nitwits! Crawl away and die!"

They only stared at him curiously and went on shoving the chairs across the room. I couldn't stand the uproar and went into the first bedroom, occupied by Frank, a retired railroad man who had had a stroke months before and was subject to intermittent seizures. He sat at our table when he was able to leave his bed, and we waited on him. He was always grateful, patting our arms in thanks. He could not talk; only grunts and groans came from his mouth.

"Mind if I sit a spell?" I asked. "It's like a boiler factory out there."

He grinned, moved his lips, and motioned me to a chair. Frank had a small radio in his room; he kept it on all day. He read a lot and chewed on candy bars, brought each week by his wife who came up from Grand Rapids to see him.

He was finicky about his room. Only Len and I were ever invited in. When one of the curious—Boy Blue, for example—poked his head inside the door, Frank gesticulated wildly and grunted and groaned. He cried when his wife came and cried when she left.

I usually talked to him about Grand Rapids, and he nodded, smiled when he agreed and shook his head violently when he disagreed. He liked Grand Rapids, but I didn't so there was much head-shaking.

It was warm in Frank's room, or I was running a temperature. A few minutes later my teeth began to chatter and I was in for a chill. I said goodbye to Frank and sought out Miss Brown, who unlocked my room and fetched blankets. The chill passed in about fifteen minutes, and I went to sleep, only to be awakened by Miss Brown, who gave me three pills.

"The doctor has it, too," she said, "and won't be in today. If you get any worse, I'll call him. Looks like just a cold."

Just a cold! I have always been fascinated by the nonchalance with which the medical profession views the common cold. I have had virus pneumonia twice, the flu countless times; and I have been dosed and waited upon, rushed off to the hospital, or ordered to bed for a week. But when I have had colds, with all the misery they breed, I have been told to take some aspirin and drink lots of liquids. There has always seemed to be a conspiracy, a hush-hush attitude that says: We know we have a bastard child among us, but let's not admit it.

I dozed again, and the pills or the temperature induced nightmares. I woke screaming. The Brat pushed open the door, surveyed me curiously, walked to the bureau, and calmly appropriated a pack of cigarettes. He fled before I could get out a curse.

The fever subsided, but I did not want dinner. I tried to read one of the books the doctor had given me and fell asleep again. When I woke it was dark; in the thin shaft of light coming from the hall I saw a man kneeling beside the bed.

"What the hell are you up to, Franklin?"

He looked up, startled, his lips still moving. In a few moments, he said, "Praying."

"For whom?"

"For you and for me, too."

"You do it wholesale?"

"You're a pretty sick man. I thought...."

"The hell I am! Just a cold. Miss Brown said so."

"Miss Brown's off duty. We've had supper."

"You mean you actually ate?"

Franklin sighed. "I know they'll electrocute me for it, but I tried some hash and it was good, so I ate all of it, God help me!"

"Well, I'm glad you're getting some sense. Don't you feel better?"

He said honestly, "Yes. Feel kinda peppy. Bowels moved, too."

It was my turn to sigh. "Oh, you're one of those! How do you expect your bowels to move if you don't eat?"

[*96*]

"I don't expect. I figure my bowels will get all tied up and then I'll die."

"Oh, God! Listen, Franklin, I thought I wanted to die, too, and I made a fool of myself. That's why I'm here."

"Oh, no, you're not. You're the inspector, I know that. But I like you anyway. That's why I'm praying for you."

"You think God's got time to cure my cold?"

"God's got time for everything. God is everywhere."

"Why doesn't God cure you?"

"There is nothing wrong with me. I just want to die, but I don't want to be electrocuted."

"You want things your own way. Maybe that's your trouble."

He got up from the floor. He spoke quietly, "No, I have never had things my own way. When I was a kid I did everything my father said. When I was in school I was teacher's pet because I never did anything bad. When I married, my wife took charge of the money; then she took charge of the store. When I wanted to put on an addition she said no, but she put it on—during the Depression. No, I wouldn't say that I have had my own way."

I broke the rule. "Why are you here, then, Franklin?"

"I don't know. I really don't know."

"Is it a refuge, maybe?"

"Might be."

"From what?"

"Well, I…." And then he pressed his lips together. "Good night, Jack. I'll pray for you all night."

I had come closer, perhaps, than the doctor, to learning Frank's secret. In the days to come he seemed on the verge of confiding in me several times but he always backed away at the last moment.

[*97*]

Art Ammidon came by to ask if I wanted anything to eat. I was feeling better, but had no appetite. Art gave me some more pills and stayed to chat.

"Two new ones came in today," he said. "Funny thing, one of 'em is Red's uncle. He's been here before. He's in a bad way, trembles all over, can hardly walk, and has difficulty swallowing his food. Can't talk, either. Carries a pad and pencil to do the work for him. You'll be interested to see how he changes in a week or so."

"What's the matter with him?"

"He got a good dose of flu in that 1918 epidemic and it did something to him. He gets so bad at home that they have to put him to bed. He can't feed himself, can't get up to go to the toilet. Then they finally send him up here. We don't do much for him, but he starts to improve the second day. It's mostly in his mind, Doc says; something at home stirs him up and he goes back to being a baby again, even to messing the bed."

"His wife, I bet. Wives are blamed for a lot here, aren't they?"

Art grinned. "And outside, too. But wife trouble does send a lot of 'em here. They probably don't know it, but that's the root of the trouble. Mothers, too. Mothers can raise hell after Sonny Boy takes a wife."

"How about husbands and fathers?"

"They don't seem to cause much trouble. I guess men don't butt in so much. After you've been around here awhile you won't say women are the weaker sex."

"I never did…. Who's the other new one?"

"Guy named Pickerel. They sent him down from D-4. Batty as they come. Drives you nuts with his wisecracking and speeches. He's always yelling. "I'm a Jew! I'm a German

Jew!" Wish Heilhitler was still here. Boy, they'd wreck the place!"

After Art left I got up to go to the bathroom. The Brat stood in the doorway, and I had to push aside to enter. He said casually, "Frank got out of bed and fell."

I ran across the hall into Frank's room. He was lying in a corner, waving his arms and legs. I got him to his feet and into bed and then called Art. "Bet he's going to have a seizure," said Art, looking worried, but Frank shook his head. Apparently he had simply toppled over after getting out of bed.

I went back to the bathroom. "You little stinker!" I said to The Brat. "You just stood there and let him struggle."

"It really was funny," he said. "His nightshirt went right up over his head!"

I'm not a fighting man—never have been—but I let fly with one that missed him by a foot. Gurgling with laughter, he slipped away into the Day Room.

I was awakened in the middle of the night by a terrific pounding overhead. Someone seemed to be throwing chairs against the walls; bed springs screeched. Then a man screamed. I got up and went into the hall. A few minutes later the night attendant let himself in from the outside staircase.

"Tough time on D-4," he explained, panting. "Two guys went at each other. Wrecked the room over you. One of the guys got his leg broken."

"What were they fighting about?"

"Dunno. Attendants upstairs say one of the guys is a pussy. That might be it."

Everyone except the old men on D-3 had heard the commotion. One by one they emerged from their rooms; most of them wore long underwear, and they made weird shadows on the walls in the subdued light. We got fire from the attendant and smoked and talked for a few minutes; he was excited and overlooked the fact that we should be in our rooms.

"You look like hell!" Len said cheerfully.

"Feel that way, too. Do they often have fights like that?"

"On D-4; not down here. Two niggers got at each other once and made hash of each other before the attendants could get 'em apart. You never know what's going to happen on D-4."

Back in bed, sleep would not come. I fetched a year-old magazine from the Day Room, asked the attendant if I could have the light on for half an hour, and tried to read. The article I turned to was a warning by a disgruntled ex-New Dealer that the United States was headed for socialism. It put me to sleep all right.

the
THIRTEENTH
day

Sunday I was worse. The chills came back and I could not eat. The doctor came, dragging his feet and looking wan. "February can't get here too soon," he said. "I get a month in Florida then."

"I'm tired of this cold weather and snow, too. Used to like it."

"That's old age creeping on. It's raining now, which won't help things. Wonder who started this bug."

I said, "I danced with a woman Thursday night and she came down with this the next day."

"You're a Typhoid Mary, eh? Well, stay in bed and (here it comes, I thought) drink lots of liquids. I'm going to change your pills, but they probably won't do much good. Best way to lick these colds is to sit them out. You get well just as fast without pills, but you can't tell a sick guy that."

Miss Brown fetched tomato juice, orange juice, and a pitcher of water. I dutifully drank, swallowed the new pills, and lay there listening to the rain beating against the window. In an hour I began to feel better and was pleased when Crispy tiptoed into the room.

"Good Lord," she said, "you must have been sick!"

"You're telling me!"

"Of course that beard makes you like a death's head."

"You're charming this morning!"

"Someone has to be charming around here. All the patients seem to have got out of the wrong side of their beds. Even Len is cross. And Ralph won't play the piano."

"It's the weather, or so they tell me."

"It doesn't seem to upset the women patients so much. I was over on C-3 for awhile, and the women were behaving nicely."

I asked if the student nurses preferred working in the women's wards.

"Fishing? Truth is we don't. Even in the regular hospitals, we'd rather care for the men. They're always more considerate, even when they're very sick. The women are so demanding; they want this, they want that. By the way, there's a woman on C-3 who's crazy about you."

"Good Lord!"

"The whole floor knows about it, and the nurses and attendants, too. You danced with her twice; she has rolling eyes."

"Lena!"

"She's the one. She's told everyone that she's going to marry you and you're going to New York on your honeymoon."

"No mention of the fact that I have a wife?"

"Oh, no. Nor that she has a husband. He's a minister somewhere down state."

"For God's sake don't spread this around! If Len hears of it, I'll never live it down."

Crispy giggled. "He knows about it already and is making elaborate plans. Thinks there ought to be a stag party for you."

I groaned. "Thanks for the warning, anyway. What's the matter with Lena? Sex-starved?"

"No more than some of the others. But she's got the idea that all men are crazy about her. And she says she hates her husband because he's not romantic."

"But she told me that no one ever asked her to dance. She was kind of hopeless about it."

"She tells all the men that. And the new ones often fall for it and are sorry for her."

"I walked right into the trap!"

"I'll say you did!" Crispy was enjoying herself. "She was writing you a letter this morning. She was on the sixth page when I left. Oh, yes, and she told the women you held her very close when you danced."

"I did not!"

"Well, you don't have to be so outraged. I just thought you'd like to know so you can be prepared."

"For what?"

"Well, she's permitted to go to the canteen now and then when a nurse or attendant is along, and she certainly means to treat you as her property when she sees you again."

"I'll stay away from the canteen!"

"Oh, no, you won't! Then you'd miss seeing your Suzy."

"She's not my Suzy. Furthermore, she's sick, too. You know, I was feeling better until you started this. Crispy, you've got to do something! Call her off!"

"Oh, come now! Surely this isn't the first time you've been in such a predicament."

"I'm not in the habit of discussing my love life with young whipper-snappers!"

"I'm crushed! I do so want to hear about your love life, sir!"

"Get out, Brat!" She went away, her shoulders shaking, and I had to laugh too. It was ridiculous, but it was rather pathetic. Whoa, better not take that line again!

I knew that Len would not wait long. He appeared in five minutes, his face wreathed in smiles. "Congratulations!"

"Go to hell!"

"I knew you were good, but I didn't think you were that good. Lena! There *is* a conquest. How'd you ever manage it, boy?"

Play it out. If you become indignant he'll never lay off. "Well, I was feeling kind of down, and she *is* a woman. Quite attractive, too, in a sexy way. I think we can probably make a go of it."

"My God, you out of your head?" Then he grinned. "Damned if you didn't have me for a moment! All right, I'll lay off. But, seriously, she's going to be a pest. She got a crush on a guy on D-1 when I was here last time, and drove him nuttier than he was. But I'll stand by you, son!"

"I bet! Who dragged me into it in the first place?"

"Just doing my good deed for the day. Want anything at the canteen? I'm going over this afternoon."

"No thanks. Think I'll get up after a bit. But they won't let me go out."

They didn't. I asked Miss Brown, just to see her reaction, if I might go to the canteen. She was horrified and was quite severe with me. But she said I might sit in the Day Room if I'd stay away from the windows.

In the Day Room the patients who were aware of the Great Romance (and Len had not been idle) grinned and nudged each other. But several came over to ask how I felt, and I was surprised when The Flash took a chair next to me.

"I wouldn't worry too much," he said. "Happens all the time here. Why, in the summer some of them women get knocked up right here on the grounds."

"This is winter," I said bleakly.

He wouldn't be put off, although he changed the subject. "You know, I was kinda pooped when I came back here, but they give me one of them electros and I feel fine now." He shivered. "Don't know if I can stand more of 'em, though. I had so damned many of 'em."

He paused to borrow a cigarette. "Been rolling my own with that state tobacco. Can't taste 'em. Nothing like a tailor made. My wife, she smokes tailor-mades. God-damned wife always smokes tailor-mades!"

He inhaled deeply, and some of the bitterness left his face. "You mind me talkin' like this?"

"No. I'm a good listener."

"Fellow's got to talk sometimes. I won't talk to Doc, though. Every time I talk he gives me one of them electros.... You see, it's like this. I'm a worker; I'm a hard worker. I work on the farms or sign up with a road contractor. Things like that. I know I ain't got brains; I got to work with my hands. But my wife, she's got other ideas. It ain't that she wants more money, though she's always yellin' about that, but she keeps pesterin' me to do something fancier. Like clerkin' in a store or sellin' cars. Things like that. I tell her it ain't no use, and she keeps pesterin' me. And then I go kinda haywire and I hear voices and I get lost when I go out. So then my wife, she goes to probate court and they send me back here. They give me some of them electros and I'm okay. Then I go home and it starts all over again."

He paused to put out his cigarette. "That's what you gotta watch out for when you go home. Every bastard in town knows where you been, and they give you the old up-and-down when you meet 'em on the street. Oh, they're polite and all that, but you know they're talkin' about you and callin' you a nut. And you can't do nothin' about it, seein' as how you *are* a nut. Christ, they make you feel like you was in a zoo!"

"I know what you mean. I felt that way when I went down town."

"Well, there ain't nothin' you can do about it except face 'em down. Act like you was the king of England. That don't go over with your wife, though. My wife, she starts the minute I come home, telling me how the neighbors talk and the like. I tell her, 'Who the hell sent me up there?' And she says, 'Who the hell wants you here?' And then we're off. We make it up later and we have a go at each other and everything seems all right, but something starts it up again next day.

"Last time I was here I got thinkin' about it and I got madder'n hell. So I took off one night. Jesus, what a trip! Took me two days to get home, and then I was afraid to go in. We got a swamp near our place, and I stayed out there till midnight. Then I sneaked in. Scared the livin' Jesus outa my wife. She was goin' to call the sheriff, but I talked her outa it. Then we got into bed, and she wanted it, too. But the next morning she went to the store and called the sheriff. Course they'd been after me in a day or so anyway."

The Flash lost interest in himself and his troubles. "Think I'll wash my feet," he said vaguely, and hurried into the Utility Room to get a bucket. I half-dozed in the chair, wondering about him and his wife. Walk along any street at night, I thought, and look at the little houses with the glow of light in the windows. See the people moving about inside. And if you're a stranger and lonesome, you'll envy them and long for your own fireside. But you haven't the least idea what is going on inside those houses.

You'd never guess, looking into The Flash's home, what was going on. All those nice little houses, and the lights glowing and, perhaps, everyone sitting down to dinner. But how do you know that the man cutting the roast isn't going to use the knife on his wife that night? You have no way of knowing; you stand on the outside and it looks homey to you and you want to be in the man's place. But you won't feel that way after you get out of here. Every time you look into someone's home you'll think of The Flash and his wife, or Len and his wife, or Franklin and his wife....

It must be the pills, I thought.

Miss Brown distributed the mail. I had two letters, one from a sister and one from my daughter in California. They were nice letters, and after I had read them I sat holding them and feeling warm and comfortable. Johnny received a letter, too. It contained an early Christmas card. Miss Brown read to him the few words written on it: "Dear Johnny: This is the first Xmas card, but I will send some more. Be a good boy and you'll be home soon. Love, Mom."

Johnny took the card and calmly dropped it into the trash can. "Poor Johnny," said Miss Brown, "he doesn't understand about letters. And he'll never go home."

the
FOURTEENTH
day

The young doctor who admitted me to the hospital came up to D-3 to invite me to dinner. I felt much better, but he agreed that it would be unwise to go out so soon. "We'll give you another chance," he said.

Frank's wife called and spent several hours with him. She brought candy and fruit, and Frank insisted that I have some chocolate-covered cherries. After his wife left, Frank mumbled something that I could not understand. I got paper and a pen and he wrote in a shaky hand: "Don't feel well. Will you look in on me?"

I said that I would stay with him. He lay with his eyes closed, his fingers kneading the bedspread. Suddenly he began to shake; his teeth chattered and foam formed on his mouth.

Miss Brown was off duty and there was no nurse on D-3. I called Goodman, and he summoned a nurse from D-2. They gave Frank a hypodermic, but he continued to shake. In an hour they gave him another, after telephoning the doctor.

I thought Frank was dying; there was a rattling in his throat, but they said that was from the seizure. I think Frank thought he was dying, too, and he fought against it. It gave me pause, watching him struggle. He hasn't much to live for, I thought, but he doesn't want to die.

I sat with him for two hours, and slowly the seizure passed. At times he clung to my arm and his eyes pleaded for help. When he was quiet again he smiled his thanks and went to sleep.

In the Day Room there was considerable excitement. The Financier, obtaining permission to go early to the canteen, had taken off. "Picked a good day for it," said Len. "The snow's all gone; it's just like spring."

Len said that The Financier probably would try to hitch-hike to Detroit. "He'll hide out for a couple of days; then the police will pick him up and back he'll come. You watch; Red'll try it in a couple of days, too."

The new patient, Pickerel, a middle-aged man with a bald head and a big belly, asked for a cigarette. "I'm a German Jew," he said, "but I got winning ways. All the nurses are crazy about me." He pointed at Crispy. "She's so crazy about me she wants me to marry her, but I can't. I got a wife; she's an old bag, but she's crazy about me, too." He patted his belly. "We raise rabbits. Make a lot of money off 'em. But that old bag, she won't send me any of the money. That's why I got to borrow cigarettes. Maybe I'll get a letter today I'll get a letter today with some dough."

He waltzed away to Crispy, but she would not dance with him. Unperturbed, he danced with himself, humming a little tune. When he tired of that he lay on his back and kicked his feet in the air.

"He won't be here long," Len said. "Sure is cuckoo."

Len introduced me to Red's uncle, Larry, a little man with thin gray hair and a sweet face. He walked with tottering steps and seemed unable to control his facial muscles. He wrote on his pad: "Did you like Red?" I said I had liked Red, and Larry nodded. "Hope he doesn't run away," he wrote.

Larry wrote many letters to relatives and, in a few days, was receiving more mail than anyone else on D-3. He enjoyed his letters, spent hours re-reading them, and always carried them with him. He liked candy bars and Cokes, too; not being a smoker, his two dollars went a long way. His wife often sent him candy; she wrote at least once a week— brief, formal letters signed "Your Wife." Larry liked to show them to Len and me; he viewed them as love letters. Yet once he was back home, she did something to him that sent him groping back to his infancy. Len and I couldn't figure it out; for that matter, neither could the doctors.

Larry was religious, read the Bible each day and copied verses from it, which he gave to any patient who would accept them. He offered one to Pickerel, but the buffoon spurned it, saying, "I know the Bible by heart; I don't need no verses. I'm a Catholic."

Len said, "Thought you were a German Jew."

"German Jew, Catholic—everything."

The doctor dropped by in the afternoon with another book, Karen Horney's *Neurosis and Human Growth*. It was rather hard-going for a layman, but I became interested in using Dr. Horney's theories to analyze myself and some of the other patients. There was one sentence that hit most of us, I thought: "Those who are proud of their unselfishness may not be openly demanding but will impose upon others through their helplessness and suffering."

I showed this to Len. "You'll *really* go crazy reading all those books." He was reading a paper-back titled *Kiss and*

Kill. "That's the kind of stuff," he said. "You can read it and not think about your troubles."

Art Ammidon beckoned to me from the doorway. "Will you help Doc and me?" he asked. "We got to give Franklin a tube-feeding."

We went into the Treatment Room. The doctor had a long red tube with a rubber funnel at one end. On a table was a pitcher of eggnog.

"Spiked?" I said.

No one smiled. Everyone, I learned later, makes the same remark in an effort to ease the tension. Franklin, sitting in a chair, struggled as Art and I entered, but Art quickly grabbed his head and held it tilted back. "Hold Franklin's hands," the doctor ordered. Franklin pushed me off, but I was able to keep his hands down and away from the tube, which the doctor inserted into one nostril. Franklin groaned and blubbered.

The doctor stood on a chair and poured the eggnog into the funnel. "This isn't orthodox," he said, "but it works."

"He can't even taste it," Art explained. "It shoots right into his stomach."

Franklin ceased to struggle. The strange part was that in the few minutes it took to empty the pitcher the color came into his face and he seemed to relax. When the doctor pulled out the tube, Franklin sighed. "That's terrible!" he said. "That's awful!"

"Another one tomorrow if you don't eat," the doctor said cheerfully.

"Now I know you're an inspector," Franklin said reproachfully to me.

"He's not," the doctor said. "He had to help us because you're such a baby."

"Feel better?" I asked. "You certainly look better."

To our surprise Franklin said, "Guess I do feel better!" Even more surprising, he listened to Crispy's urging and played the piano for five minutes. Played it well, too, while Ralph frowned in his corner. Crispy was called away, and Franklin, minus his prop, ceased playing and wandered back to the urinals. He ate most of his supper but would not admit that he enjoyed it.

They brought in a new patient after super, a youth of seventeen with an unruly shock of hair whose first name was Teddy, but we couldn't understand him when he spoke his last name. "Write it out," said Len, who had taken a fancy to the boy.

Teddy hung his head. "Can't write. Can't read, neither."

"That's tough," said Len. "Maybe Larry here could teach you."

Larry nodded eagerly, got out his pad and pencil and took Teddy over to the big table near the piano. The first lesson lasted nearly an hour, and Teddy's face was wreathed in smiles when he returned. "Oughta get it in a coupla days," he boasted.

Teddy had spent most of his seventeen years in juvenile homes. His father disappeared when he was an infant, and his mother apparently couldn't be bothered with him. He liked the last juvenile home because there was considerable farm work to be done.

Len said bluntly, "Why'd they send you up here then?"

"Dunno," said the boy.

"Get into some kind of trouble?"

"No... well, I did sass the superintendent's wife, the old bitch!"

"We don't cuss up here," said Len, whose every other

word was a curse. He had really taken to Teddy, who followed him everywhere.

Teddy arrived with chewing tobacco, two cigars, and a pack of cigarettes. He said he took up chewing when he was two and had his first cigar when he was three. "I smoke a pipe, too, but it ain't got the kick it used to have. And I like gin."

"All right," Len said mildly, "we know you're a he-man!"

But Teddy was not to be put off. "And I can hump a girl, too! I ain't never been in love, though. That must be kinda different!"

"I wouldn't know," Len said stonily.

"I'd sure like to try it."

"Maybe you'll meet the girl of your dreams at the dance— if they let you go. You got to behave yourself, or no dance."

"Len will fix you up," I said bitterly. "He certainly fixed me!"

I must have been psychic, for Art beckoned to me again. "Visitors," he said briefly, but he seemed to be grinning to himself. At the entrance to the neutral space stood a pretty attendant from C-3, and—Crispy had been correct—with her was Lena, looking just as she had at the dance.

"Lena has a letter for you," the attendant said, and *she* was grinning.

"Darling!" breathed Lena into my ear. I gulped. Boy Blue, passing on his shoeless rounds, paused to stare, the first time he had evinced interest in me. I heard Len and Art laughing down the hall.

"I told them you were a kind of a relative," Lena whispered, "so they let me come in for a minute with the attendant. Here's a letter for you, darling. You'll write me, too, won't you?"

[*113*]

"Oh, sure," I said, feeling like a fool.

"Come on now, Lena," the attendant called. "Say goodbye to your relative!" She giggled. Of course they all knew that I was no relative, but they had sidestepped the rules to have a little fun. I said goodbye to Lena, and she seized my hand.

"My," said the attendant, "aren't we in a state!"

The letter was eight pages. It began: "My darling precious," and glowed with Lena's assumption that we were to elope to New York. She said that she might have some difficulty getting off C-3 "for they're watching me pretty hard," but she would manage it somehow. Then she went on: "I will now tell you my life history." Her husband was a minister, she wrote, and they had two children, but she couldn't live with her husband because "he isn't a good minister. I can preach circles around him."

Before coming to the hospital "for a rest" she had been with the FBI; then she had gone to France and joined "the French FBI." In her spare time she wrote poetry and detective novels. And would I please send her a pack of cigarettes when I wrote?

"Steer clear of her for a few days and she'll forget all about you," advised Art, seeing my face. "She'd rather write about herself than eat."

"I felt sorry for her at the dance. Still do. But Lena *is* on the ardent side!"

"Doubt if they'll let her go to the next dance," Art said. "They usually keep her in when she gets worked up."

Len, of course, was delighted and kept rubbing it in until bedtime.

the
FIFTEENTH
day

The doctor said I could go outdoors but warned against staying too long in the canteen. Then he invited me to attend staff, as an observer this time. I got in line early and was in the first group to be taken downstairs to the barber. Heretofore I had shaved myself, with an attendant standing nearby, or had gone downtown. But shaves were fifty cents down town, and fifty cents was a lot of money in a state hospital.

We were taken to the hospital barber in groups of ten. There were two chairs in the barber shop, and a patient sat in each while the barber quickly lathered their faces. Then he shaved one while the other lay with a hot towel over his face. It took the barber only twenty minutes to shave ten of us. He gave each man a quick once-over; there was no soothing shaving lotion, no powder. Some of the patients said that the barber was a butcher, but I thought that he did remarkably well considering that all the men had stiff beards.

We had to wait until all ten were shaved; then the barber called D-3. Bates or Goodman or a nurse came down for us, bringing along another group of ten.

"You won't believe this," said Len in the elevator, "but the barber's name is Trimmer!"

At ten A.M. I went to staff and sat in a corner with The Reverend. Other members of the staff greeted me pleasantly and did not seem to mind an outsider. Crispy risked a wink.

My doctor explained the first case before the patient was brought in. It was the case of Lloyd. The D-3 doctor sketched briefly what Lloyd had told him, which was virtually what he had told us but in more polite terms. Then the doctor said, "What appears to be important but what he skips over, is that his wife recently had a miscarriage. She had been warned by her physician not to take long drives in their car, but one day they took a ride over a bumpy road. The miscarriage followed.

"Now, the patient admits that neither he nor his wife wanted the baby. His attacks of what he calls stomach cramps followed the miscarriage. Evidently he has a feeling of guilt, and these attacks are the result. There is nothing wrong with his stomach; he eats like a horse. Hints around about having a drink to settle his stomach, but gives no indication of being an alcoholic. I have met his wife; she is the stronger-minded. Told me that she would rather see him dead than have him take one drink."

Lloyd was brought in. He was ill at ease and smiled foolishly most of the time. When he told about the miscarriage, he held his head down and rubbed his palms together. After he left, it was suggested by several members of the staff that he be given some electros. The D-3 doctor agreed and added that town parole "with a couple of drinks thrown in," might be of benefit. "Especially if he'll take them in front of his wife. He needs to stand up to her."

Teddy was next. The doctor had not had much opportunity to talk to him, but reported that juvenile authorities said Teddy was apt to lose his temper and strike the nearest person. He was too much for them to handle.

Teddy enjoyed staff. He had borrowed a tie from me and pointed proudly to it when he came in and saw me. He was inclined to take the whole affair as a joke; said he wouldn't mind spending the rest of his life here "if I could have all the chewing tobacco and cigars I need." He also said that he had fourteen dollars in a savings bank and would the hospital please have it sent to him right away?

There didn't seem to be much to do about Teddy. It was decided to keep him on D-3 and watch developments. Teddy walked out with cocky step, and I remembered with a wince my own day at staff.

The third and last patient was a young man from D-4 whom I had noticed talking to himself on my visits to that floor. He was quite a serious case; said that he heard voices all the time and "saw people out on the window ledge." That was about all he would say, except that he couldn't understand why he was in the hospital.

The doctor said that he had struck an attendant on D-4 last night, but the young man could not, or would not, recall it. The doctor said that this was another case in which strong-willed women could be held partly responsible.

"The boy was ruled by his mother until he broke away and married a Catholic girl. He became very religious after the marriage and joined the Catholic church, which outraged his mother. Her letters to me have insinuated that their child is not his; she obviously hates the wife. The wife obviously hates the mother; writes that they could be happy if the mother would mind her own affairs and stop talking against the Catholics. The boy does not want to go home; he has had enough, but he is becoming worse."

Electros were recommended for the young man. I thought: There is going to be a furor on D-3 tomorrow when the little machine which gives the electro-shocks is fetched in.

I thanked the doctor and the superintendent for permitting me to sit in at staff.

"Gives you a different picture, doesn't it?" asked the doctor. He grinned. "Now you know how we talked you over."

"I can imagine!"

"Come down again. I want you to understand how all these people are trying to escape something or...."

"Trying to get attention?"

"That's right! This kid Teddy is a show-off, which is all right if it doesn't go too far. Understand that Len is being the big father to him. Bet anything Len will be sick and tired of him before long."

I said, "I think Len's homesick, even though he jokes all the time."

"Yes, but he'll stick it out. He's a stubborn cuss."

I told Len about it as we walked to the canteen over grass that only a short time before had been buried under snow. Len sniffed the spring-like air. "Like to be at the camp now." He had a summer cottage at a nearby inland lake. "Maybe I'll go there, anyway, and be a hermit the rest of the winter. Yes, I guess I am stubborn; that's why I'm staying on. I'm not drinking, and Doc says he'll put me on a diet to take down the belly."

"That I want to see—you on a diet!"

He grinned. "You get better food that way, but not so much, of course."

The canteen was surprisingly quiet. Most of the younger people, a clerk said, were down with colds. "It's been real peaceful," she added.

Suzy sat on a Coke crate eating ice cream. She seemed paler, but the tip of her nose was red and she carried a bundle of tissues in her hand. We compared sickroom notes and blamed each other for passing around germs. "I get it every winter and now and then in summer," Suzy said. She smiled suddenly. "Am I too late to offer congratulations?"

"You heard, too?"

"News travels fast around here. They're talking about us, too."

"That's different."

"Yes. I don't mind if you don't. Should we go up the hill today? That'll really make them talk."

"I've been waiting for it."

"You wouldn't want a third person?" suggested Len.

"Of course," Suzy said.

"Of course," I said.

"I was just kidding, and don't get your feet wet."

Suzy led the way through a rear door and up a stairway to the main hall of Center. "We aren't supposed to be up here, are we?" I asked.

"Oh, they have so many rules you can't remember all of them," Suzy said impatiently. "Anyway, you don't look like a patient, having your own clothes and all. They'll think you're a visiting legislator."

"I don't know just how to take that!"

"I know what you mean. Some of them are pretty disgusting. The Governor comes up now and then. He's nice. I shook hands with him, but I wasn't especially thrilled."

We went out the front entrance of Center and then over to Suzy's hill. It wasn't a steep hill, but I was panting by the time I got to the top. Huge pine trees were all around us, squirrels were frisking across the grass, coming to abrupt stops as they located caches of food, buried when the snow was piled high. Below us a brook rushed under a small rustic bridge and splashed into a large pond that had been frozen solid when I arrived.

"It's lovely here; I don't wonder that you like it."

"I like it better when the snow's on the ground. Then it really is beautiful; it does something to me. I'm trying to write a poem about it."

"You write poetry?"

"No, I'm not so very good at it. But sometimes just looking at things doesn't seem enough. So then I try to write poems about them."

I said on impulse, "Are we going to talk today, Suzy?"

"About us being here, you mean?"

"Yes."

A frown passed over her face. She wielded the tissue with violence and her nose became redder. "There isn't much to tell about me, but somehow I don't mind—with you. I lived on farms until I was twenty-one and came here."

"You're twenty-nine then? A mere child! That's what a lot of people say. They say that I have the mind of a child."

"You've only seen me this way.... Well, yes, that one day in the canteen when I was angry. Sometimes I can't talk straight or write straight. Sometimes they lock me up."

"Why should they do that?"

"I guess I get too excited, make scenes. Once I hit another

patient. . . but she *was* going through my room. You become awfully possessive here; you don't want anyone else to touch your things."

I thought of The Brat. "I know; I've had that feeling."

Suzy said thoughtfully, as though she, too, was puzzled by her being here, "I remember when I was a little girl they said I was queer. I remember aunts and uncles saying that, and the other children in school. My father said it, too. My mother is dead, but my father is working his farm near Detroit. I don't see him very often."

"But what do they say here, Suzy? The doctors and all?"

"They don't say much to me. They say, 'Now, Suzy, you stay a little longer with us.' They've been saying that for eight years! But I guess they know best."

Her eyes grew large and tears welled in them.

"I'm sorry, Suzy, I didn't mean to dig the past out of you."

She smiled through the tears, using the last of the tissue. "It isn't the past; it's the present—and the future. It isn't pleasant to know why you are here and yet not really to know why. This isn't a bad place at all, but sometimes I feel I must get out." She hesitated, then rushed on, "Once I decided to throw myself into the pond."

"Oh, no, Suzy, you wouldn't do that!" Before I realized it, I was telling my story. I told it rapidly, and there was a puzzled frown on her face part of the time, but when I was done she said, "Thank you, Yack. I think I know why you told me." She considered for a long time, then said, almost shyly, "You must have loved them very much."

"Yes, possibly too much."

"Was she pretty—your first wife?"

"Very pretty. And little. She had hands like yours."

"And your daughter?"

"Pretty—and tall, or so she seemed in comparison to her mother. And both were lots of fun."

"I have fun with you. I don't know why; we've talked so seriously so far."

"We'll have fun. After all, there's the canteen; there's the dance...."

"And the hill."

"The hill, of course."

"You won't be here much longer, though, will you?"

I said that I had no idea how long I would be on D-3, but that I would make no attempt to leave until the doctor said I was ready. I must have talked earnestly, for Suzy said when I was done, "You sounded like The Reverend."

"Well, I am sincere about it; I do mean it."

"I know you are, but don't let them keep you too long. Sometimes I wonder...." She looked to the north to the ugly brick building where Ward 11—her ward—was. "I wonder if some of us don't depend too much on those walls. I wonder if we would miss them—outside."

"Some people might, but not you."

"Once an attendant took me down town at night. It was Christmas Eve. I liked the lights in the stores and the Christmas trees everywhere. But I didn't like the people; they were too happy."

"For Christmas Eve?"

"You haven't spent a Christmas Eve here. You don't see many happy faces. I was glad to get back to Ward 11 that night and see the faces that rarely change. You understand now what I mean about the walls?"

the
SIXTEENTH
day

During the night they moved Frank down to D-2. After breakfast I was there with Bates, carrying laundry that each day seemed to become more mixed up. I peered into Frank's room and spoke to him; he smiled feebly but could not give the usual wave of his hand.

Another patient was moved into Frank's room on D-3, a good-looking man in his thirties who spent his days wandering around the Day Room speaking to no one. Bates said that his name was Elmer; he had been an insurance man in Lansing, had a fine wife and two children and no money worries. He had been here for four months and showed no signs of improvement.

Elmer perked up, however, when he was assigned to Frank's room. He had been in a three-bed ward. The new privacy accorded him seemed to loosen his tongue. "I can be real happy here," he told Bates. "Couldn't stand the other guys in that ward."

Elmer's trouble in the ward had been his inability to hoard the boxes of candy, cookies, and cakes that his wife sent to him each week. He could not eat all of it, but he could not share it, and his room-mates solved that by simply appropriating the foodstuffs while he slept.

Now he became suddenly generous, carrying two boxes of cookies to the Day Room and passing them around. They were excellent cookies, small but rich. "My wife made them," Elmer told each patient. He actually seemed happy until Boy Blue, greediest of all, snatched two cookies after having munched on a handful. Elmer turned swiftly, knocking down Boy Blue's hand and spilling the cookies on the floor.

"You're a God-damned thief!" shouted Elmer, bursting into tears. Boy Blue got down on his knees and carefully picked up the crumbs and ate them.

Len had a handful of the cookies and was gobbling them. "Go on my diet at noon," he explained. "Don't want to have Doc see me eating these."

It was a languid morning. Franklin again surprised everyone by playing the piano for ten minutes. The new nurse, Miss Love, sat with him, and they played a duet. The new nurse was pretty and slender; she joked with the patients, especially Len, and she was the only one who could tame Pickerel. He waltzed with himself while she was at the piano or pestered the student nurses. When Miss Brown entered with the mail, he shouted, "Anything for old Pickerel, the German Jew? Anything from the old bag?"

There was a letter from his wife, and he insisted on reading it aloud. The letter contained a dollar bill. Miss Brown took it to place in his account, which until then had contained thirty-one cents. Pickerel was unconcerned by the dollar bill. "Take it!" he cried. "Buy yourself a pretty!"

It was a strange letter that Pickerel read. It began: "My dear, darling Husband," and ended, "with Oceans of Love, your Adoring Wife." Below her signature was a line of XXXs and OOOs. The letter told how much she missed him, said the rabbit business had fallen off, that she was desperate for money to buy coal but enclosed please find one dollar for cigarettes.

"Watcha think of that, boys?" yelled Pickerel. "Pretty good for the old bag, huh? All the women do that. All the time sendin' me love letters and dollar bills. Nothin' too good for old Pickerel, the German Jew!"

He was still in high spirits when the dinner bell rang. Filling his tray, he joked with Mary, the patient from C-3 who always had a good-natured retort for the men. But not for Pickerel. "Shut your mouth, you damned old fool!" she told him. Her attendant shushed her, and Bates moved Pickerel on. He was preparing to seat himself at a table when Mary picked up an apple from a tray in front of her and hurled it. It whizzed by Boy Blue's nose, missed Pickerel by less than an inch, and spattered against the wall.

Pickerel fell silent. But Boy blue was entranced. "That woman sure can throw good, can't she?" he shrilled.

Len had to leave our table and sit at the first table, reserved for patients on diets. I paused to examine his plate: cottage cheese, a tiny slice of lean meat, canned cherries, half a slice of unbuttered toast, and tea. My tray was loaded with Polish sausage, creamed potatoes, string beans, two pieces of bread spread with honey, a baked apple, a glass of milk, and a large square of spice cake.

"Trade?" I asked.

"Go to hell!"

He finished in five minutes and got a second cup of tea. Then he got a slice of the cake. After dinner he dug out a

[*125*]

chocolate bar from his coat pocket and gulped it. "Got to start off easy," he explained, seeing my grins, but he had the grace to turn red.

In the Day Room, The Flash was tremendously excited. Somehow, probably with the aid of attendants, he had borrowed a banjo from a patient in another building and was tuning it.

"I can really go to town on this!" he said jubilantly, and he could. Len and I worried a little at first about Willie's reaction; we thought that he might be considerably upset by this rivalry. However, Willie fooled us. He sat up straight when The Flash began playing; then he clapped his hands in a pleased way and got out his guitar. He played along with The Flash; rather, he played at the same time. Faster and faster went The Flash, and faster and faster went Willie until his little hands could no longer pluck at the strings. He sat back, exhausted but at peace with the world. "Sure is good to have someone accompany me!" he said blissfully.

The Flash played for two hours until he, too, was exhausted. But he was a changed man. He wiped the perspiration from his face, borrowed a tailor made, and beamed when we complimented him. He made no more dashes that day at the wall, and he was light-hearted with everyone. He even tried to give The Brat a banjo lesson, and for once The Brat was quiet and respectful.

Because we had enjoyed The Flash's concert so much, all of us ground parolees were late at the canteen. Len, grinning sheepishly, ordered a hamburger; Lewis had one, too, and poured drifts of salt on it. Larry was with us for the first time, drooling at the candy counter and pointing to the bars he wanted. Curly came in, looking for his once-a-year wife, and stayed to drink a Coke and twist his curl morosely. I wasn't hungry; I stood by the window, waiting for Suzy.

The superintendent made one of his frequent calls at the canteen and was promptly greeted by shouts of "Dr. Sheets! Oh, Dr. Sheets!" This one wanted to know if she could go home for Christmas. That one demanded why the hospital was keeping all his money. Dr. Sheets smiled upon them all, spoke quietly to some, joked with others, and the buzz of excitement continued while he was there.

He asked about my health, and we chatted. I wanted to inquire about Suzy, but decided that the time and place were wrong. The hospital had put my car in a heated garage on the grounds, and I thanked him for that. He said that he was sorry that I could not drive it, but that if I had even the most minor accident it would reflect on the hospital. I could see that, of course. I didn't know why, but there it was. Were the walls getting to me, I wondered aloud.

He understood what I meant and laughed. "I don't think you're in any danger of that. You like life too much!"

Dr. Sheets said that he hoped eventually to enlarge the canteen, to put in many more tables, even a juke box. "I like the idea of a social club for our people," he said. "It helps them, just as the dances and the movies do. We want them to have all the freedom possible."

He left as Suzy entered. "Well, Suzy?" he said pleasantly. She backed away and came over to me.

"What's the matter?"

She shrugged. "I don't know. He's been awfully nice to me, but I feel timid talking to him. I feel that way about our ward doctor, too."

"Probably a doctor complex. You've had so many doctors giving you tests that you shy away at the sight of one."

"Probably. Silly, isn't it? Want to walk?"

We started for the door, but we didn't get through. From the outside hallway burst Lena, followed by four other women patients and two attendants. "Darling!" she gushed, seizing my hands.

From Len came a roar of laughter, Others in the canteen stared; then they joined in. Even the clerk and the women attendants laughed. And in this moment of horrible embarrassment I could see that Suzy was bent over with merriment.

"Lena, please!" I protested. She lowered her voice but continued to cling to my hands. "This isn't the place!"

"What do I care about the place?" She rolled her eyes roguishly. "We know what we know, and that's all that counts!"

There was nothing to do but wait it out. I died a thousand deaths standing there listening to Lena's hoarse whispering. "You didn't answer my letter.... Did you like my letter?... You look better when you're shaved.... Write me a letter tonight, Precious...." She kept it up until the two attendants became sorry for me and pushed her over to the counter. There she made a few purchases, but ran back to ask if I had a pack of cigarettes for her. I bought the cigarettes, the attendants pushed—bumped is a better word—her to the door, and she was gone, blowing kisses with one hand and slapping at one of the attendants with the other.

"Rape of the Sabines was never like this!" bellowed Len.

"Oh, Yack! Oh, Yack!" gasped Suzy.

"A fine pair you are! Neither of you lifted a hand to protect innocent manhood!"

"Your face, Yack; it was wonderful!"

"'You look better when you're shaved!' Dear God, no wonder I can't leave this place!" Len squeezed his stomach. "My belly actually hurts from laughing. Tell me, Gorgeous, have you ever tried a poodle cut?"

"Listen, boys and girls, the party's over." But I had to laugh, too, and we kept it up until even Len tired of it or became worried about his belly. By then it was time to go back. I walked with Suzy as far as her building. "This has been a wonderful afternoon," she said, "even if you have been the goat. The hill tomorrow? Lena can't go there."

"Utopia! The hill by all means."

"Will you tell me about your travels?"

"Why, I haven't traveled much. Never been out of this country, in fact, except to Canada and Mexico."

"But you lived a long time in New York. You could tell me about New York. I always wanted to go there. Did you like it?"

"More than any place in the world, but, of course, I haven't seen much of the world. It gets you, though, Suzy, after you have been there awhile. Not when you're just spending a few weeks. Then you think it's a cruel, lonely place. But after you get to know it...."

"You *will* tell me?"

"Of course."

Would I? Go over it all again—the good times and the bad times? Back to the past once more? Live for the present and the future, the books warned. But couldn't I go back now, bringing the wonder of it and the loveliness of it to someone who had always wanted it and could never have it?

I thought I could now. I knew I could. "Of course," I said, meaning it. And walking on alone to Receiving, I thought: Suzy is right; it *has* been a wonderful day, and perhaps I am not the goat after all.

the
SEVENTEENTH
day

The November spring did not last long. When I woke, snow was piled on the windowsill, the smaller pine trees were bowing under its weight, and it was still falling in lazy, cottony flakes. Suzy will be happy, I thought, for the hillside was draped in a sheer counterpane of white.

At breakfast Jacob, who had taken Len's place, bemoaned the fact that walking down town would be difficult. "I simply have to go," he said, "because I'm out of bread and syrup." Throughout the meal he whined about the hospital food, and he kept it up while we were sweeping. I hurried to Bath, expecting to help Bates, but Goodman also was working, so I was excused.

"Red took off last night," Bates announced. "He and another guy tied sheets together and slid down them. It must have been tough getting to a main highway because it was snowing two hours before they took off. Both of 'em were wearing only sweaters."

I hurried to the Day Room to tell the news to Len, but he had heard about it. "Damned fool! It'll go hard with him when they catch him this time." Larry was distressed; he scribbled on his pad: "He'll head for home. He always does."

I thought about Red most of the morning. What drives him to do these things? Does he want attention, too? Is it that he simply adopts a different means of getting it?

Did The Financier want attention? No, he wanted new clothes. And yet, all that talk about gangsters and going to the police for protection. Wasn't that an effort to gain attention? I gave it up; I told myself that it was none of my affair, but I wished that I knew more of the strange urges that are in all of us.

By noon the snowstorm had abated. Miss Brown was dubious about permitting any of us to go to the canteen, but she gave in finally and stood over us while we pulled on rubbers and donned extra sweaters. The tractor-plow had been through, and there was a wide path leading to the canteen. I left the group after a few steps and waded through the snow to the hill. Len raised his eyebrows but said nothing.

There were deep footprints leading up the hill, and Suzy was waiting at the top. She had swept the snow from a fallen tree and was sitting on it, looking far away. For a moment it seemed that she did not recognize me; then she smiled and patted a cleared space beside her.

"Isn't it beautiful? You see what I mean now?"

"I know it's beautiful, but do you have to go into a trance?"

She laughed. "Did I really look that way? I was dreaming that I had a sled and was going to bellyflop on it and slide down the hill."

"You're still a little girl. My bellyflop days are over, I'm afraid. We coasted all winter long when I was a kid on The Farm. We even coasted at night, in the moonlight on Howe's hill, with the dogs racing down hill with us, barking and scooping up snow with their muzzles. When we were tired, we went to someone's house and had apples and doughnuts and played Post Office."

"Post Office! I remember that, too. But I always got our Sunday School teacher. One letter for Suzy! He kissed too hard and his lips were wet."

We sat for a little, watching the trudging figures below us. I don't believe that we thought of much of anything, and we might have sat in silence for a long time but for a sneeze behind us. I turned around, and there was Jacob, half-hidden behind a pine tree. He was holding a can of syrup and a loaf of bread, and the syrup had smeared his chin.

"I wasn't spying, really I wasn't!" I thought this would be a good place to come to have my snack, but I'll go right away."

"Suzy, this is Jacob. He and I do the sweeping on D-3. He's an excellent sweeper."

"Oh, nothing special, really!" But he was pleased. He shifted from one foot to the other, then hastened down the other side of the hill.

Suzy said, "No one else ever came up here before."

"Don't worry, he'll never come back. He hates women."

"Did you ever hate a woman?"

"Only one. She poisoned my first dog. Or so I thought she did. I have never ceased to hate her."

Suzy said shyly, "I wrote the poem about the hill this morning. I looked out the window and it seemed to come easy then."

"I'd like to hear it."

She took a crumpled piece of ruled state paper from her pocket. She read slowly:

> *White is the hillside,*
> *Covered with snow.*
> *Clear are the footprints,*
> *Where we must go.*

"That's nice. I like that."

"It's not too vague?"

"Well, the footprints leading up the hill, and we like the hill...."

"Oh, I didn't mean that! It's kind of symbolic." She rushed on eagerly. "When I looked out the window there were no footprints, but in my mind I saw them, one set leading up the hill and one leading down. Don't you see? Mine go up the hill because I am staying here, and yours go down and away because some day that is what you will do. You see now?"

"Yes, but I don't feel elated about it."

"But it is very true! The footprints *are* clear. We know which way we must go, and we must not try to fool ourselves. That would upset everything you have learned here."

Her eyes met mine and did not waver. "Thank you, Suzy," I said. "Thank you, dear."

Only then did she look away, but she said briskly, "Now tell me about New York. You promised."

Yes, better get on to New York. But where to begin? How to describe it? Well, why try to describe it? Better story-tellers than I had tried and failed.... Tell about the little things, and perhaps through them the city will come alive.

"When we arrived in New York with two babies we had eighty-five dollars. We went to stay with my sister-in-law, who had a two-room apartment in Greenwich Village. Rather, my sister-in-law gave the apartment to us, and she moved in with a friend. There was a divan in the living room, which was both kitchen and dining room. We had to pin Jackie, the younger one, to the mattress, but somehow she managed each night to crawl, dragging the mattress, to the stove. She put her head under it and went back to sleep, and each morning we found her that way, her head under the stove and her bottom and the mattress sticking up in the air....

"The first day we took a ride on the Hoboken ferry. When we reached the upper deck, Jackie broke away from her mother and waddled to the rail. Both of us flung ourselves at her, but it was too late...."

"Oh, no!"

"Not what you think. She couldn't have gone overboard, but she could see overboard, and all that water rushing by the bow was too much for her. There, on deck with scores of passengers looking on, she solemnly but whole-heartedly wet her pants!"

"Yack, how cute!"

"We didn't feel that exactly, but we weren't bothered by it. She stayed wet while we stared at the skyline and got goose pimples because it was so big and beautiful. And we glimpsed the Statue of Liberty rising out of a haze, and passed close to the Mauritania slipping out to sea with flags flying and people waving from her decks. Years later I followed her one night in a police boat; all her portholes were closed and covered; there were no flags; there were no happy-go-lucky vacationers. She was stealing out to sea that night to go back to England which had just declared war on Hitler....

"It was fearfully hot and humid in New York that summer. It is every summer, no matter what the New Yorkers say.

[*135*]

We used some of our precious dollars to buy an electric fan, and I took to sleeping on the living room floor, which was cooler. One night we left the fan on. A breeze came up and blew a curtain into the fan, which short-circuited the motor and set the curtain ablaze. I woke to find the soles of my feet scorched. I aroused my wife, got the children out into the hallway, and then returned to pull on my trousers. Always the gentleman! In the meantime my less modest wife had picked up my mattress—how she did it I'll never understand—and heaved it out to the sidewalk....

"In a few minutes a fire truck arrived. And the firemen had a wonderful time breaking windows and squirting chemicals on the walls. When it was all over, Mary Alan, the older one, clapped her hands and pleaded, "More fire, Daddy; more fire!"

"It took me three months to land a newspaper job. The papers weren't taking on new men. Everyone was keeping cool with Coolidge, which meant everyone was hanging on to his job and to hell with the other guy. My wife got a job making puppets; she was paid twenty-five dollars a week, and we lived on that for three months. Three months and two weeks, to be exact, for when I drew my first week's salary it and my wallet were taken by a pickpocket while I was riding home on the subway. We were crushed, but my wife went out to an Italian bootlegger and bought a bottle of gin. My sister-in-law came over, and all three of us had cocktails, stepping carefully over the babies when we went into the kitchen. My sister-in-law, who had studied voice, stood at the open window and sang 'Ave Maria': she sang it beautifully, too. She wasn't being funny about it; she simply wanted to sing it. And the Italian children and their papas and mammas out in the street trying to escape the heat stopped their screaming and chattering as though a giant wave had engulfed them, and they listened until she was done, and some came over and thanked her. We forgot all about the stolen salary and the wallet....

"Each Sunday we spent the day with a couple we had known in Michigan. They had a big, cool basement apartment on Twelfth Street, off Fifth Avenue, and it had a yard and grass in back. The babies played out there, or napped, and we grown-ups talked; we talked about everything under the sun and some things above it. We talked until we were hoarse, and if there had been television then, we would have scorned it.

"When the streets were beginning to cool, we walked farther down in the Village to Johnny Monte's, where we had delicious Martinis and squab en casserole. We always were guests during that period; it was understood, without a word being spoken, that eventually we would be hosts....

"Some Sundays all six of us would go for a ride on the Staten Island ferry and then ride home up Broadway on an open trolley car. One sweltering Sunday while we were racketing up Broadway a sudden rainstorm struck. The rain pelted down, cooling the burning pavements and skyscrapers and drenching everyone on the trolley car before the curtains could be pulled. But no one cared, and in the streets men took off their straw hats and tossed them high in the air, and some of the people danced in the middle of the street because it was cool and they could breathe again....

"When I finally landed a job we moved into an apartment in what had been an armory. It was like a fortress. The steps were of cement and wound around and around between each floor. The hallways were gas-lit, but there was electricity in the apartments. A middle-aged couple across the hall from us

[*137*]

were drug addicts; they wandered along the hall and up and down the stairs and were ghostly in the gaslight. They turned on their own gas one night, and the people who next took the apartment were tap dancers, and they were going day and night. But they threw their garbage out the window into Christopher Street because they didn't want to walk down three flights of stairs....

"And I'm slightly worn out, too, Suzy. But it has been fun, telling you about the early days. It never was fun before— because I wouldn't let it be, I guess."

"I could listen all day, Yack, to such nice, warm memories!"

"But I couldn't talk all day, even though I'd rather talk than eat."

"Some other time you'll tell me more."

No reluctance now. "Of course. And Suzy...."

"Hm?"

"Could I have the little poem?"

Her face became radiant. "You really want it?" She dug into her pocket and her impish smile appeared. "If you hadn't wanted it, I'd have been miserable. Because I wrote it for you."

the
EIGHTEENTH
day

The doctor borrowed a cigarette. He provided the fire and we smoked in silence. "Well," he said finally, "what's the viewpoint now?"

"Fine. Maybe it's time for me to leave?"

He thought awhile. "No, I wouldn't say that. You can walk out, of course, whenever you feel like it, but you said you'd wait until we gave you the okay."

"I'll wait. But I *would* like to be out before Christmas."

"Why?"

"Well...."

"What I thought. You don't know why. Christmas is all mixed up with sentiment—in your case. Where would you spend it?"

"I thought of taking a little place in town. I want to do some writing...."

"And you'd sit in your little place Christmas Eve and Christmas Day, with no turkey and no family, and you'd be happy? The hell you would!"

"You think I'd be happy sitting in this God-damned Day Room on Christmas Day?"

"Yes," he said, "I think you could be happy in the Day Room on Christmas. Or New Year's, or the Fourth of July— if you'd let yourself be happy. Jack, I've given you some books to read, and I've talked a bit with you, and you've come up with some conclusions that are good. But you'll have to work at it all the time; if you let down your guard you're in for it again. You'll probably have to work at it the rest of your life, but you should have a pretty sound platform before you leave here. And it isn't sound if you want to get out just because Christmas is coming."

"I can see your point. But Christmas always meant a lot to me."

He smiled a nice smile to soften his words. "Too much, perhaps! We don't want that foot to start hurting again."

"You win!"

"No, you'll win—if you stay. Think it over." He walked on with Miss Brown, and I vaguely overheard him arguing with Len about something. Think it over, he said. All right, I'll think it over. He'll be sorry.

But it didn't run out that way. I thought of the past Christmases when the children were no more than babies, yet still got us up at four in the morning. I thought of them in their bathrobes, their eyes popping when we turned on the Christmas tree lights, their hands shaking as they fumbled through their presents. I thought of their mother, pink-cheeked and pretty even at four A.M., bending over them and laughing softly over their *oh*'s and *ah*'s.

I thought of Christmas when they were older, and I spent most of the night in the basement trying to put together their first bicycles. And how their mother came down at intervals with a highball and a patient look. And how, when the blasted things finally were in working order, the two of us had a private—and late—Christmas Eve party in front of the tree and laughed and joked and dreamed aloud of our daughters' futures.

But why wasn't I all choked up inside? Why was I smiling to myself over the memories? Because they were good memories—nice, warm memories, Suzy had said—and now I could view them as such. Would I have that view if I left the hospital and spent Christmas in a flat or a little house? Had I learned enough to risk that? Something inside me said no; something told me that I was still in kindergarten, and that graduation was far away. I knew then that Christmas would find me in the Day Room. That damned doctor, wasn't he ever wrong?

Len flopped into a chair next to me; his face was beety red and he was biting hard on a cigar, which he rarely smoked.

"Well, little Sunshine?" I said.

"Christ!" He pulled out the cigar and hurled it across the room. Teddy, always lurking near him, retrieved it instantly, and circled the room looking for fire. "I told Doc I want to go up to the cottage and bach it, and he sat hard on me and said I ought to stay here until I hear from my family. He knows he's got me; I can't leave until that wife of mine sends some money."

"He sat on me, too. I wanted out for Christmas, but he was against it. Guess he's right again."

"By God, I won't be here Christmas! I'll walk out without a dime if I have to!"

"I could let you have some money if the doctor would okay an order."

Len relaxed. "Say, that's damned decent, but I wouldn't

[*141*]

take it. Matter of principle. Wife's got to come through. After all, it's my dough. I wouldn't need much up at the cottage; just enough for beans and tobacco...."

"And a bottle?"

He grinned. "Sure I'd have a bottle. Used to have 'em hidden all over the damned place—in rotted stumps, out in the woods, even in the lake. That's the hell of it; if my wife didn't scream bloody murder every time I took a drink, maybe I wouldn't drink so much."

I had heard that story many times. "There's a reason for your drinking, Len. Why don't you let the doctor try to find it for you?"

"To hell with that!"

"Maybe it goes back to the time your wife tied up your money."

"No, I drank before that. I've been a drinking man most of my life. It got worse, though, after I sold my canning plant and decided to be a retired guy. Not enough to do, I guess. I really like to tie 'em on."

We walked to the canteen, with Teddy dancing alongside, boasting that now he could write his name. "That Larry's a swell guy," he said. "He knows a lot, too. Say didja notice he's beginning to talk?"

Len said, "He always gets better fast. Can't wait to get home to his wife. All the good it does him."

"If I had a wife I'd beat the hell out of her it she tried to boss me," Teddy said, prancing.

"Aw, dry up!" Len said. Then he softened. "Don't mind me, kid; here's a dime to blow."

The center of attention in the canteen was Jeanne, whom

I had noticed before and about whom I had heard many stories. She was only about four feet in height, was in her late thirties, yet appeared, even close up, to be only a child.

Her eyes sparkled as she showed some of the Christmas presents she had bought. "The stores are decorated already," she said happily. It's really wonderful down town; I'm going down every day until Christmas, even if I can't buy anything more."

Lil sniffed. "Home's better on Christmas."

Jeanne eyed her coldly. "You know damned well I haven't got a home. What you going to have this time, Lil? Boy or girl?"

"You can't tell ahead of time," said Lil, laughing. She could not be insulted. "Maybe twins, who knows?"

Teddy stood like a statue, watching Jeanne; he could not take his eyes from her, even to spend his dime. "Golly," he whispered to Len, "I'd sure like to know her. She's so little. Golly, she's cute!"

Len introduced them; then he introduced me. But Teddy, seizing Jeanne by an arm, hurried her to the counter. "What you want?" he demanded. "I've got a dime!"

She laughed up at him. "My treat! I've got some Christmas money left."

Teddy shifted from foot to foot while she ordered hot dogs and coffee. He could hardly eat, he was so entranced. Other patients in the canteen began to giggle.

"Kid's got it bad," said Len. He gave me a glance. "Seems to be a month for romances around here."

A group of C-3 women entered and I ducked behind the Coke machine. But Lena was not among them. I stayed behind the machine, however, looking out the window hoping to see Suzy. She came shortly, along the path from Eleven; she walked slowly, kicking at the snow. When she saw me at the window, she beckoned.

I joined her outside. "I don't want to go in there," she said abruptly.

"Why? Everyone's having a good time. Teddy's fallen for Jeanne."

"It's too noisy in there. I want to get some air."

"Up the hill?"

She said, almost crossly, "I don't want to go up the hill today."

"What's wrong, Suzy? Have I done something?"

"Oh, leave me alone!" She began to cry. "I'm going back," she said, and ran along the path to Eleven. I stared after her.

Lil, coming out, chuckled. She rarely missed anything in or around the canteen. "Suzy got another tantrum?"

"I don't know," I said, still staring.

the
NINETEENTH
day

The night was long and laced with bad dreams—when I slept. I dreamed of people I had not thought about in years, and in each dream the person involved was trying to kill himself. Each time a nightmare awakened me I began to worry about Suzy. I worried about money. I worried about the state of the world. When the brain tired, I went back to sleep, and the bad dreams began all over again.

At 5:30 in the morning a new attendant turned on the lights and shouted, "Up, you bums!" He pushed open my door and glared at me—or at any rate I thought he glared.

"Get out of here, you lousy bastard!" The venom in my voice startled me, but I couldn't stop. "You have to scare the pants off a guy? You stinker, you!…" I burst into tears.

He started for me, his face going all red, but when I began to weep he stopped, and a look of contempt replaced the flush. "Oh, one of those!" he said, and wheeled and walked out, slamming the door.

I got up and dressed slowly. I kept saying to myself: What the hell is this all about? Somewhere, deep in me, I knew, but

I wouldn't let it come to the surface. Instead, I let myself do whatever impulse led me to do.

At the urinals, when Franklin came fawning and mewing, I told him to go screw himself, and he slunk away. "All you need is a tail between your legs!" I called after him. Boy Blue, patting himself with a few drops of water, looked up in admiration. "Say now, he does, doesn't he?"

"Why don't you wash your face?" I said. "Really wash it? Wash all over. You stink!"

He thought it over and nodded. "Guess I do," he said complacently and wiped his dirty hands on a dirty towel.

The Brat came out of the first toilet. "My, what a temper!" he simpered. I slapped him in the face, and he ran, blubbering, out to the Day Room.

The other men, pausing in their morning chores, looked curiously at me, but no one interfered. Larry, shuffling anxiously away, accidentally knocked a tube of toothpaste from my hand. I turned on him, but something held me back. Not that little June bug, I thought, and the thought calmed me. I washed quickly and went back to my room.

I was sitting there, smoking, which was against the rules, when Len poked his head in. "Thanks, pal. The Brat's really taken it to heart. Just sitting in a corner and stroking his face."

"I don't want to talk about it."

"It's that way, is it? Okay. Everyone goes stir crazy now and then."

"I'm not stir crazy. I'm...." Again the tears; they came unexpectedly—a flash flood of emotion.

"I'll scram," Len said softly.

Teddy was the last straw. He burst in as though it was his room; his boyish face was aglow from his morning scrub. "Say would you write a letter to Jeanne for me? I wanta tell her we oughta get engaged." His eyes widened when he noticed my wet face. "Oh, you sick or somethin'?"

"Get out! Get out!"

"Yeah, yeah. You wanta doctor or somethin'?"

"Get out, God damn it!"

He scuttled from the room. The breakfast bell rang, but I didn't move. I sat there waiting for the new attendant to come. I heard him shooing Franklin and Johnny along the hall; then he came back.

"You going to eat?"

"When I get good and ready!"

"That's okay with me."

"Your breakfasts stink, anyway!" After all my arguments with Jacob about how good the meals were.

"I guess they do," he said mildly. He had control of himself and wanted to skip the earlier scene, but I wouldn't let him.

"The whole God-damned hospital stinks! And the attendants. I don't like to be called a bum," I said righteously.

"I don't like to be called a lousy bastard."

My voice was tender-sweet. "Well, aren't you?"

"Listen," he said, still calm, "I can't beat you up, but I'd like to. It's against the rules to beat up guys like you. But I can twist your arm behind your back or I can get a nice choke hold on you, and you won't be calling me a lousy bastard. But I ain't going to do that. You know what I'm going to do? I'm going to lock you in until breakfast's over, and you can have another nice cry, babykins!"

I made a rush for him, which was what I figured he wanted. He slipped out and locked the door. "And don't break up the furniture or there'll be hell to pay!" he called.

He was back in ten minutes. "I'm unlocking the door.

[*147*]

Guess I got a little sore." He smiled as a mother smiles at a naughty child who has been punished. The smile said: Now let's forget all about it and be good.

"Sore isn't the word for it," I said, "You're a stinker!"

"Seems to me you're a stinker yourself this morning. But some of the guys told me you're all right. Just off the beam today, huh?"

"Listen," I said, "I know what this is all about. You're afraid I'm going to squeal on you. Well, I'm no squealer."

"Oh, sure. I figured you wouldn't be doing that." Relief was all over his face.

"But I don't like you a damned bit. All right, I started it, but I still don't like you a damned bit."

"That's okay. That's fine. We don't have to be pals, but we don't have to hole no grudges, now do we?"

"Skip it. And you skip, too. Then we'll both be happy."

"That's it. That's the way to talk." He went out, giving me a wet-mouth smirk.

I felt a small glow, a glow of victory. Victory over that lout? But there it was, and it was enough to jerk me back, so that in a few minutes I was disgusted with myself for feeling that I had won anything. He was a lout, one of the few among the fine attendants I had come to know, but what had I been? And why?

After that it was fairly easy to bring it out into the open. Suzy had been cross; Suzy had walked away from me without any explanation. And the little boy of five hadn't liked that; he had sulked, he had had bad dreams, he had wept, he had struck out blindly, not caring whom he hurt. Because he was hurt and he wanted to hurt others; then he would get attention and perhaps his hurt would go.

It was a relief to admit it, but with the relief was the despairing thought: It isn't licked yet. I thought I had come a long way, but I haven't.

The doctor did not come to D-3. He was in Detroit attending a convention, Miss Brown said. I decided not to say anything to him about the nightmares and the scenes. I had figured them out for myself, and that was what he wanted. The doctor, I said to myself, shouldn't be used as a crutch.

Miss Brown was curious; so was Bates. Somehow they had heard, but not, I knew, from the new attendant. They said nothing, yet I noticed that when they were not too busy their eyes followed me. Or was that my imagination? Was I still wanting attention? I asked Bates about the new attendant, and he said the man was a farmer who worked only part time at the hospital.

"I don't like him," I said.

"I can understand that. Some people don't take to this work; they just want the extra money. Had trouble with him?"

"No," I lied.

"He's here only now and then. I wouldn't let him bother me."

The office phone rang. When Bates hung up he said, "Well, what do you know! Lloyd's wife come to see him. She's got the okay to take him down town."

That was big news. Anything like that, anything outside of routine, was big news on D-3. I was like a child who had been told that Auntie's coming for a visit! I hurried into the Day Room and informed Len.

"We got to see her," Len said. "I can't sleep nights unless I see her."

"They'll show her into the Visitor's Room. We can't barge in there and just stare at her."

"You'd be surprised what I can do!"

Without shame we followed Lloyd down the hall when Bates summoned him. Company manners were forgotten, and I was glad to forget them. I wanted to look through a peek-hole at someone else. I was tired of peeking at myself.

Len swerved into the Utility Room and got Jacob's sweeping brush from a locker. "Take a broom," he told me, "and for God's sake look as though you know how to use it."

"I've learned the hard way, which is more than you can say, you polishing plutocrat!"

He looked over his glasses in mock admiration. "Nice phrase! Feeling better, eh?"

"Yes."

"Well, grab that broom and let's get going."

We strode, businesslike, down the hall. Bates, coming back from the Visitors' Room, eyed us but said nothing. Miss Brown was busy in the Treatment Room and did not see us. Len pushed open the door to the Visitor's Room.

"The trouble with this hospital," he said loudly, is that they want to work you all the time. Sweep, mop, polish, dust…. Oh, I beg your pardon! Why, hello, Lloyd!"

"Gee," said Lloyd, "you sweeping this time of day?"

"Orders," said Len. "But we don't want to disturb you."

"Oh, you ain't disturbing us. We're going down town."

Len said, "That's nice. I bet your sister will like Traverse City. It's a nice little town."

Lloyd's jaw dropped. "Sister? She ain't my sister. She's my wife." He did not introduce us; he stood there grinning.

We bowed as though we had been introduced, and then we stared. Years ago I had stared, as I was staring now, at a woman about the age of Lloyd's wife. That woman was sitting in the witness chair in a Long Island City, New York, courtroom. Her name was Ruth Brown Snyder, and eventually she went to the electric chair with her lover, Judd Gray, a little corset salesman, for the murder of her husband. I think that every man in the courtroom had his secret thoughts about Ruth Brown Snyder. She was not beautiful; she was not even pretty, and she had a dumpy figure. Her ankles were thick and her hair was stringy, yet she had something that made men think things. She had something that dragged shy Judd Gray from his suburban complacency, from his wife and small daughter, into the death house Sing Sing.

Lloyd's wife had the same something. There were thin streaks of dirt on her neck and her hair needed shampooing. Her nose was shiny; there were food stains on her shabby dress; her stockings were wrinkled at the ankles. Yet Len and I, standing there staring, were instantly aware of the woman in her. There, I thought when I began to think, is a female who believes she was put on earth for one purpose. And perhaps she was.

She did not speak to us; she merely smiled, but her smile said: Yes, gentlemen, I know, but we can't do anything about it.

"We'll leave you alone," Len said lamely and walked out.

"Yes," I said, "we'll leave you alone." And I followed him.

Halfway back to the Utility Room he stopped and leaned on Jacob's brush. "Whew!" he said.

"That's mild for you."

"I don't feel like cussing. I'm pausing to pay tribute."

"To her?"

"To Lloyd. Just think of living with that woman, going to bed with her every night…."

"I'm trying not to think of it."

"And only now does he wind up in the nut house. My God, we did him an injustice! What a man!"

I said, "Stir crazy or sex crazy, you'd better calm down. You'll have a stroke."

"You're one to talk! You were raping her with your eyes."

"Yes, and I have bi-focals!"

We sat in the Utility Room on upturned mop buckets and got bawdier and bawdier. Curly left the window to protest, "Say, you fellows shouldn't talk that way. Say, a lady's a lady. A lady's a lady in any language."

"A lady's a lay in any language!" Len bellowed.

We had a wonderful time.

the
TWENTIETH
day

More snow—so much that several of the faithful church-go-ers, peering out the windows and shivering, decided to re-main in the Day Room. On impulse I gave my name to Miss Brown.

"You're going to church?" She smiled. "Well now, that's a good idea. But—"

"I know. I'll wear my rubbers."

"You should wear a hat, too, what with all this snow."

"I haven't a hat and I haven't worn one in years, summer or winter."

"We could give you a state hat."

"Please, Miss Brown!"

"Well, if you catch another cold, don't blame me." She shook her head over me. Miss Brown always bundled up when she went out, and so did Miss Love. I had to admit that they rarely came down with colds.

Bates took us over to the auditorium. We were snowmen before we got there, the flakes were falling so fast. Other lines of men were marching along the paths; the procedure was the same as that for the dances.

It was the same in the auditorium, too, with the men sitting on one side and the women on the other. A side aisle was between them. I took a chair near the aisle. The Financier was next to me. He wore an entirely new outfit, and he even had a silk shirt.

"Glad to see you back," I said formally.

"Many thanks. I had a little business to transact in Detroit." He seemed quite happy.

"They didn't put you back on D-3?"

He coughed. "No, I'm in one of the cottages." He didn't say which one, but I learned later that he had been put with a group of old men who listened gravely while he told them, hour after hour, of his stock market deals.

"How did you get away?" I asked.

"Oh, borrowed some money from a friend down town and took the train." He chuckled. "They never thought of looking for me on the train. I'd still be in Detroit, but those gangsters got after me again and I had to go to the police about 'em."

A man in back of me tapped me on the shoulder. He had a winning smile, and I smiled vaguely in return, although I couldn't recall that I had ever seen him before.

"Good to see you again," he said. "Glad you're feeling better."

"Thank you," I said.

He offered me a package of gum. I opened it to extract one piece, but he said quickly, "Oh, no, take the whole package. Glad you're feeling better."

"He does that all the time," The Financier whispered. "Thinks everyone's been sick except himself. Must spend a dollar a week on gum."

It seemed to be the thing to chew gum during the services. Ralph, at the piano on the stage, was chewing vigorously, and I suspected the choir of men and women patients of also indulging in the vice, for they sang listlessly, and some did not sing at all. They stared into space and had to be nudged when it was time to sit down.

After two hymns The Reverend walked out to the pulpit. He appeared to be tired. It must be a strain, I thought, to preach to these people, many of whom do not even hear him. They must come here from habit, not knowing why—and not caring. But there were others who were enthusiastic. Their *Amens!* Could be heard all over the auditorium; some bowed their heads in their hands throughout the sermon; some wept; some jumped up and down. One woman patient had to be led out by an attendant. She was moaning, "Christ is coming! Our Saviour is coming!"

With Christmas approaching, The Reverend spoke of the Prince of Peace, but there was a note of hopelessness in his voice as he said, "We may never have eternal peace in this world." Then his voice rose and the hopelessness was gone. "But there is no reason why you good people here cannot have peace of mind and soul."

Peace of mind? Here? I thought: What a thing to tell a group of people in a state hospital! They wouldn't be here if they had peace of mind.

But then I thought: You're finding peace of mind, slowly perhaps, but you're finding it, and if you can find it, so can countless others, even those who have to be shocked into it by electros and insulin. Why, I thought, The Reverend isn't just mouthing words; he's giving hope, and he knows more about these people than I'll ever know. Perhaps he knows more about me than I know myself.

"A wise person, The Reverend," said The Financier. He rubbed the sleeve of his new brown topcoat with tender, womanish hands. "Yes, peace of mind, that's it. Did I tell you I brought six silk shirts in Detroit?"

An attendant shushed him. Peace of mind, that's it, I repeated. Some find it through God; some, like The Financier, find it in silk shirts. Well, I cannot turn to God and I do not like silk shirts. Perhaps the way they have outlined for me is the best for me. Finding my own peace of mind and hanging on to it, not letting it go for an instant. Yes, even if I have to pretend at times that there is peace of mind.

When we filed out, I thanked The Reverend for his sermon. I told him a little of what I had thought while he was preaching, and his face lighted up. "That will make my day," he said. "I've been worrying about you. I'm glad, I'm mighty glad, you don't think life is hopeless."

As the others filed by him they bowed or smiled; some shook his hand; others gave him little offerings: strips of paper, a gum wrapper, a penny, a cork from a wine bottle. He thanked them all and put the offerings into a coat pocket.

"I accept everything they give," he said. "I know the spirit behind their giving."

As we came down the auditorium steps, slipping and sliding, I saw Suzy, half hidden behind a tree. A red mitten beckoned. I glanced at Bates; he had seen her, too. He nodded. "But make it fast; we got to get back."

It didn't matter that scores were watching. I stumbled through the snow to the tree, and I felt good inside because Suzy was smiling, although her eyes were anxious.

"Yack, I went to D-3, but they said you were at church. So I came here. Yack, I'm so sorry; I didn't mean to."

"I don't know what you're talking about!"

"Yes, you do. But it's over now. I'm all right now, Yack."

"Good! We'll go up the hill this afternoon?

"Please, yes!"

Bates called…. "I have to run now. One o'clock, Suzy?"

Her eyes no longer were anxious. I pressed one of the red mittens and floundered back to my group.

"Ahem!" said Bates and let it go at that.

In the Day Room, Len wanted to carry on from last night. "You know what? Lloyd told me all about it; smug as hell, he was. They drove out towards Acme yesterday and parked off the road and tossed one off in the car. She wanted some more, but Lloyd wasn't up to it. They came back to town, and he got out and went into a tavern and had two straight ones. She raised hell, so he told her to scram back home and he walked back to the hospital. Maybe the guy's got a little backbone after all."

Lloyd's sex life and his momentarily defiance failed to interest me, despite the hilarity of yesterday. Len sensed how I felt and dropped the subject, but in a few minutes he went over to Lloyd, half dozing in a rocker, and pumped him for more information. Teddy pounced on me; he had writing paper and a pencil.

"Listen," I said, "you hardly know the girl. And, furthermore, she isn't a girl; she's a woman. If you have to send her a letter, we'll make it just a friendly one. You can do your proposing later—in person."

His face fell, but he said, "Maybe you're right."

I took the paper and pencil. "Now tell me what you want written."

He thought it over. "Well, something like this: Dear

Jeanne, How are you? I am fine. Thanks for the hot dog. Can I dance with you Thursday night?"

"That seems to cover it," I said, "and it has the beauty of brevity."

"Then sign it, Yours truly."

"No sooner said than done. Now where's the envelope?"

"Oh I ain't goin' to mail it. I'm goin' to give it to her tomorrow at the canteen!"

Well, I was seventeen once, too.

Miss Brown could not understand why I wanted to go out in the afternoon, and I didn't want to tell her about the hill.

"You're too keen about this fresh air," she chided me. "It'll be your undoing some day."

"More factors than fresh air have entered into my undoing." I meant it as a feeble joke, but Miss Brown looked concerned. "You're not upset—again?"

"Well, the pork roast doesn't sit too well...."

"Oh!" She was relieved. For all the paper work she had to do, the doling of pills and countless other tasks, Miss Brown somehow found time to mother her charges. She had a smile for every patient who appreciated a smile—albeit at times a harried one—and most of us depended on it.

"Well, then, on your way! You're the only one who wants to go out. You must be crazy!"

"What a way for a state hospital nurse to talk!"

She blushed and laughed. "Get!"

Perhaps she isn't far wrong, I thought, as I struggled up the hill. Only a balmy person would come out in this snow. It got into my shoes; it made a white crown on my head and, when I slipped and fell, it poured eagerly up my coat sleeves. My glassed came off and I had to dig to find them. But I got to the top of the hill and walked in a circle, making a path and trying to keep warm.

The juniper bushes were bowed under the weight of the snow, and they brought back the winters on The Farm when I dug a tunnel under our juniper bushes, covered the scraped earth with straw from the barn, and crawled in with my favorite Airedale, Peggy. We spent hours there, sometimes napping with an old horse blanket over us, sometimes nibbling on cookies or pie wrested from a mother who couldn't say no. On the coldest days I had a kerosene lantern for warmth, although Peggy was a little pot-bellied stove all by herself. When we weren't sleeping or eating, we dreamed with our eyes open. All the dreams a boy has—of being a policeman, a fireman, an engineer. But most pronounced was the dream of some day going to sea. I must have inherited the love of it from my grandfather. It was a game that Peggy and I often played, Going to Sea. Of course I was the captain and I stood outside the snowy tunnel and issued orders to Peggy, the crew. She seemed, in her tolerant, loving way, to understand what it was all about.

I wondered, standing on the hill, if perhaps I should have made Going to Sea more than a game. If I had turned to the sea when I was young and breathed deeply of salt air instead of printer's ink, would I be here now?

Wonder, little boy; wonder all you wish. But do not dream, for your dream days are over.

I wouldn't have admitted that a few weeks ago. A little more progress, I said to myself, but in a small voice.

I waited until two o'clock, but Suzy did not appear.

the
T W E N T Y - F I R S T
day

The sputtering snow tractor awakened me at five A.M. It had toiled all day Sunday clearing paths; that it was back at work so early indicated more snow during the night. I stood at the open window watching it gouge another path from Center to Receiving, until it occurred to me that Miss Brown wouldn't like that…. And I had developed the sniffles.

The Day Room was still locked. I walked the hall looking for the night attendant and fire, but he wasn't on the floor. Teddy darted from his room. "You lookin' for fire? I got some matches!" He acted like a Parisian vendor of dirty postcards.

I accepted a match, but said morally, "You shouldn't take a chance with those. If they find out you've got matches, they'll crack down on us. Might even ban smoking except at certain hours."

Then I became a co-conspirator and shooed Teddy near the toilets so that we could toss away our cigarettes if the attendant suddenly appeared. Having been off the floor, he would know if he caught us smoking that one of us had matches. Despite our precautions he walked in on us.

He was the attendant who had routed me out the first morning, and I hadn't seen him since; they seemed to switch the night attendants like freight cars.

But he joined the conspiracy. "You guys want some fire?" he asked, straight-faced. As straight-faced I took some fire from him for my already burning cigarette. "But five up the matches," he said. "I can't go too far."

To my surprise, Teddy handed them over without protest. The attendant pocketed them and didn't scold. He unlocked the Day Room and we went around closing the windows. Even I shivered.

"It's about ten below," the attendant said.

Teddy and I huddled near a wall radiator. He seemed nervous and I asked what was wrong.

"Well, I done somethin' you won't like, maybe."

"Such as?"

"Well, I got to thinkin' that letter wasn't so hot. So I asked Len to write another, and he wrote a dilly!"

"I bet!"

"Here, you can read it." He thrust a sheet of ruled paper at me. I read:

Darling—Now is the time for all good men to come to the aid of the party. Now is the time ....

It went on and on that way. I handed it back. "A work of art," I said. "Really impassioned!"

"Yeah, that's what I thought. Len read it to me a coupla times. Bet she'll be surprised."

"True, very true!"

When I saw Len after breakfast, I said, "What's the idea of pulling a fast one on the kid?"

He grinned. "Showed it to you, did he? Hell, we can't let him send out the guff he wants to. She'd laugh at him."

"Think she won't laugh at this masterpiece?"

"She won't get it. Teddy wants me to deliver it, so I'm just going to tell her the state the kid's in. She'll understand; she'll pretend she got the letter and let him down easy. Boy, you should've heard me rattle off the stuff I pretended to write. Didn't know I was such a hot lover. Teddy ate it up. What the hell, it makes him happy."

It seemed the best way out at that.

"Of course," said Len, "if you want to hire me to write *your* love letters, I'll have to be on the up and up. Teddy can't read, but I presume you can?"

"Just Mother Goose stuff. But it wouldn't hurt you to read some of the books the doctor gave me."

"You keep on with those books and you'll be analyzing all of us. Say, maybe they'll give you a job here. Doc could use some help."

He'll always make a joke of it, I thought. They'll never get him to try it—any more than I can ever get him to vote Democratic.

It was time for the cleaning squads to go to work. As Jacob and I pushed our brooms down the hall, the door to the neutral space was unlocked and Goodman came in. He saw me and grinned. "Attendant on C-3 gave me this for you," he said, handing me a folded piece of paper. I knew immediately. Lena! The note read:

Precious Darling: Please come for me in a chariot driven by snow white Steeds. Lena

"I've only got a Chevrolet!" I murmured.

"What's that?" asked Jacob.

"Nothing." Why explain to Jacob, the woman hater? But wait until Len sees the note. Should I show it to him? Let him laugh at Lena whom I wanted to avoid but said I was sorry for? I put the note in my shirt pocket. I'd get rid of it later.

My gesture of gallantry was that and no more. Halfway back to the hall, Len met us with the polisher. "How you like my chariot?" he said, going into a Ben Hur attitude. Of course someone had read the note before it reached me. Goodman! I looked accusingly at him, but he said solemnly, "I don't know what's got into Len this morning!"

"Apes!" I said, and we all fell to laughing.

"I don't see," whined Jacob, "what there is to laugh at on cleaning day!"

Shortly before noonday dinner I had a caller. I was hesitant to go down the hall, fearing that Lena somehow had squeezed in again, but the caller was Eloise who, The Reverend had said, wanted to see me.

We stared at each other, for many years had passed since I had left The Farm, and she had been no more than a baby then.

"Well!" she said finally.

"Am I as much of a shock as that?"

We laughed, and then we began talking as people talk who have not met for years. She told me about her sisters, Ina and Isabel, with both of whom I had been madly in love—at the same time—when I was no more that fourteen. I told her about my sisters. And then we started on: What ever happened to so-and-so? Do you remember when... ?

Willie, passing by on his way to the drinking fountain, smiled at us. "Nice to have your wife visit you, ain't it?" he said.

I smiled back and nodded. "No point in explaining," I said to Eloise. "It would take hours."

She said, "Well, now that I'm Mrs. Kerkhoff you can tell me about yourself."

I told a little of it; she was interested and sympathetic. "I'm sure they'll help you here. We have fine doctors and nurses. It's a wonderful place, really, but it still scares me."

"Scares you?"

"Yes. Even though I work in the business office and see a lot of the wards, I'm scared every time I leave my own desk."

"There's nothing to frighten you up here. We're all calm and peaceful on D-3…. Well, most of us are."

But I could see that she was nervous, and when she left I walked down the hall with her, shooing Boy Blue and The Brat away when they came too close. Eloise let herself into the neutral space with her own key; she said that she would come up again before Christmas.

"My husband and I are going to Indianapolis to spend the holidays with Ina and Isabel," she said. "Providing we aren't snowed in."

"Tell them I'm still in love with them. Has Ina still got her freckles? Are Isabel's eyes still beautiful?"

"Yes—to both questions. But you've changed. You were always gay and romping around, as I remember it."

"My dear young lady, I was no more than fourteen at the time! One does slow up, you know."

"You were thin and you didn't wear glasses and you didn't have a moustache."

[*164*]

She was so earnest about it, I said, "The next time you call I'll shave off the moustache and throw away the glasses. And I'll go on a diet today."

"Mother always liked you," she said, still serious.

"I liked her, too. She told me some wonderful stories. Funny ones, mostly. And your father made my first pair of skis; they were made of barrel staves and I damned near killed myself on them."

"It doesn't seem right."

"What?"

"Your being here. But if anyone can help, they can here. Well, goodbye."

People *can* be good, I thought, going back to the Day Room. Eloise didn't have to come up here to see me, but she wanted to make the gesture despite all the years that had gone by. How many years? Oh, Lord, too many—too many to count.

Suzy was waiting at the top of the hill. She sat sedately on the fallen tree, again brushed clear of snow, her mittened hands folded in her lap. I was so relieved to see her that I wanted to turn a somersault; in a quick flashback I saw myself doing that in front of Ina the day we played in the hayloft. I wondered: Does the male child ever grow up?

I sat on the fallen tree. "I missed you, Suzy."

"I'm all right now," she said, speaking low.

"Want to tell me about it?"

She looked down at the mittens. "There isn't much to tell. I had one of the spells, that's all. I thought it was over Sunday, and that's why I got out to let you know. But when I got back to Eleven it started all over again."

"Tell me more about it—if you want to."

She looked up then; she looked directly at me. "I lose my temper; I kick things. If there's a chair in my way, I don't go around it. I kick it out of the way."

"Lots of people kick chairs. Lots of people kick dogs that are in their way."

"Oh, I wouldn't kick a dog! I love dogs."

"Well, then...."

"But I throw things, too. And sometimes I swear at the attendants, but not often. And something happens to my voice... I talk baby talk."

"I don't think that's so bad. Something's troubling you, probably, and you let yourself go...."

"No. I didn't tell you the other time we talked, but I've heard them discussing me, and they say I was born that way and I'll never be different."

"You're all right now."

"Yes, but it'll come back, maybe tomorrow, maybe in a week, maybe in a month. I never know. Oh, Yack!"

I put my arms around her and held her close. There were snowflakes on the tip of her nose and on her eyelashes; there was a scent about her of the snow and the pine trees. I pressed my lips against her hair, wet from the snow, and she turned her face to me.

the
TWENTY-SECOND
day

The doctor returned from Detroit. He had another cold, and I whispered to Miss Brown, "You should make him wear his rubbers!"

"Doctors are the worst of all," she said primly.

After the doctor made his rounds he called me into the Treatment Room. He said abruptly, "I wrote your wife under Dr. Sheets' name, which is our custom here. I wrote her that you probably had been a problem and that I could understand her reactions. But I wrote that you were developing a new outlook on life and that I thought you'd keep on developing. I wasn't trying to patch things up for you, but I thought she should know."

I said, "I know what's coming. My wife wasn't impressed?"

"She wasn't. I debated whether to show you her letter in answer to mine. I guess you've learned enough to take it."

The letter said that she did not believe I had changed. She wrote that the doctors should not be fooled by my "charm," and that she believed I should be kept in the hospital indefinitely.

"Well?" the doctor asked.

[*167*]

I felt a little sick. "I really don't know. I've been going along with your opinion that both of us will be better off apart. But I resent that letter—and I suppose I shouldn't. Is that the boy of five speaking again?"

"I don't think so. The letter should end it, once and for all."

"It does."

"And I wouldn't be bitter about it."

"I am—for the moment. But that'll go."

"That's the way to talk! You'll have some pangs, of course, perhaps months from now. But what I want you to do is analyze those pangs. Ask yourself: Do I really feel them or do I think that I *should* feel them? You'll come up with the right answer."

On impulse I told him about Suzy. He looked at me over his glasses. "Not getting hot and bothered?"

"Nothing like that!"

"Well, you never know. Don't see anything wrong in it. Maybe you can help each other."

"She's helping me—I know that."

"Yes. You've been surrounded by women since you were an infant. You probably need one now to listen to you, and if you give a little too, that won't hurt you by a long shot. But don't go having dreams. Suzy'll be here for a long time, probably forever. Not much we can do for her—in the way of a cure, I mean."

"What is her trouble, if you don't mind telling me?"

"Hysteria. Form of neurosis. Her condition is called multiple personality. One day fine, normal, logical; the next, an entirely different person. It dates way back, as I recall her case. Hers is a fairly mild form; she has fits of temper mostly. Some patients afflicted with hysteria become paralyzed;

others become half blind; still others live in a sleep-walking world. It's hard to reach them. You might reach Suzy; I don't know."

"I'm going to try!"

"That's okay with me. As I said, maybe you can give each other a boost, but don't become too involved."

"Involved?"

"Well, you'll be leaving after a bit, and she won't."

"She's emphasized that several times."

"If you got too emotional about it, you might have another problem when you leave. Not fair to her, either."

"We have good times together—when she's all right."

"Try to keep it that way." He got up, sighing. "Blasted cold's really got me this time." But he was able to go back to the Day Room and play some boogie-woogie before going up to D-4.

The Flash and Pickerel were moved today to Cottage 34, a work ward. Bates and I took them over, and I was surprised that they were not downcast. Pickerel played the clown all the way over, but The Flash was pleased by his transfer.

"What I need," he said. "They'll put me to shovelin' snow and I'll work it off. No more electros, Doc said. Might even get home for Christmas."

"I'm dreaming of a white Christmas!" sang Pickerel, dancing in the snow. "I'm a German Jew, but I like Christmas!"

"They'll take some of that pep out of him in Thirty-four," said Bates. "Funny thing, when the peppy ones are sent over there and put to work, they seem to snap out of it."

"Maybe that's where I belong."

"You've done more than your share on D-3. Pickerel

didn't do anything to help, and neither did The Flash, but over here they'll work like hell—and probably like it."

Thirty-four was old and dreary compared to D-3, but Pickerel and The Flash took to it immediately. "We been here before," The Flash explained. "We know the ropes."

The Flash shook hands with me and thanked me for the tailor-mades he had borrowed. Pickerel didn't bother to say goodbye; he recognized some of the Thirty-four men and promptly deserted Bates and me for them. I felt that I wouldn't miss Pickerel, but I was sorry to see The Flash go. There was something about him—and he *could* play that banjo.

He had not been permitted to take it with him to Thirty-four; it was returned in a few days to its owner. But when we were back on D-3 I noticed immediately that Willie had appropriated it and was strumming it with the same devastating effects. They took it from him finally, and he went back to his battered guitar. But he had trouble with it; the pieces of rag that held it together were loose.

"It don't feel right," he complained.

The Brat, of all persons, went to the rescue. He spent more than an hour removing the rags and replacing them with surgical tape. He actually appeared to be happy. Willie thanked him and permitted him to strum the guitar for a few minutes. Then Willie put it back of the piano, and they sat together chewing gum and talking as the young and the old often do. I doubted that Willie heard a word The Brat said, but he nodded and smiled.

Bates asked me to help sort the latest supply of laundry. Crispy and two other student nurses were sewing in the Clothes Room.

"I thought you'd eloped," I said. "Where've you been?"

"On C-3," she said drearily. "We had to help out with the womenfolks. But that's over, praise be! We'll be here until after Christmas."

"And then?"

"Then back home. More training. More exams. Then graduation."

"We're going to miss you here."

"Oh, there'll be a new group coming in. I think they're from Saginaw—or Lansing. You won't miss us!"

There was a touch of bitterness in her voice. When Miss Love called the other students and Bates moved into Bath, I said, "What the hell goes on, Crispy?"

"Nothing."

"Come on, give."

"It's really nothing."

"He's found another girl friend?"

Her eyes widened. "You're a mind reader—and I don't like it!"

"No, I'm not, but sometimes I used to outguess my daughters when they said, 'It's really nothing!'"

"He's going to marry her, and they're going to stay over there."

"Honey, that's tough. That's God-awful tough!"

"I'll get over it."

"Of course you will. You've got gumption, Crispy, and you know about things here and—well, you don't want it to build itself up into something too big for you to handle."

"No, doctor!" She looked up with a fleeting smile.

"That's better!"

Bates came back, and Crispy returned to her sewing and

I to the laundry. Poor little Crispy! He must be a stinker. He could have Crispy, but he wants someone else. But who are you to judge? You can't even help her.

I remembered that I couldn't help my daughter in a similar situation. She came out from New York to visit us, and I knew at once that something was wrong. It came out one night: She had been deeply in love with a young lawyer, and he had jilted her for another woman—for his mother, who had ruled him all his life and wanted him to marry the girl next door in Scarsdale.

My daughter sat on my lap and wept it out. What could I do? Say that it didn't matter—that someone else would come along? As my father, meaning well, said when my first dog was poisoned, "We'll get you another." I couldn't think of a thing to say that would make sense, and so I began to ramble on about the day she was born. I told her how I paced the floor for hours and how I worried about her mother. I told her how I heard the doctor spank her bottom when she was born, and how it meant nothing to me until a woman friend said, with a wonderful smile, "That's your baby!" I told her how pretty she was, even in those first few minutes, with her face pink and white—not red—and only the tiniest birth mark showing on one cheek. And how awed I was by the supreme contentment on her mother's face after all the hours of agony.

Perhaps I did help a little. The tears finally ceased, and we sat for a long time talking about the funny things and some of the sad things that happened when she was little. But one thought beat at me: If only her mother could be here. I can settle the affairs of the world; I can advise the White House at a moment's notice, but I can't solve this.

She solved it in her own way. Someone else did come

along, and she married him. Six months later she suddenly died, and with her died the baby she wanted so much.

As I went over it all again, all the defenses I had built up in the hospital collapsed. You're up one day and down the next, I thought. It's hopeless. Give up—give up as Collar Button did.

the
TWENTY-THIRD
day

The simplest way, I said after a night of thinking of the difficult ways, is to go down to the bay and walk in. There'll be ice along the shore, but you can still walk in. You have town parole, and no one will suspect a thing.

I ate a small breakfast, but went through the sweeping with Jacob. Then I asked Miss Brown if I could go down town.

"So early?"

I lied, "I want to do some Christmas shopping. The doctor advanced me some money." That was true; he had.

Miss Brown said that I could go, but she was suspicious. I considered writing some letters explaining it, but I knew that there was no explaining it. I avoided Len and Bates. I wanted to see Crispy, but she was on duty with the insulin boys. I had a glimpse of her while I was pushing the broom down the hall; she was sitting calmly at the bedside of one of the boys. He was in shock; his face was lathered with perspiration and he was straining at the straps that held him down. I felt a moment of shame. She is suffering but she can do her work. You can't do anything; you give up. But I pushed the thought away.

Miss Brown let me out. "Thank you," I said meaning: Thank you for everything. Her eyes were worried and I could not meet them. I hurried down the stairs.

I'll go up the hill once more, I told myself—just once more. They'll be watching me from the windows, but I'm going up just once more.

Suzy was there. I must have felt that she would be there, and yet I was surprised, or pretended surprise. I sat beside her, and I was stiff and formal until she said, "The little boy is back."

I wanted to hurt her; I wanted to say something that was bitter and cutting. Instead, I buried my head in the gray coat and, as the red mittens stroked my face, I wept as I never had wept before. Great gusty sobs that caused physical pain. I cried out that I was no good, that I never would be any good and that I couldn't go on.

"Tell me, Yack; tell me all about it," she said over and over until the gusty sobs were whimperings and I could speak.

"Tell you what?"

"About them. Tell Suzy."

Tell Suzy! You've never really told it to anyone. Tell it, tell it! But I couldn't, just then. "I didn't think you'd be here," I said. "It's so early."

"Didn't you? You think just because I'm in this place that I don't feel things? You think I didn't know?"

"What, Suzy?"

"That you were troubled again. I guess women feel those things—all the way across the world maybe. If you'd been in China and I'd been here, I'd have felt it. Even if I am different, even if I am queer."

[*175*]

"Little Suzy!"

"Tell me, Yack! Tell Suzy."

It came spilling from me: "I was going to a cocktail party after work. I got into a taxi and gave the address, but something made me change my mind. I told the driver to go to my home. I hurried up the stairs to our apartment. My wife was lying on the bed; she was in a coma. My daughters were there with her, and so was our landlady. My wife's hands were icy. I rubbed them; I slapped her face. I whispered into her ear, 'Eleanor! Eleanor!' Then I called the doctor. He was there in ten minutes. He said that Eleanor should be taken to the hospital. We lived around the corner from a police station, and he said he'd call the police ambulance; it would be quicker.

"The ambulance came, and they put Eleanor in one of those wobbly stretchers. The ambulance driver took one end of the stretcher, and I thought the policeman who rode in the ambulance would take the other, but he told me to take it.

"I took it, but I don't know how we got down the stairs; I don't know how we got her into the ambulance. There was an intern inside smoking a cigarette."

"What we got now?" he said to the policeman.

"'You sons of bitches!' I said. I fumbled in my pockets and finally found my police card, which all newspapermen carry. I'd never had much use for it before.

"'Get going!' I said. 'And cut out the wise talk, or by Christ I'll turn you in for the lousy, cold-blooded bastards you are!'

"The policeman backed down immediately. The intern stared, but he put out his cigarette. He did nothing for Eleanor; he just stared at me all the way to the hospital.

I think of him often, and hate him, yet I tell myself: He was so young.

"They took Eleanor into an emergency room, and another intern and a nurse came in. They were asking me questions when she began Cheyne-Stokes breathing.

"'Why, that woman's dying!' the intern said. There was a shocked expression on his face. I begged them to do something, but I knew that it was hopeless. They gave her a hypodermic, but they knew that it was hopeless, too. They were kind, and when she died, the intern said, 'We'll leave you alone for awhile.'

"I kissed her cheek. She was wearing a plain white nightgown, and for some reason I smoothed it until it was neat. Then I left her, and I never saw her again. I did not go to the undertaking rooms, where some of her friends went. They said that she looked beautiful; they said all the things that people say.

"The funeral services were brief. I don't remember what the minister said. But I remember the scent of the flowers; I'll always remember that, and it makes me sick inside. That's because I'm a neurotic and no God-damned good to anyone."

"My little boy!" Suzy said. "My little boy! What I want to say is my darling...."

"Say it, then! Say it over and over!"

She did say it, and it was good to hear the words again. Then she said, "Now tell about the other one—about Mary Allan."

"She and her husband were at our house one night, and we had a gay time until she complained that she wasn't feeling well. It was some kidney trouble that pregnant women have.

She telephoned her doctor, and he said it was nothing to worry about. He said he'd leave some pills for her on his front porch. They stopped on their way home and picked up the pills, but the next day she was worse. They lived in the country, and the doctor wouldn't come out; he still said that it was nothing to worry about.

"They got a local doctor, and he said she should be taken to a hospital. They brought her back to town in an ambulance, and she seemed to pick up, once she was in the hospital. But that night her husband telephoned me that she was dying; she had developed what they call galloping pneumonia.

"I couldn't face it; I couldn't go to the hospital and see her die. The office knew about it, and a reporter I liked came up. He brought a fifth of whiskey with him. We sat there drinking and waiting. In an hour my wife came back with some friends who had known Mary Allan when she was a baby. They meant well; they said that they believed Mary Allan already was with her mother. They hinted gently that I shouldn't be drinking at such a time. I took another drink. I drank for two days and then I went back to work. For several weeks her husband and I met each night after work and went to a tavern, but we couldn't talk about it. We drank and talked about everything else, and then we said good night...."

I felt almost calm again and for once was not ashamed of the tears. Was that because I had got what I wanted? Attention? Swallow the bitter pill again, I said, and I did. I knew that I would not go down to the bay—at least not that day. And, after years of keeping it inside me, I had finally got it out. Perhaps I should have told it to the doctor, but it would have been difficult. Yet I could tell Suzy. Because she didn't try to analyze it; she simply let the little boy talk.

Suzy said, "You feel better now, Yack? You'll feel better for a long time."

"Yes, I feel better." I smiled ruefully. "And I told the doctor I was going to try to help you!"

"We can help each other. It helps just being together, doesn't it?"

"It helps so much!"

"And you aren't going to think any more about what you were thinking?"

"How did you know? How did you guess?"

She said simply, "Women don't guess those things."

the
TWENTY-FOURTH
day

Helping in Bath, I whistled and joked with the men. I was even polite to Ralph when he littered the floor with his clothes trying to find a pair of socks that suited his fancy.

Crispy came into the Clothes Room for needle and thread.

"You're not supposed to be in here on bath day," I said. "No peeking, please!"

"I have no desire to peek, sir."

"How's it going?"

"All right. I'm not the type to torture myself."

"Meaning I am?"

"I saw you when you came in yesterday. Your eyes were all red."

"Too much dissipation." But why lie to Crispy? "Got a bit sunk, but it's over now."

"Good! They can't get us down, can they?"

"You sound like a cheer leader at a football rally." But we smiled at each other understandingly. Brave little Crispy! I wished I had half her gumption.

When Len came in for his shower he had news. "Red's

back. They picked him up in Jackson. They got him on Six—and in a nightshirt! Figure he won't take off in that."

"Why do they always put him on Six? Maybe if they'd left him here he wouldn't have taken off."

"When a guy takes off they always put him back on the ward he took off from. But Doc told me they'll probably move Red after a few days. Six isn't good for him; makes him sore."

"I'd like to see him."

"In a nightshirt? We might walk by Six this afternoon."

We went by on the way to the canteen, but there was no sign of Red at the windows. However, an attendant from Six was in the canteen, and told us that Red was taking it all tight.

"He's really subdued," the attendant said. "Something must have happened while he was outside. Says he's ready to do anything we say. Can't figure out what's come over him."

Jeanne joined Len and me for coffee. Len told her about Teddy and the letter, but she was worried. "He's such a child," she said, looking like a child herself. "I don't want to hurt him. I was hurt too many times when I was a child."

I was curious about her, and she sensed it. "I don't mind talking about myself," she said. We drank coffee and she talked.

"I was the ninth in a family of twelve children. Because of my size I wasn't to play with children my age. That bothered me and I came to dread school. So I began skipping classes, and when I was twelve my parents put me in a girls' training school. That didn't help. I soon learned how convenient it was to be surly and non-cooperative. When I was that way people left me alone.

[*181*]

"I stayed there for two years. When I got out I was in the same grade as a sister who was two years older. I was in the second year of high school, but my parents wouldn't let me go out at night to parties or basketball games because they said I was too small. I began to have spells of depression. For three years I moped, and then suddenly I discovered that I could sing. I couldn't get a job singing in my home town and my parents didn't want me to leave home, so one day I ran away.

"I went to Cleveland and right away got a job in a night club. I was happy for three months. Then an attack of appendicitis put me in the hospital. After leaving there I went to Buffalo and got a job that lasted three years. But the moods came back and I began to drink. Finally I wound up in a New York state hospital where I took six months of shock treatments. Then I came out here. I've been here for fourteen years, still taking treatments."

Len said, "It's hard to believe. You always seem so happy-go-lucky."

"I am—until a mood hits me. We all have moods or we wouldn't be here. And if you two don't ask me to dance tonight, I'll go into a mood. I love to dance, but few men ask me because I'm so small."

"May I have the first?" said Len.

I said, "No, I'll have the first."

She laughed. "I'm overjoyed to have you two big hulks fighting for the first dance." She flirted with her eyes. "But I'll take Len; I don't want to make Suzy jealous. Or Lena."

"I forgot to tell you," Len said. "Lena won't be at the dance. Got in a row with some other woman, and both of 'em have to stay in. You're safe tonight, my boy!"

"There's going to be a Christmas play," said Jeanne. "And I'm in it. I play the part of a little girl; I always play the part of a little girl." But she said it without bitterness.

"Christmas!" said Len, and he *was* bitter.

Art Ammidon made out the list of those who wanted to go to the dance. There were ten of us. "What goes on?" he said. "You all getting to be social butterflies?" But he was pleased that ten of us wanted something more than sitting in the Day Room waiting for bedtime.

At the last minute, when we lined up at the door, Franklin said, "I want to go, too." We stared at him. Art looked worried. "He's so weak he can hardly stand up," he said in an aside to me.

"Let him go," I urged. "I'll keep an eye on him, and maybe the change will do him good."

Art was reluctant but gave his consent, and we waited while Franklin got out his long unused overcoat and hat. I walked with him to the auditorium and chatted of this and that, but he said nothing. I found a seat for him near one of the radiators. "You're sure you don't want to dance, Franklin?" I was relieved when he said no, for I knew how exhausted he was.

Len didn't have the first dance with Jeanne. Teddy seized her as the orchestra began to play; she protested mildly, shrugged her tiny shoulders at Len, but danced with Teddy. He wasn't a good dancer, but she was gentle with him, showing him the steps. He came back to the men's side looking as though he had just won a million dollars, but all he could say was, "Gosh! Gosh almighty!" Even Franklin permitted himself a feeble smile.

Suzy was late. I was dancing with Crispy when she came

[*183*]

in with the group from Eleven. She wore a new dress—a Mexican print, Crispy said it was—and there was a red flower in her hair.

"I give up," said Crispy.

"Now what?"

"I can't compete with Suzy. My Lord, she *is* beautiful!"

"I told you she was."

"Well, if you could stop staring long enough to watch your feet you'd save an awful lot of wear and tear on my shoes. They're white, you know, or rather they were white."

"I'm sorry. And she's not the only beautiful woman here."

"Don't be gallant! On second thought, go ahead. I could use some gallantry."

So I went ahead until Crispy burst into laughter at my fumbling efforts. "Well tried!" she said.

"Well, anyway, it made you laugh."

"You like to play, don't you?"

"Play or play-act?"

"None of that! No, what I meant was that you like to make jokes and awful puns. I eat 'em up. Keep on doing it."

"Yes, doctor!" For the second time that day we smiled with understanding.

When I danced with Suzy I told her how beautiful her dress was. "Do they sell Mexican dresses in Traverse City?" I asked. "Especially in mid-winter?"

"I made it. The skirt's of Mexican lunch cloths, and the waist part—well, that's just a frilly waist." She pressed my hand. "You look happy tonight."

"I am. Thanks to a certain person."

"A certain person is happy, too. Let's be happy, Yack, while we can."

"Yes, but what do you mean by while we can?"

"We won't talk about it," she said, knowing that I knew.

I sat out two dances with Franklin, and he tried to be nice. He even said that he was enjoying himself. "I used to dance a lot," he said.

"Go ahead—if you feel up to it."

"Oh, no, I couldn't do that."

"Why not?"

He said lamely, "I don't know, but I couldn't." Although he was close to the radiator, he pulled his overcoat tighter around him and lapsed into silence.

I danced with Jeanne, who said that Teddy was behaving well and that she didn't think he would be a problem. Then there was a square dance and I had that with Suzy. I hadn't had a square dance since the days on The Farm, and I missed many of the calls. But Suzy knew them all and pushed me here and there and somehow we got through it with everyone laughing at us and our laughing with them.

"Oh, Yack, wasn't that fun?" Her cheeks were flushed and her eyes were dancing.

"Grand fun!"

We had to wait, then, until the last dance because of the three-dances-with-the-same-person rule, but it was a long dance. We didn't talk; there seemed to be no reason for conversation. And I was silent on the way back to D-3 because I didn't want the singing within me to escape.

The only discord was: *While we can.*

the
TWENTY-FIFTH
day

It didn't seem possible that more snow could fall, but it did. The little tractor sighed and went back to work. There was sighing, too, in the Day Room, for some of the patients were going to their homes a week before Christmas, and they were worried about the blocked highways. Miss Brown didn't sigh. She said happily, "The snow will make it real Christmasy."

"Good heavens," I said, "we've got about ten feet of snow now. How much do you have to have to feel Christmasy?"

"The more the better! I think I'll get out that poster."

She disappeared somewhere, returning with a large canyon drawing of Santa Claus. "A patient did it two years ago. He's doing well now, down in Florida."

She got out some surgical tape and fastened the poster to the center pillar in the Day Room. "There, that gives us a start. The students are coming in tomorrow and we'll get up the decorations."

"Do we have a tree?"

"Oh, yes. There's a tree for every floor here and for all the wards and cottages. And then they have lights on that big pine in front of Center."

There was a faint stirring among the men when the poster went up. Some walked over to admire it; others fixed it with sour glances. It was an excellent drawing, and I could understand why Miss Brown had saved it for two years and doubtless would have it two years hence.

"I've also got the tree ornaments tucked away" she said. "They're rather bedraggled, but they'll do. Lights? Oh, the electricians come around and put them on."

I began to feel a tingle of the Christmas spirit. It's not going to be so bad, I thought, and they'll probably tell me I can leave a few days after Christmas. Because I *am* better; I feel good, and I'm not going to slip back into those moods again.

Feeling at peace with the world, I even gave The Brat a cigarette. He was surprised but took it.

"I gave Art a hell of a time last night," he said cheerfully. "Threw all my clothes out into the hall."

"What was the point of that?"

He seemed astonished. "Don't you ever want to throw your clothes away?"

"No. And why pick on Art? He's a pretty decent sort."

"Oh, he's paid for it." The Brat sauntered away, flicking ashes on the floor. Then he came back to thank me for the cigarette. Apparently he had forgotten about my slapping him.

Len was down with a cold. I peeked into his room, but he was asleep. Jacob cornered me near the Visitors Room and began to complain again about the food. I listened patiently.

I *must* be in a good mood. First, The Brat, then Jacob.... You're a little Boy Scout today, all right.

Elmer asked me into his room; he, too, had a cold. He gave me a handful of cookies that had arrived from his wife the day before. He was in the dumps.

"I don't know how I'm going to stand it here on Christmas," he said. "Christmas is nothing, anyway, without kids."

"Miss Brown seems to think that we'll have a good time. I suppose we'll have to pretend a bit, though."

"Pretend is right! It's the kids I think of. Fine Christmas they'll have with their father in the nut house!"

He wouldn't be cheered up, so I ate his cookies and left. I sat with Willie for awhile and heard his story all over again. When I told him that it was snowing hard, he shuddered.

"You ever been in Florida?" he asked.

"No."

"Always wanted to go there. They say you can keep real warm there, even in winter. But I'll never get there."

The student nurses came in for a few minutes and asked Ralph to play some Christmas songs. Willie was delighted by their singing and got out his guitar. But they had to leave for a class, and he put the guitar back and resumed his rocking.

Boy Blue was the next to test my patience. He told me about his farm and his deer hunting, and then he said, "They want me to go home for Christmas, but I ain't going."

"They?"

"My wife and my other son. I like it fine here; I'm going to stay right here for Christmas. We're going to have turkey."

"I'd think you'd be tickled to pay a visit home."

"Safer here," he said vaguely. "Well, I got to exercise." He took off his shoes and padded away.

I was becoming bored. It was the same thing, day after

day. I hunted up Bates and asked if he had something for me to do. He said he was taking Ted, the Montgomery Ward catalogue boy, to Cottage 32 and that I could go along.

"It's bad out," he added. "We'd better take the car."

Ted, whom I had almost forgotten, evinced no interest as we skidded through the snow, but when we checked him in at the office of the cottage, he burst into tears.

"This isn't a bad place," Bates said, trying to comfort him. But Ted would not be comforted.

An idea occurred to me. "Bet I know what's wrong. He forgot to bring his catalogue."

Ted nodded eagerly. So we drove back to D-3, unearthed the catalogue, and carried it to Ted. He hugged it to him, and walked away, happy again.

I was the only one to go to the canteen in the afternoon. It was still snowing, but the tractor had cleared a wide path. Halfway to the canteen a group of men passed. They were a surly lot, forced to take some exercise and not liking it. Last in line was Red.

"Well," I said, "thought you were in a nightgown!"

He laughed; he was in high spirits in contrast to the others. "I'm a good boy now. They gave me my clothes when I promised not to take off again."

I turned and walked along with him; the attendants glanced at me, but said nothing.

"What's come over you, Red? You aren't the same."

"Hell, I just decided it wasn't worth it—fightin' the whole damned world, I mean. I'm goin' to be an angel-face from now on, and then I can get outa here legitimate."

"Makes sense. Hear they picked you up in Jackson."

"That's wrong. I gave myself up. Got home all right and saw the wife and kids. Spent one night with 'em. Then I went to Jackson to scare up some dough from a buddy and I got to thinkin' I was all wet carryin' on a feud with Doc, and the hospital. Don't know what gave me the idea, but I went to the police before I could change my mind. Goin' to be a regular Boy Scout from here on in."

"This must be Boy Scout day," I murmured.

"What's that?"

"Nothing. Just talking to myself."

"Doc was damn decent when I got back. He's goin' to bat for me at staff, and he says he'll get me off Six pretty soon."

"Swell!" The doctor doesn't seem to work hard on any of us, but he gets results, I thought. That is, where there's an even chance of getting results.

Red asked, "How's that old bastard Len?"

"Got a bad cold. I'll tell him about you. He'll be pleased."

He grinned. "Kinda pleased myself!"

I saw The Flash and Pickerel on a snow shovel gang, and I said goodbye to Red. He walked on whistling.

The Flash was a different person, too. He greeted me lustily and leaned on his shovel while he asked for news of D-3.

"Miss the gang there," he said, "but this workin' outside is sure fixin' me up. Oughta see me eat!"

"How's the head bumping?"

"No more of that! Never even think about it."

Pickerel was not so enthusiastic, but he had lost weight and he worked steadily and silently. It would be difficult to play the buffoon on a snow shovel gang.

The canteen was virtually deserted. Lil, sitting alone at the table, brightened at the prospect of company. She said that she was going home tomorrow and had come over to say goodbye. "Guess the sissies are afraid to come out."

[*190*]

I wished her a merry Christmas. She laughed her big laugh.

"Oh, it'll be merry all right! Bet I'm plastered by tomorrow night. Then you know what? My old man'll try to beat the hell out of me and I'll get sore and shack up with some guy…. Say, I shouldn't talk like that to you. You're supposed to be a gentleman!"

"That's libel!"

"What? Well, it's the dope that's gone around. Oh, hell, what's it matter? Men are all alike."

"You really think so?"

"Yeah; specially when it comes to a big woman like me. Men don't fall in love with big women. All they want is… all they want is one thing."

I thought of the contrast—Jeanne and Lil. One was here because she was so little and the other was here because she was so big. And when they brooded about it too much, they let themselves go. Just as I did; all three of us wanting attention. And Red, didn't he want attention? And Len, waiting for his wife to make the first move?

"Hey!" said Lil, "You going into a trance?"

"No. I'll tell you, Lil, I was thinking that men and women are a lot alike."

"Aw, nuts!"

the
TWENTY-SIXTH
day

The student nurses arrived early, eager to help put up the first decorations. Miss Brown, beaming, gave them yards of red and green tissue streamers, which they draped from each corner of the Day Room to the center pillar. Because of the solid walls and pillar, they used surgical tape to hold the streamers in place. Nails and hammers were frowned upon D-3, anyway.

"We'll have lots more in a few days," Miss Brown said, "but I thought we'd get these up early. Makes the Day Room more cheerful,"

Most of the men regarded the proceedings with bleak looks, although they liked having the student nurses in the Day Room. I helped put up the streamers and enjoyed it, even when the stepladder wobbled under me. Larry, permitted to twist the tissue into streamers, gurgled with delight. Willie also was pleased by the gay colors. We three appeared to be the only patients who were having fun.

Len, up and around but still groggy, grunted, "Lot of damned nonsense!" And Ralph, injured because he was not

asked to help, sulked in his corner. The Brat was more interested in pawing the students than in being of assistance.

Len brightened, however, when I told him about Red.

"Maybe the guy'll come out of it after all. Wonder if
seeing the wife and kids did it?"

"He could have figured it out for himself."

"Could be," Len admitted, surprising me.

I had to help Bates in the Clothes Room. When I returned
in an hour, the students had gone, and two of the streamers
were trailing on the floor. No one had made a move to pick
them up. Larry was agitated; he tried to tell me what was
wrong, but I couldn't understand his words. Finally he wrote
on his pad: Tape melted. Too hot in here."

I told Miss Brown about it. "Oh, dear," she said, "that
happened last year. We'll have to get some Scotch tape; that
doesn't melt."

"Of course," I said, 'if we let a little air into the Day Room
maybe the surgical tape wouldn't melt."

"Don't be sarcastic. You know we have to keep it warm.
You run over to the canteen before it closes and get the other
tape—that is, if you want to."

I hurried to the canteen and bought two rolls of tape. I also
sneaked a quick hamburger. As I was leaving, Suzy came in
with a large order for the women on Eleven. I waited until it
was filled and carried the carton containing the order.

"Do they do anything on Eleven besides eat?" I asked.
"This weighs a ton."

She laughed. "We eat all the time when we have the
money. The men eat a lot, too, don't they?"

"Some of them. The old ones eat so much at meals that
they don't care about snacks. They just sit there bloated most
of the time."

[*193*]

"I like snacks. We used to have them on the farm all the time. Do you like to take sandwiches to bed with you?"

"Among other things."

"Idiot! I like you when you're gay, Yack."

"And when I'm not?"

We had reached the gate to Eleven. She looked up at me, her face serious. "Then I love you. I guess I love you when you're gay, too. That's an awful thing for me to say."

"Why?"

"Men are supposed to say it first, aren't they?"

I put down the carton. "It really wasn't necessary for me to say it. You must have known all the time."

"Yes, but a woman likes to hear it."

"I love you, Suzy."

We did not see nor hear the woman attendant who came out the gate. She spoke sharply, but she was smiling. "SUZY, they're waiting for all the stuff." She walked on.

I picked up the carton for Suzy, and she slipped through the gate. I called after her, "The hill?"

"Not today. I have to work on the floor. Tomorrow."

She waved a red mitten; the carton teetered, then dropped. Upside down, in the snow. I went through the gate, which was against the rules, and helped her pick up the stuff. We giggled and made jokes about iced coffee and cup cakes with snow frosting. Finally the carton was intact again and I lifted it for her.

"You'd better run, darling," she said. "If they catch us here we'll both be in trouble."

When Miss Brown let me in she said with mock severity, "Did you go to the North Pole for the tape?"

"I was delayed by circumstances beyond my control."

"I wonder! Well, let's get up those streamers again."

[*194*]

We got them up, and I sat with Larry and admired them. He told me about other Christmases, and I could catch only a word here and there, but his meaning was clear. He was boyishly happy; he had fetched a tiny radio from his room so that others could enjoy it, but few paid any attention to it. Willie responded immediately, however, and beat at his guitar. Then The Reverend appeared bringing a portable record player and long-playing discs of Christmas carols.

It was a weird concert we had for the next hour. Willie strummed away on one side of the room. On the other, Larry's radio, frequently troubled by static, grumbled and squealed, and in the center of the room, near the windows, The Reverend's carols vied with both.

I chose the carols. I sat close to the player, which The Reverend left with us while he made his rounds, and I thought: they are beautiful, but they are sad. I had always thought so, but now I could see that beauty and sadness often went together. If not, why did so many people weep at the opera? Why did strange silences fall when people gazed into the setting sun or watched the waves rolling in from across the world? Why did mothers cry at weddings?

I remembered a little scene in the Twelfth Street apartment where we used to go on Sunday when we were new in New York. I remembered our hostess, whom we both loved, putting on a smock and going out into the back garden and sitting in the grass and holding the hose upright, letting the water shoot into the air and fall on her in a fine spray, She sat there, dreamy-eyed, until she was drenched, and I think that she forgot all about us.

I remembered that I felt choked up, watching her, because she was beautiful—a China doll. Some time later she died. Perhaps I had seen ahead.

The Reverend, returning, interrupted my thoughts.

"You like the carols?"

"Very much."

"They do something to people this time of year. I'd like to leave the player here, but there are other floors...."

"We always have Willie!"

He smiled. "I appreciate your being nice to him."

"I haven't done anything."

"I've seen you talking to him—and listening. It helps to have someone who will listen."

"I know. I've learned that."

He disconnected the player. "You seem to be coming along fine. The doctor says you are."

"I feel that I am—now. But I'm staying until after Christmas."

"Probably wise. What are your plans? Going home?"

"No, that's over."

"Sorry to hear it, but you don't seem bitter about it."

"I'm not bitter—any more."

He rose to go. "That's splendid! Well, easy does it!"

I wondered if The Reverend ever despaired. He always seemed cheerful, even when he was tired. Yet day after day he saw the hundreds of hopeless cases in the hospital. A man would have to have faith to see those cases and never doubt. And The Reverend never doubted; perhaps at times there was something akin to despair, but never doubt. And he was God's messenger, not His advertising agency, for he never tried to force his belief on others.

I was half-dozing in my chair when a big man with both arms swathed in bandages burst through the door from the hall.

"I'm Santa Claus!" he shouted. "Here's Santa Claus!"

He strode into the room, smiling and bowing, and took a seat next to Lewis, who looked horrified. All of us stared—it was so unexpected. And I thought: What was it I said about the same old routine?

Art hurried in looking harassed. "Just be quiet now," he said. "We'll fix you up in a jiffy."

The big man ceased to be Santa Claus. The blood surged into his face and he screamed, "Get me outa here! God damn it, get me outa here! I'll call the sheriff! I'll call the governor!"

Two attendants, whom Art had called earlier, came down from D-4. They tried to soothe the big man, but he wanted to fight. The two attendants and Art finally seized him, as gently as they could because of the bandaged arms, and hustled him off to D-4. We could hear him screaming up there.

When Art, dripping perspiration, returned, he told Len and me that the big man's seven-year-old daughter had been raped and the big man had plunged his arms into boiling water when he was told about it.

"In God's name, why?" Len and I said together.

Art said, "Some guilt complex. Probably felt he'd failed her somehow. Her mother's dead."

"Merry Christmas!" Len growled. But he looked sick.

the
TWENTY-SEVENTH
day

At breakfast I heard that Pickerel had tried to take off from the snow shovel gang. But he was caught a few blocks away. He came back, pleased with himself and boasting, "I'm a German Jew, but I made the headlines!" Well he had, in a way, on D-3. I never saw or heard of him after that; like so many who make the headlines for a day, he seemed to vanish.

No one talked about the man who had believed for a moment that he was Santa Claus. No one talked about his raped daughter. I thought about him and about her, and probably others did, too, but no one mentioned either of them. I wondered: If that story were in the tabloids would the "normal" people be as restrained over their morning coffee cups?

Even The Brat was remarkably silent. He ate no breakfast—he usually gorged—and he looked like a choir boy as we lined up to leave the dining room. But as he neared the door he walked a few steps to the woman who scraped the dishes and spat into her face.

Five minutes later, The Brat was on D-4.

Len was elated. "High time they got that little bastard out of here!"

I thought so, too, for he had been a thorn in everyone's side. I had slapped him and I had hated him at times, but I felt only pity for him now. That's half your trouble, I thought, you spend too much time pitying people, including yourself.

"Let's skip it." But I thought often during the day of The Brat among the tough ones on D-4, and probably wanting his mamma.

As Jacob and I pushed our brooms by the insulin ward, Crispy poked her head out.

"Your troubles are over," she said. "Lena's been transferred to a cottage—I don't know which one."

"How does that end my troubles?"

"She won't be allowed out for some time, Don Juan!"

"What a day! They seem to be moving all the people who got into my hair."

"We aim to please!"

Jacob, waiting anxiously, said, "We'd better be going. I don't want them to think I'm loafing. If they think I'm loafing they'll give me something harder to do."

"Back to the mines, then! Thanks, Crispy."

Safely out of hearing, Jacob said, "I don't trust her. I don't trust any of those students."

"Why not?"

"They're young and pretty, and you can't trust 'em when they're young and pretty."

"Oh, God! Go lap up some canned syrup!"

He took me seriously. "I couldn't do it up here. They'd be mad."

I dropped the subject; it was the simplest way out.

When we were back in the Day Room Len was bending over Willie who was having one of his crying spells.

"He's cold again," Len said. "It *is* damned cold. Bates says it must be ten below."

I found Bates and told him about Willie. We went through the Clothes Room and found a state fleece-lined jacket.

"That ought to fix him," Bates said.

I suggested a blanket, too, and he got one from the Storage Room. We put the jacket on Willie and wrapped him in the blanket. In a few minutes he stopped crying, but he sat all day next to the radiator with his hands covering his face, rocking and rocking. Not once did he touch his guitar.

Shortly before eleven o'clock, Boy Blue's wife was admitted to the Visitors' Room, and Bates called Boy Blue.

"I don't want to see her," Boy Blue protested.

"Oh, come now! Better put on your shoes, too."

Boy Blue thought it over. Reluctantly he put on his shoes. Reluctantly he followed Bates down the hall to the Visitors' Room.

He was back in five minutes. He seated himself at the big table, removed his shoes, and began to thumb through the magazines.

Larry wrote on his pad: "That was a quick visit!"

"Something funny there," I said. "Something more than his son's death."

"What, professor?" asked Len.

"All right, all right! But I'll bet there *is* something else." I had no idea what it could be, and I never found out.

Boy Blue jumped up fifteen minutes before the dinner bell was to ring and gave us the time reports with his usual gusto. When the bell rang he was first in line again. Not once did he look into the Visitors' Room, the door of which was open. But the rest of us did, and we saw his wife, a stolid farm woman sitting comfortably in an easy chair and staring out the window.

Boy Blue gulped his dinner and was the first out. He sailed by the Visitors' Room and into the Day Room where he threw himself on one of the benches and had his customary after-dinner ten-minute nap. Later Bates tried to coax him into the Visitors' Room, but he wandered away from Bates.

Boy Blue's wife left a few minutes later, leaving a large box of cookies which Bates gave to him. He seemed pleased, thrust both hands into the box, and ate greedily. He didn't offer the cookies to anyone else.

"Wish I had a wife," said Teddy, eyeing the cookies. Later he sat down with Boy Blue, listened to the same old stories, heaped praise on him, even straightened his tie for him. Boy Blue, glowing from all the attention, finally offered him some cookies. Munching them, Teddy came back to us.

"He's nuts," he mumbled, his mouth full.

We looked at him coldly.

Miss Brown was off duty, but when I went to the Clothes Room for my rubbers and overcoat, Miss Love proved equal to the occasion.

"And where do you think you're going?" she asked with her prettiest smile. Miss Love reminded one of the nurses on Red Cross posters.

"Out," I said.

"In this weather! Don't you know it's ten below?"

"I'm at my best when it's ten below."

"Why do you want to go out? No one else is. There's no place to go; the canteen's closed."

I almost told her, feeling that she would understand if anyone would. But I didn't tell her. I said I needed fresh air and that I wouldn't stay out long.

"Well…." She didn't like the idea at all. "But you'll have to wear a hat."

"You and Miss Brown have a hat complex."

"No hat, no out!" She meant it, too, so I gave in. She found an old state stocking cap and she wrapped a state muffler around my neck. She also made substitute state galoshes for my rubbers. I looked like a character in *Way Down East*.

"If you have a St. Bernard and a cask of brandy handy, I'd better take those along, too," I said.

She laughed, but she said, "At least you won't have to go to bed with the flu again. And don't stay out long."

When she let me out she said, "Give her my love!"

"Love from Miss Love—I'll remember. Say, how did…?" But she had closed the door, and I could hear her laughing to herself. Oh, well, probably everyone else knew, but they didn't know about the hill. Only Lena and Jacob knew about that.

It seemed to me that it was closer to thirty below outside. The telephone wires were singing and the snow was crunchy underfoot. My nose tickled when I drew a breath.

Suzy was ahead of me; she was flaying her arms to keep warm. She looked at me in amazement.

"Mr. Peary, I believe?"

"No, Dr. Cook. I had to fake to get out. This outfit is Miss Love's idea.

"I had to fake, too. Said I'd left my pen on C-1. I can only stay a minute. And who is Miss Love?"

"Nurse on duty. And a very nice person, except for bundling me up like this. Bundling! That's an idea!"

"Sir!... Anyway, I think the book of rules is again it."

"Don't tell me they thought of that, too!"

We carried on light-heartedly until Suzy's time was up, and we were happy that we could be that way for a change.

I had to knock on the door to D-3 for ten minutes before Miss Love unlocked it.

"Well," she said, "about time!"

"If the hired help was more alert," I said, "I could be busy at a picture puzzle by now."

"I was in the Colonic Room. Didn't hear you until Boy Blue yelled at me."

"High colonics on the Sabbath! Nothing is sacred around here!"

"You *must* have had a good time! Christmas presents are coming in, and we have to open them and examine them and tie them up again."

"But in the Colonic Room!"

"It's the only room large enough where you nosey people can't get in."

"I don't know what Santa Claus is going to think—coming down the chimney and landing on the colonic table!"

"I think," said Miss Love, trying hard to be prim, "that we have gone far enough."

I sneezed. I sneezed three times.

"Oh, no!" she said. "Not that again!"

"You made me wear a hat. The onus is yours."

By nightfall I was running a temperature.

the
TWENTY-EIGHTH
day

It wasn't a bad cold, but I drooped most of the day. When Miss Love came back in the morning she was all for my staying in bed.

"Your guilty conscience, no doubt," I said. "But I don't need to stay in bed."

"Regardless of my conscience, you stay there until the doctor sees you. Did you eat breakfast?"

"No."

"Like some tomato juice?"

"I loathe the stuff."

"Orange juice?"

"I thought that was for babies."

"Well, aren't you a baby? All men are babies when they're sick."

When she went for the orange juice, I admitted to myself that she was correct. Most men when ill, I thought, either deny that anything is wrong while they limp around looking like martyrs, or take to their beds and groan and whine. But most women don't. Perhaps it has something to do with child-bearing; after one has experienced birth pangs, what matters a little cold?

I obediently drank the orange juice and found it good.

"Of course," I said to Miss Love, "if I'm so ill that I can't get up, then I can't do the sweeping. And this is Monday— the super-cleaning day."

"That's all attended to. Lloyd took your place."

"No! That guy hasn't done a lick of work since he came here. He's all worn out, though."

"From what?"

"His sex life."

"You go to sleep!" said Miss Love.

I did. The doctor and Miss Love were there when I woke. He said that I could get up.

"Do I have to wear a hat?"

"What!"

"Miss Love and I have a secret formula for preventing colds. It has to do with wearing hats."

He pulled up a chair. "I don't know what this is all about, but I'll have a cigarette with you."

Miss Love went out, pausing at the door to shake a fist at me. The doctor said, "You seem pretty chipper for one who was running a temperature last night."

"I don't feel chipper, but I feel good, if you follow me."

"I follow you. You're coming along well. Given much thought to where you're going when you leave?"

I said that I thought a place in town was still a good idea, but he was hesitant to approve. I said that I also had considered going to California and living near my daughter and her family, but that I didn't want to use them as a crutch.

"No, you don't want to do that. Well, it's something you'll

have to decide for yourself. Wherever you go, if the old feeling comes back, you can always return here."

I thanked him. "Do you think that it will come back?"

"No doubt about that. For a time, anyway. All we can do is bring you to a point where you will recognize it for what it is. The rest is up to you."

"I almost didn't recognize it the other day."

"I know. I heard about it."

I asked, curious, "From whom?"

"That doesn't matter. What does matter is that you got out of it. What was it—the wife and the daughter again?"

"Yes. But I didn't get out of it alone. Suzy did most of the work."

"I don't give a damn who did the work. You got out of it. I think you're going to get out from it from now on. But, as I said, if you think you're losing ground, come back here."

He paused at the door. "I could put you on D-1 for a couple of months. You could do your writing there. The rooms are unlocked all day and you could come and go as you pleased."

I thanked him again. "But wouldn't that be a crutch? I'd be putting off a decision—taking the easiest way."

He grinned. "You *are* coming along! You'd have jumped at the chance a few weeks ago."

I said, "The damnedest thing is that I want to leave—and I don't want to leave. And it's not only because I feel safe here."

"What is it then?"

"Suzy."

"I told you not to get too involved. Well, there's another decision you have to make."

"Just one decision after another!"

"That's right. Five-year-olds can't make 'em. Grown-ups can—or are supposed to."

"Yes, Doctor!"

I dressed slowly, thinking it over and getting nowhere. Well, there's no hurry, I said, putting it off. Even grown-ups need a little time to make decisions. Damn him, I suppose he felt he had to stick that barb into me.

When I reached the Day Room I found Len in a rage. D-1 had kept the polisher for hours, and Len was just getting down to work.

"Fine institution! One polisher for four floors. Well, they got two, but one is always on the blink."

"Polishers cost money," I said.

"Well, what the hell! Can't the state afford a few more polishers?"

"It so happens that the state is in the red. It so happens that the legislature is as stingy as hell when it comes to state hospitals. And it so happens that the legislature is Republican."

"We got a Democratic Governor."

"And he can't get to first base with his budget because the Republicans won't let him. And the newspapers, which are Republican, too, won't let him. Cut, cut, cut—that's their slogan, and they don't mean cut only the budget. They mean cut the Governor's throat because he happens to be a Democrat."

"Say, what started you off?"

"You did. You and your polisher."

"Well, me and my polisher'll go to work, if you don't mind. We can take up the political situation later. There may be something in what you say, though…. *May* be, I said."

"I never thought I'd live to see this day!"

"Move aside, radical! We Republicans got work to do."

He started the polisher and it slithered across the floor with Len deftly guiding it. Behind him, carefully keeping in step and holding the electric cord out of Len's way, was Larry.

"Got myself an assistant," Len said on the return trip. "Big help, too; that damned cord was always getting in the way. Larry's really picking up, isn't he?"

Larry's little face was beaming. It did one good to watch him and his happiness. Therapy with an electric cord! And that narrow-minded Republican, Len doubtless thought it up and coaxed him into it. Oh, to hell with politics!

By dinner time I was hungry and ate two servings of chop suey while Jacob clucked and shuddered. I still felt droopy, but I was restless and wanted to go out. I suggested to Miss Brown that it wouldn't hurt to walk to the canteen and back. She gave me a withering look.

She withered all of us a few minutes later in the Day Room.

"I was at the dining room door when you left," she said. "No one asked me for fire. Yet all of you are smoking Now, who has the matches?"

It was obvious, of course. If no one had asked Miss Brown for fire, then someone *did* have matches. I had got my fire from Len, "Where'd you get yours?" I whispered.

"Damned if I remember."

We stared at Miss Brown. She repeated, "Now, who has the matches?"

Ralph jerked up in his chair. "I got 'em!"

Miss Brown was taken aback. "Why, Ralph! Well, you come to the office, Ralph."

He hurried out ahead of her, his music roll under his arm.

"There's something wrong with this picture," I said. "That guy never gave anyone fire, and he never took fire from any of us. He always got it from the nurses or the doctor."

"Just what I was thinking," said Len.

I looked at Teddy. "Did you start us off with the fire?"

"I ain't got any matches," he said, "Honest!"

Bates came into the room. "Listen, fellows, Ralph hasn't got any matches. He just spoke on impulse, I guess. Now, Miss Brown says that if the matches aren't turned in, no one can go out this afternoon. She means it, too."

He didn't like his role; his voice was apologetic. "I'll give you five minutes." He went out.

Len reached into a pocket and brought out a half-used book of matches. "Haven't used 'em today," he said. "I'll turn 'em in, though, so we can get out of this mess. But I'd like to know who in hell did give the first fire."

Larry shuffled up to him and gave him a note. It read: "I did."

"You don't smoke," I protested.

He sputtered some words, but we couldn't make them out. He scribbled on his pad: "Found them in the can. New man asked for fire. Gave it to him."

"Let me have them," I said. He handed them over, his eyes anxious.

I said, "Len has a book. We ought to have one more guilty guy. Who's volunteering?"

A newcomer named Smitty tossed a handful of wooden matches on the table. I threw in Larry's book, and Len followed with his a moment before Bates returned.

"There's the contraband," I said. "Len, Smitty, and I are the guilty parties."

"It's funny." Bates said, "what this cold weather does to your ears. I can't hear a thing, off and on."

He picked up the matches and went out.

At dusk I stood by a window looking up the hill and not thinking much of anything. Suddenly a huge pine in front of Center began to glow with dozens and dozens of red, blue, green, and yellow lights. I had looked upon many municipal Christmas trees: New York's, with its background of steel and concrete; Grand Rapids', with the YMCA for its backdrop; and a pathetic, emaciated tree in Uniontown, Pennsylvania, that was black from coal dust. But never had I seen such a tree as this.

It towered even above the giants that New York imported, and its mighty arms were generously spread as though protecting the baby pines that huddled nearby in the snow.

The snow itself reflected the lights, as does the sea on a calm night; there was a circular rainbow that danced over the drifts and flirted with the fringes of the baby pines. In back rose the hill—no skyscrapers here; no blast furnaces—with its own piney forest outlined against a blue-black sky.

I feasted on it, feeling a warmth steal over me, a nourishment of beauty, until someone said, "Say, isn't that wonderful?"

I hadn't heard Curly come up. "Yes," I said, "it's wonderful."

He sighed. "Say, you know I like Christmas trees. I like 'em outdoors. My wife does, too. Say, I bet she's out there now looking at that tree."

"I don't think so, Curly. It's awfully cold out there, you know. You wouldn't want your wife to be out in the cold."

He considered. "That's right; she doesn't like the cold. She never liked the cold. Say, maybe they'll let her in for Christmas and she can stand here and look at the tree. I bet she'd like that."

"I wonder, Curly. I wonder."

But he had pressed his face against the window, going back to his everlasting search, and he did not hear me.

the
TWENTY-NINTH
day

The student nurses arrived early to complete the Christmas decorations. They had cardboard letters covered with silver paper to spell out MERRY CHRISTMAS and HAPPY NEW YEAR. But against the yellowish walls the letters were drab and forlorn.

Crispy, making a face, said, "Some great mind should be able to solve this problem."

I said, 'It doesn't take a great mind. Just mount the letters on squares of that red tissue paper and the letters will stand out."

"There must have been a sign painter among your ancestors," she said, busying herself with the tissue paper.

"No, but I had an uncle who had a naked woman tattooed on his navel, and…."

"Some other time!" said Crispy.

Bates brought in a stepladder, and I put up the MERRY CHRISTMAS and HAPPY NEW YEAR letters. MERRY CHRISTMAS was taped to the wall near the piano; HAPPY NEW YEAR on the wall in the opposite corner where Ralph usually sat.

It took an hour to get them placed just right. I had a critical audience. Len said that the Y in MERRY was unbalanced; Teddy said that CHRISTMAS should be spelled with an X; and Larry scribbled on his pad: "First P in HAPPY doesn't match second P."

"You can all go to hell," I said, standing back to view my handiwork.

"That's the Christmas spirit!" Crispy said.

Miss Brown brought in more posters, all of them of Santa Claus, and taped them to the walls. Then she suggested that patients who had received Christmas cards tape them to the center pillar.

"We can make the pillar real gay," she said.

Larry was the first to offer his cards. He already had more than a dozen. One, from his wife, was the cheapest of all; cheap in price, cheap and thoughtless in the sentiment printed on it.

May All Your Christmases
Be as Merry as This One

It was signed in pencil: "Your Wife."

"Wonderful!" Larry sputtered, and for once I could understand him. "Wonderful wife!"

Elmer also had received many cards, but as he taped them to the pillar, he wept. Willie had a card from his school-teacher friend but would not part with it. Johnny dropped his in the trash basket and went back to the ping-pong table. I dug out the cards and taped them to the pillar.

"You're really enjoying yourself, aren't you?" said Len.

"Yes, and if you got off your fat can and joined in you'd enjoy yourself, too."

"Not me! That's stuff for kids."

[*213*]

"There's a kid in this room, and he's talking to me! Why don't you grow up, you old bastard?"

He chuckled and walked away.

Three of the insulin boys caught the spirit and fetched a sprig of mistletoe from their ward. They taped it over the door leading into the hall, and the three of them caught Crispy under it a minute later. The old men laughed to themselves while Crispy was being kissed, and Franklin deserted the urinals to watch, his lips twisted in a crooked smile. The other students took advantage of that to lead him to the piano, and he played for a few minutes, but his hands trembled and so did his knees.

"That guy's no good to anybody," Boy Blue announced to the room in general. "Better take him out and shoot him!"

The doctor arrived then, and Franklin staggered from the piano and back to the urinals. After the doctor came four men from D-4, including The Brat.

"Oh, God, he's back!" groaned Len. "And look at those other three pot-bellies!"

They were a sorry lot. Among them was the big man with the burned arms; he was quiet and sat with his arms outstretched and his head bowed. The other two had wild eyes that glared at us.

One by one they were led into the ward; the students were summoned by Miss Brown, and Bates and Goodman went into the ward, too.

"That means electros," I said. "Bet The Brat's going to get one."

The electros interested me, and I had asked the doctor if I might watch some day. He considered, but shook his head.

"You aren't up to that yet," he said.

The doctor explained that they weren't so bad, but that

most of the patients built up a fear about them. "It's just a little shock," he said. "I know, because I've tried it. It's a poor doctor, you know, who won't swallow his own medicine."

"What's the point of them?"

"Well, we know that they straighten out some people and do nothing for others. What happens inside them we don't know yet. But we know that nature is the best healer, and it is our theory that when the electros shock the brain, nature goes right to work to repair the damage. That's only a theory, though; we don't know. Same thing goes for insulin."

Goodman and a D-4 attendant came for The Brat. He was poking among the decorations on the big table, and when he saw them coming, his legs collapsed under him. They picked him up.

"No, no!" he moaned. The color seeped from his face and his lips trembled. In a moment a veteran of the Battle of the Bulge became a terrified little boy. They half-carried him from the Day Room.

I was glad then that the doctor had said no.

Both Miss Brown and Miss Love were on duty. Miss Love said definitely that I couldn't go out, but a few minutes later she was called to help in surgery and I appealed to Miss Brown.

"I did help with the decorations, you know," I wheedled. She gave in, but insisted on the stocking cap. I took it off the moment I was outdoors.

Suzy was at the canteen and was glad to see me. I told her about my cold, but she was inclined to side with Miss Love.

"You should dress warmly up here," she said. "The cold and wind go right through you if you don't."

We were talking about the Christmas decorations when

the door burst open and a huge woman wrapped in a fur coat strode in. She wore long, tinkling earrings—and she was smoking a cigar.

"Good Lord, who's that?"

"Queen Deborah. Or that's what she calls herself. She's been down with the flu; that's why you haven't seen her before."

"Does she always smoke a cigar?"

"When she can afford them. And she loads herself with jewelry, mostly glass. She's always looking for a man to play king with her, but so far she's been unsuccessful. There's your chance, Yack!"

"Don't believe in monarchies. Beside, she must weigh three hundred pounds."

Queen Deborah descended on Len with glad cries. "Didn't know you were back," she puffed. "You're looking good, Len. Same old trouble?"

"If you are referring to my over-indulgence in alcohol, the answer is yes."

Queen Deborah chuckled. "That's what I'm referring to all right. I could over-indulge right now. Just getting over the flu."

Len said, "Yes, I can see that Your Majesty is wasting away."

She whacked him on the back, nearly knocking him from the Coke crate. "Wasting away, hell! Put on ten pounds while I was sick; never missed a meal."

Len introduced us. She looked me up and down, the fur coat open and her hands on her hips. She wore five neck-laces, one of coral and four of glass beads. There were rings on seven fingers and bracelets clanked at her wrists.

"Not bad," she said. "You'd make a good king."

I said, "I appreciate the honor, Your Majesty, but I think I'll remain a commoner. Being a king is too much work."

She nodded. "Affairs of state—I know. Gets me down at times. That's why I need a king—someone to share the royal duties." She lost interest in me and turned back to Len.

"Does she actually think she's a queen?" I whispered to Suzy. "Or is she just putting on?"

"Oh, she believes it all right. You should have seen her at the Halloween dance. She made all the women curtsy to her. She was going to knight one of the men, but he began tickling her. That broke up the court session; both of them were taken out."

Suzy told more stories about the Queen: How she hoisted herself into one of the swings outside Receiving Hospital, and it broke under her. "She couldn't sit down for a week," said Suzy. How she fell in love with a man half her size and wanted him for her king. He was coy about the matter and fled across the grounds, but the Queen, despite her weight, caught up with him and, highly insulted, tossed him into the pond.

"Funny thing about that," Suzy added, "is that he's boasted about it ever since."

We didn't go up the hill but stayed in the canteen until closing time, listening to the Queen. It was dusk when we left. I kissed Suzy good night at her gate, and she said, "If the Queen saw you, you'd be beheaded."

"For this I wouldn't mind being boiled in oil."

"We both probably will be. We're supposed to be in by four and it's nearly four-thirty."

I got to D-3 just as Art was rounding up the men for supper. He said nothing about my being late. I hoped that Suzy fared as well.

[*217*]

the
THIRTIETH
day

Teddy was getting on everyone's nerves. Full of youthful vigor, he raced up and down the hall until Miss Brown warned him. For all his vigor, however, he did no work. Len finally told him off, and he condescended to pick up the throw rugs in the bedrooms before Jacob and I went through with the brooms. He was forever borrowing cigarettes, chewing tobacco, and money. Len cut him off when, after giving him a quarter, Teddy spent all of it on one cigar.

"Here I am smoking state tobacco half the time and that little bum buys a twenty-five-cent cigar. I'm through!"

So Teddy turned to me. "I gotta buy Jeanne a Christmas present. I gotta have five dollars."

I still had some of my Christmas-present money, but I wasn't putting out five dollars for Teddy.

"Listen, kid, that's damned big money in these parts. And you're making yourself damned unpopular asking for dough all the time. You act as though it was your right."

"I'll pay it back when my money comes."

"I don't think your money ever will come, but it's not that. It's your attitude."

He whined, "I gotta give somethin' to Jeanne. She's going to give me somethin'."

"But it won't cost five dollars." I fingered my Christmas-present money. "I was going to get you a little present, but if you want a dollar to buy something for Jeanne, you can have it. And don't spend it on twenty-five-cent cigars."

He thanked me so profusely that I said, embarrassed, "Don't cry about it; it's only a buck."

He sped down the hall to find Len and was back in ten minutes. "Len says for me to buy her a pair of panties!

"Len would! Kid, you don't buy panties for women you hardly know."

"Why not?"

"Question of taste, that's all."

"I gotta get her somethin'."

"Well, candy's the best bet. No, you can't get a good box of candy for a dollar. How about one of those ball point pens? Or a handkerchief? You can get a nice handkerchief for a dollar."

"That's it! I'll get her a handkerchief. I'll go down town this afternoon."

I said, "You haven't town parole, have you?"

"Naw, but I been down a coupla times."

"Kid, you're riding for a fall. They'll raise merry hell with you if you keep on breaking the rules."

"You broke the rules last night. You come in late. I seen you."

He had me there. "Better let me do the shopping for you. I'm going down in the next few days."

But he said no, he'd do it for himself.

Just before dinner they carried in a Christmas tree; it looked stunted and moth-eaten when compared to the big pine outside. Then two electricians came with the lights, hooked them up, and draped them over the tree. Miss Brown dug again into her treasure chest and provided ornaments— silver rain, little balls of cotton, and ringlets, made of colored paper. Larry and I did most of the trimming; he was excited about it and attached so many ornaments to one branch that it bent to the floor.

Elmer watched us for awhile, but shortly burst into tears. As he left the Day Room he paused to kick Johnny in the ankle. Bates saw him and rebuked him.

"That's his trouble at home," Bates said. "He's nuts about his children, but they say he loses his temper ever so often and sails into them."

Johnny rubbed his ankle and his lips quivered, but a few moments later he was staring into space again, the incident forgotten.

When the doctor arrived on the floor, four or five men rushed up to him clamoring for permission to go home for Christmas. But only one received permission—a drug addict whom we all disliked because he was forever complaining. We were surprised that he was allowed to go, but presumably the doctor was testing him: If he returned without having gone back to his dope, then he was on the road to recovery.

Lewis begged the hardest of all, but the doctor shook his head. "I can't let you do it, Lewis," he said. "You aren't ready for it yet." He never would be ready, for he was getting worse each day, crying over his wife's letters, demanding more and more pills for "my God-damned bowels," and lashing out at anyone who dared to sit on the bench he had appropriated for himself.

"I'll kill myself—that's what I'll do!" he shouted.

"I wouldn't talk that way, Lewis," the doctor said. "You don't want your ground parole taken away, do you?"

Teddy rushed up. "Can I have town parole, Doc?"

"No, young man, you can't. Not until you calm down a bit."

Teddy went into a corner and sulked.

All of the insulin boys were told that they could go home for Christmas—in fact, could stay until after New Year's. And there would be no electros during the holidays, the doctor said. Those who had been receiving them became animated at once; even Franklin, who hadn't had an electro for a long time, came out of his corner.

"Maybe I could have a drink of water now?" he suggested.

I said, "I think it's safe."

He went to the fountain and gulped water and air. Willie, feeling his way to the fountain, chided him, "You shouldn't drink thataway. Just a little bit at a time." He took several bird-like sips. "You don't wanna let the air in; gives you cramps."

They solemnly discussed their insides until the dinner bell rang. I thought that Franklin might give up his hunger strike as well, but he only pecked at his food.

I reached the canteen early, but I had a premonition that Suzy would not be there. Another woman from Eleven handed me a note from her. It read:

Darling: They're boiling me in oil! No ground parole for two days because I was late. But I'll be at the dance. I love you. Suzy.

"Suzy's all right, isn't she?" I asked the woman from Eleven. She was a motherly person, plump and pink-cheeked.

"Oh, my yes! She just has to stay in for being late. They do that all the time."

"Well, she says she'll be permitted to go to the dance."

"Oh, did she write that? Don't you know there's no dance this Thursday? They're having a Christmas show Friday night instead."

I had seen the posters but had forgotten about them. It would be Friday afternoon, then, before I could see Suzy. Damn Queen Deborah!

One of the men who had asked to go home for Christmas approached me after supper.

"I don't know you," he said, "but I seen you around."

I had noticed him several times, but he spent long hours working in the kitchen and I knew little about him. He was about twenty-eight, had only a few teeth left, but boasted a tremendous belly.

He said, "Wonder if you'd do me a favor?"

"Sure. Go ahead."

"Well, I can't read and I can't write. I gotta get word to my wife. Teddy says as how you helped him once."

We went out to the big table. He said that he wanted to tell his wife that he wouldn't be home for Christmas. "Reckon she knows that already," he said dismally.... "Well, tell her 'bout the weather and say I could use a few bucks and them cigars is all gone. Tell her I send my love to the kids."

I wrote the letter. He wanted to end it with "Love and kisses." Then he laboriously signed his name, Mannie, in block letters.

I can do my name all right, but that's all, he said proudly.

He didn't know how to spell the name of his home town, and I had never heard of it, so I looked it up on a map.

Thanking me, he reached into his pocket and brought out a dime.

"Forget it," I said. "Glad to do it for you."

He looked the dime over carefully and finally put it back.

"I sure figured I was goin' home," he said. "Guess Doc, he's got it in for me."

"How's that?"

"Well, it's this way. You see, a coupla months ago I was driving my wife and one of the kids to the store, and when I was makin' a sudden turn the door on their side flew open and they was spilled in the road. I asked my wife, 'you wanta doctor?' She said she wasn't hurt bad. Kid wasn't either. But they was some people in the store, and they seen it, and they told the sheriff I pushed the wife and kid outa the door. Can you figure that? Tryin' to kill my own wife and kid!

"I told the sheriff how it was, but no one would believe me. I don't know what my wife done, but anyways they sent me up here. And the Doc, he won't believe me neither. He says I did it on purpose. I tell him, 'You get that car up here and I'll show you where the catch's loose.' But he won't do it."

He seemed so mild-mannered and so honest that I was impressed by his story. He said casually, as an after-thought, "You know what I'm goin' to do when I get outa here?"

"No."

"Goin' to kill them bastards what was in the store! Say, you goin' to see this here new Christmas play?"

the
THIRTY-FIRST
day

Another new man was in the Day Room when we filed in at 5:30 A.M. He was a skinny little man with thin gray hair, virtually no teeth, but bright blue eyes. He was so thin around the waist that his state pants slipped down each time he stood up. He spoke in a squeaky voice.

"Hello, fellers," he greeted us. He went right on, "You fellers don't have to worry none now. Arthur's here. Arthur's goin' to take you out."

The old men turned away from him; they were interested at the moment only in their breakfasts. But Len, a few others, and I listened curiously.

"Plane's outside," Arthur piped. "Right on these here grounds. We'll take off whenever you fellers are ready."

He explained that the plane could carry forty persons; then he changed that to four hundred persons. "And she's loaded with food and clothes and everythin' you fellers need."

"Whiskey, of course?" interposed Len.

Arthur beamed. "All you can drink. Bonded stuff."

Teddy had to be in on it. "You got women, too?"

"No," said Arthur, frowning. "We don't want no women. They're trouble-makers."

"Where are we going?" I asked. "If and when we go."

"Every place—all 'round the world. I gotta stop in Ludington first and we'll have a good feed there. Then we'll go to Chicago and then out to Los Angeles. I'm figurin' on hitting Japan and China. Be a nice change for you fellers."

"Who's paying for all this?" asked Len.

"Me. I got hundreds of thousands. You want some money?"

"I could use a few nickels."

"No nickels. Just thousand-dollar bills. Soon's we get out to the plane I'll fix you up, too."

"How about me?" begged Teddy, taking it seriously.

Arthur frowned again. "You're pretty young, but you can have some. Enough for all," he said, waving his right arm grandly.

When we went out for breakfast, Art, who was on the early shift, told us that Arthur had been brought in during the night. He was a paresis case, Art said, with delusions of grandeur, common in such cases.

"Offered me fifty thousand for the keys," Art said.

All through breakfast Arthur talked about his plans for a wholesale delivery of the men on D-3. He said that he would get the keys all right; there was sure to be someone he could bribe. He talked of the cities we would visit and seemed to know something about them, except that he placed the Golden Gate in Los Angeles. He was so happy about it all and so sure of himself that no one had the heart to ridicule him. Only Teddy drank in his plans without question, and when Len told him what was wrong with Arthur, Teddy's face fell.

Goodman also was on duty, so I was spared working in Bath. I asked Miss Brown if I might go down town to do my Christmas shopping, although I didn't have much money left.

"Thought you had done it," she said.

"It was too cold that day."

She consented and I walked down town, enjoying it. I also enjoyed the crowded stores. In one of the stores I met some of the student nurses and treated them to coffee and doughnuts. Then I was nearly broke but had enough to buy a box of candy and a tiny cedar chest for Suzy to keep her letters in. Jeanne had told me that was what Suzy wanted most of all. I got a box of gum for Willie and candy bars for Johnny. Len and I had agreed that we wouldn't spend money on each other. "Unless, of course," Len had said, "you want to smuggle in a bottle."

The crowds were gay in the stores and along Front Street. I felt a momentary pang, thinking: They've got homes to take their presents to, and I'm taking mine to a state hospital ward. But I was able to dismiss the pang and say: You're a big man now!... I walked down some side streets on the way back until I could see the bay. It was calm, but it looked bitterly cold. It occurred to me that would-be suicides wouldn't think about its being cold, and I went on my way with a lighter step.

But something kept nagging at me, and I didn't know what it was until I was in sight of the hospital and saw the hill. Then I knew what was wrong—indecision. I still had to make up my mind where I was going when I left D-3.

Although knowing that Suzy would not be there, I went

up the hill and sat for an hour trying to think it out. If I stayed on in Traverse City I would be near Suzy and perhaps they would let me see her now and then. If I went to California, I would be near my daughter and I would like that. But what if the dark moods came back? What would they do to her? I thought of New York, but instantly said no; I wanted no more of New York, much as I had loved it. I wanted no more of Grand Rapids, which I never had loved. The choice, then, was between Traverse City and California.

But I couldn't decide. I put it off again.

The long hall was gay, even gayer than the Day Room, for while I was gone Miss Brown, Bates, and Smitty, the new man, had taped bunches of pine branches, tied with red ribbon, on each door.

"We waited for you.," said Miss Brown, "but you took too long."

"I'm crushed. I wanted so much to put a wreath on the Colonic Room door, but I see that you've gone ahead and done that, too."

"No reason why we should leave out the Colonic room, is there?"

"No reason at all. But now I can't tell my grandchildren: 'The great day in my life was when I reverently taped pine branches and red ribbon on the door of the highest of high— the Colonic Room.'"

"I daresay," Miss Brown said, "that you will be able to think of something just as ridiculous to tell your grandchildren."

Ten minutes later all the door decorations save the one on the office door were lying on the floor. None of us had seen them fall and we couldn't understand.

"It's not hot in the hall," Miss Brown worried. "See, the tape hasn't melted."

We put back the decorations, and Miss Brown and Bates left the floor to attend to something on D-1. A vague suspicion began to form in my mind, and I stationed myself in the Utility Room to watch. The door to neutral space had hardly closed behind Miss Brown and Bates when Teddy glided from the Day Room. He walked casually along the hall, and as he passed each door he brushed his shoulder against the pine branches and they plopped to the floor. He went down the right side and came back on the left; for some reason he side-stepped the office door.

As he passed the Utility Room, I grabbed him. He let out a yell and fright spread over his face.

"Don't tell on me!" he begged. "Don't tell on me!"

I wanted to slap him hard, but I didn't. "What in hell made you do that?" I was indignant, but I was curious, too.

"I dunno." And then, his courage returning, he said, "Yeah, I know. I'll tell."

We went over to the Utility Room window, and I asked Curly, as usual maintaining his vigil, if we could be alone for a few minutes.

"Say, of course. Just keep looking outside, will you, in case she comes?"

"Go ahead," I told Teddy.

He gulped a few times. "Well, it's somethin' I gotta do. I see somethin' hangin' on the wall like them things—pictures or plates, you know, in them wire holders—I gotta knock 'em down."

"But why?"

"Well, when I was a kid—about six I guess—I was out in the barn one day and I was lookin' at a lot of ribbons my pa had hung up. He won 'em at the county fair for his hogs. I kept lookin' at 'em and all I could think of was knockin' 'em down. So I went ahead and done it. And my pa, he come in and caught me. He knocked me half-way 'cross the barn, and then he got a big leather strap and he beat the livin' Jesus outa me. After that I did it all the time. I couldn't stop. You think I'm crazy or somethin'?"

"No, I don't think you're crazy." My thoughts went back many years: "When I was a kid, too, on the Farm, I went out on the Point one winter day with pals. Something hit us all at once and we went along the whole Point, throwing stones at the windows of the resorters' cottages. I don't know how many we broke, but there must have been dozens. And we weren't crazy."

"Gosh, you musta got a whalin' for that!"

"No. They held a meeting in the school after the damage was discovered. One of my pals had confessed. My father came home after the meeting and awakened me. He asked me to tell the truth, and I did. He didn't whale me. He talked to me quite awhile about it. He said he understood the impulse—all boys have it, he said—but he explained why it was wrong and that it was going to cost him a pretty penny.

"I've never forgotten that night. My father and I weren't too close—I was a mamma's boy—but after that I had respect for him and we were much closer. The other boys were whipped by their fathers—but they broke more windows later on. I never did."

"Gosh, I wish my pa was like that. He was always lickin' me."

"Maybe that explains a lot in your case. I don't know, though. Did you tell the doctor about all this?"

"Naw!"

[*229*]

"Might help if you did. You can tell him things; you can tell him anything that's bothering you."

"You goin' to tell on me?"

"No. But you'd better watch yourself. If it happens again, I'll have to tell. Now get the hell into the Day Room and stay there. When you have to go down the hall, walk in the middle. And if you touch anything in the Day Room I'll whale you myself. No, I won't. But you'll go up to D-4, sure as shooting."

"I won't do nothin'. I promise. Gosh, you're swell!"

"No, I'm not. I'm just a neurotic."

His eyes were adoring, like those of a little boy listening to a war hero. "Gosh, I wanta be a neurotic some day, too!"

the
THIRTY-SECOND
day

I was deep in sleep when my door flew open and a shrill voice called, "All right, fellers, time to go!"

I groaned. Usually when the attendant routed us out at five-thirty I was ready to get up, but today I wanted a few more hours. I got up, however, and dressed. On the way to the toilet I noticed that the Day Room door was still locked, which was unusual. And the hall lights were not on. There was no sign of the attendant.

The others straggled in, yawning and complaining. But we washed and lined up in front of the Day Room door. The attendant—the pink-cheeked one—came up from D-2, and stared at us in bewilderment.

"What the hell goes on here? You guys can't sleep or somethin'?"

Len said, "Yeah, what the hell does go on? You got us up didn't you?"

"Not me! You guys know what time it is? Three A.M.!"

It was our turn to be bewildered. But not for long. Around the corner from the hall leading to the insulin ward pattered Arthur. His face was wreathed in smiles as he came up to us.

"All ready, fellers? Takin' off just as soon as I get them keys."

Len looked at me, and we both looked at the attendant. Then we began to laugh; the others joined in, although some of them didn't know why, and we had a 3:00 A.M. laughfest that must have been heard even down on D-1.

"Arthur, you'll be the death of me yet!" Len said, and the little man beamed.

"Get the keys," he said. "Get 'em from that guy."

That sobered the attendant. "All right, fellows, turn in again. And as for you, Arthur, get into your room. I'm locking you in."

"No, you ain't," said Arthur.

The attendant grabbed him. Arthur struggled, but he was locked in within a few seconds. We could hear him weeping. Then he stopped and we could hear crashing noises. The attendant unlocked the door. Arthur had pulled out the bureau drawers and was smashing them against the broad windowsill.

"Stand by, fellers!" he called. "I'll get you out!"

The attendant went in and got him. He didn't need help from other attendants, Arthur was that small. He took Arthur up to D-4 and we went back to our beds.

All of us were a little groggy during the morning because of lack of sleep, but we came alive in the afternoon when the nurses and attendants gave us a Christmas party. It was a nice party—all the ice cream we could eat, four kinds of cake, and hot chocolate with marshmallows.

The old men were delighted. Willie was especially enchanted; he ate two helpings of everything and licked his lips and patted his little belly. Johnny wouldn't eat; neither would Franklin, but the rest of us made up for them—so much that there wasn't much left for the nurses and attendants.

Miss Brown poured the chocolate; Miss Love spooned out the ice cream, and Goodman cut the cakes—which was his privilege because his wife had made them. Bates and I passed the heaped plates to those who couldn't—or wouldn't—stand in line. In between serving and eating, I kept my eye on Teddy, but he was too interested in the ice cream even to think of brushing things off the wall. I had told Miss Brown and Bates, when they returned from D-1 the day before, that I thought we should use Scotch tape in the hall, too, and they accepted the suggestion without suspicion.

A new snowstorm blew up while we were feasting. Big flakes fastened themselves to the windows and we could see nothing outside. In addition to watching Teddy, I watched the clock, for I wanted to go to the canteen before closing time in the hope that Suzy would be there. At three-thirty I asked if I might leave.

"The party's still young," said Miss Brown.

"Jack thinks he is, too," said Miss Love, getting back at me for the hat business. "Well, go ahead. But bundle up." Neither said anything about the stocking cap.

It was beautiful outside. The snowflakes were feathery and there was that hush that always comes with a soft snowfall. Hardly any green showed on the boughs of the pines, and all the cars parked outside Receiving were alike with a thick coating of white. The seagulls were not aloft, and the squirrels had tucked themselves into the tree trunks.

Suzy met me halfway to the canteen. She smiled happily and smoothed my arm.

"I thought you were sick again. I was going to Receiving to ask."

"We had a Christmas party. I couldn't walk out in the middle of it. How's it feel to be out again—or don't you like to be out in this? Did they scold you much?"

"No. They just took away my ground parole."

We turned and walked along the soft paths—it was too snowy to go up the hill.

Suzy said that snowstorms always made her homesick for her father's farm. "We got up at five in the morning, even in winter," she said. "All of us—my sister and my two brothers—helped to milk the cows. I liked to go to the cow barn on winter mornings; it was always warm and steamy, and the cows seemed to welcome us after a long night. We had two barn cats, and they came out of their nests in the straw to greet us. I don't know whether they liked human company or were eager for the milk. We always fed them the warm milk before we settled down to work.

"I liked the breakfasts in winter, too. When the milking was done, we had fried eggs, pancakes, sausage, and mounds of home-made bread. All the others drank gallons of coffee, but I was the milk drinker. My father said that all the profits from the cows went down my throat."

I said, "Both of us are nostalgic about farm life. I especially remember The Farm in winter; there's something about winter on a farm that one never forgets. I thought about those winters many times when I was in New York wading through the dirty slush."

"I never had enough of it," Suzy said, "because they sent me away when I was sixteen."

"What! You never told me about that."

"No, but I'd just as soon tell you now. It wouldn't make any difference now, would it?"

"Nothing would make any difference."

She hesitated but went on, hunched a little against the flakes that bit into our faces as a wind suddenly came down from the north.

"I was sent to a country school when I was six. I loved school; I even loved home work. I went to the same school until I was in the sixth grade, but all the time I knew that I was different. My family never stopped talking about it. One of my brothers caught me reading in bed long after midnight, and he told them about it and I was scolded, but not too much. They said I was queer, as though that explained everything.

"When I lost my temper I wasn't punished. They said I was having a spell, and they locked me in my room. I'd stay there for days, just brooding. I didn't know why; I still don't know why. Finally, when I was sixteen, they sent me to a training school for girls. I didn't like it there, but I did like studying. They had a wonderful library and I read every chance I had."

She looked up, smiling. "But I was a miserable failure in arithmetic and I never got to algebra."

"Meet a fellow flop! At no time have I been a menace to Einstein."

Suzy continued, "They kept me there for five years and then I was sent here. Now maybe you understand what I mean about the walls."

"I understand. I've felt that way, too, at times." I wanted to say more, but what was there to say? That everything would come out all right eventually? Tell that to someone who had spent thirteen years in state institutions?"

What I did say was, "I love you, Suzy."

She nestled closer, looking up again, her eyes and her mouth smiling softly.

"Why?"

"Because you're sweet and beautiful. Because you like the snow and you like cows. Because you have a sense of humor. Because, despite all you've been through, you love life. Because—isn't that enough?"

"There is never enough of that—for a woman."

Only a few of us on D-3 went to the Christmas entertainment in the auditorium. Most of the men didn't want to venture out; the snow was still falling and the north wind was lashing it furiously, driving it against the windows and whipping it around the corners of Receiving.

We were late reaching the auditorium. I saw Suzy in the front row on the women's side and we waved to each other. The lights were turned low as we found seats, a spotlight was turned on the stage, and a group of student nurses sang "Joy to the World." They sang beautifully, and they themselves were beautiful in their newly starched uniforms, with their faces solemn yet eager; their figures so girlish yet eager, too. I could see in the dim light that several of the older men near me were feasting their eyes on them, and I thought: Those men have daughters somewhere.

Next, the students sang "Winter Wonderland," followed by the gayer "We Wish You a Merry Christmas." Then they filed down to the floor and took front seats while the audience applauded wildly. There were many patients who carried on feuds with the registered nurses and the attendants, but none I knew who had anything but affection for the student nurses.... Except Jacob.

Next came Jeanne, singing "Rudolph the Red-Nosed Reindeer," singing it playfully yet with the charm of a little girl. Jeanne brought down the house. Teddy whispered, "Gosh, ain't she noble?" That wasn't quite the word for Jeanne. I didn't know where Teddy picked it up, but he used it from then on.

A former night club singer sang, "If it doesn't snow on Christmas." Halfway through she forgot the words and, bursting into tears, fled behind the curtain. But everyone applauded.

The play was titled *Don't Open Till Christmas*. The actor-patients had been rehearsing for days, but panic seized all of them, except Jeanne, when the curtain went up. They frequently forgot their lines and stared miserably over the footlights. They forgot their entrance cues and their exit cues, and at one time there was no one on the stage. Jeanne again stole the show; she not only remembered all her lines, but made up extra ones to fill the gaps. Even Len, who pretended to be bored, was impressed.

"What the hell's she doing here?" he said. "She ought to be on Broadway."

The entertainment ended with the audience, led by the student nurses, singing "Silent Night." There was weeping, then, on the women's side, and some on the men's side, too. No one seemed to want to leave, to break the spell, but when the attendants beckoned, all rose obediently to their feet and filed out into the storm.

[*237*]

Half an hour later, peering out my window, I saw the vague lights in the other buildings go out, and I knew they were going out in Receiving, too. Silent night—except for the wind and the snow slashing at the window. Silent night— safe within these walls....

the
THIRTY-THIRD
day

When I woke this morning my mind was made up. I don't know whether it was a result of a dream or my thoughts functioning while I slept. But my mind was made up: I was going to stay in Traverse City.

Because it was Saturday and the canteen closed at noon, we were permitted to go out early. I hurried over to tell Suzy—that is, I tried to hurry over, but the drifts were like miniature mountain ranges, and the little tractor hadn't been through. It's probably fed up, I thought; it can't take any more.

Suzy came in a few minutes after I arrived. Her cheeks were glowing and she laughed at herself as she shook the snow from her.

"I went headfirst into a drift," she said. "My, it was fun!"

"You look as though you went in headfirst and then turned around and went in the other way."

"I went completely under, except for my nose and eyes. Wait until I take off my galoshes; I must have a bushel of snow in 'em."

While Suzy dug herself out, I ordered Cokes. There were

only two other persons in the canteen, and they were at the counter drinking coffee, so we had the table to ourselves.

"And now," said Suzy, straightening, "What is it you want to tell me?"

"I wish you'd stop being a mind-reader. Or is it woman's intuition again?"

"Darling, you're so obvious. You haven't a poker face. Are you a good poker player?"

"I've learned to be honest here. The answer is no!"

"What is it, Yack?"

"I'm going to stay here. Made up my mind this morning."

"Oh, no! No, Yack, you musn't stay here!"

"I don't mean in the hospital. I mean in Traverse City somewhere. Then I can be near you. That's all I want, Suzy, more than anything else."

"Yes," she said, "that's what I want, too." But all the glow was gone from her face and she didn't look at me. She looked down at the table and moved the Coke bottle back and forth. "Yes, that's what I want. I've thought sometimes, at night, that maybe you wouldn't get better; I've wished it, and then I've been ashamed. You can't do it, Yack; you've got to go away."

"Why?"

She looked up, then, and the pain in her eyes cut through me. "Do I have to explain? You know as well as I do how impossible it would be. Loving each other, yes. I think we'll always love each other. But if you stayed on in town... oh, darling. I don't want to hurt you."

"You've made a pretty good start."

"Don't be bitter. Please! You've been bitter too many times. Yack, you've got so much you can do outside. You're starting a new life—and there's no new life for me. You said that you learned here to be honest. Let's be honest then. You know I'm speaking the truth."

"I can start a new life in Traverse City. It's not necessary to go to the North Pole to start a new life."

"You *aren't* being honest. Even if we could see each other now and then, we'd both be miserable. We'd be living on—what do they call it? Half-rations."

"We wouldn't be starving, at any rate." As I spoke I realized how childish I sounded. Suzy knew it, too, but her smile was tolerant.

"We don't have to starve. We can write to each other. We can have memories—the warm memories you've learned to have, Yack. There's only one war for us. 'Straight are the footprints.' Remember?"

"Yes, but things are different now."

"That's true. We *know* now that we love each other. All the more reason why you should go away. Because it's hopeless; you know it's hopeless, my darling."

I said coldly, "It seems strange to me that you know exactly what I should do, but you can't do anything for yourself."

Suzy winced; then she smiled forgivingly. "You weren't going to be a little boy any more!" That went home, but before I could answer, the door banged open and Lil strode in. She plopped into the remaining chair and leaned her big arms on the table.

"Hello, folks! What the hell is this—an assignation?"

We gaped at her. Suzy was the first to find her voice. "My goodness, Lil, you aren't back already!"

"It ain't my ghost you see. Damned right I'm back and glad of it, too!"

I said, "It turned out the way you predicted?"

She laughed, but it wasn't her usual booming, hearty

laugh. "Just the way I predicted. Say, treat me to a coffee, will you? I'm busted. Yep, just the way I predicted. I tried to fool myself when I got home. I said I wouldn't drink and I didn't for twenty-four hours. But my damned family got on my nerves. They kept saying how much nicer I was. Jesus, nicer! But they kept hinting that I shouldn't plan to stay home too long. I might have one of my spells; I might do something to disgrace 'em. A little visit was all right, but of course I was better off up here.

"The second time my father pulled that line—we were having dinner in the kitchen and I was feeling good—I got up and threw my plate at him. I said, 'You're God-damned right I'm better off up there!' I went upstairs and packed my bag and I walked out. They tried to stop me. 'What'll the neighbors think?' they said. 'Screw the neighbors!' I said.

"I went to the nearest tavern and started loading up. There was a fellow there I used to know and we got chummy again. He had a cabin near Manistee, and we went over there at two in the morning. We took along a case of beer. I was all right while the beer lasted; then he got on my nerves, too. I said I was going back to the hospital. You know what? The bastard wouldn't drive me up here—a lousy sixty miles. I had to take a bus."

She gulped her coffee. "Pretty story, ain't it?"

Suzy said, "It's a shame, Lil. You counted on it so much."

"Yeah. Mostly my fault, I know, but they don't understand us outside. They don't try to understand." Her thick lips trembled. "They think we're freaks."

I said, "How about three freaks having some hamburgers?"

"Serve 'em up, buddy!" Lil was suddenly at home again. "My belly's collapsed!"

She wolfed her sandwich and I gave her mine. Something had happened to my appetite. I got another cup of coffee for her. When she was done she wiped her mouth on her coat sleeve and leaned back. She belched contentedly.

"Say, what's wrong with you two? You don't look so hot."

"It's the humidity," I said.

Her eyes were all-seeing. "Jesus, I didn't mean to barge in on you. Lovers' quarrel, huh?"

"You didn't barge in," Suzy said quietly. "I think you've helped. And it isn't a lovers' quarrel, Lil. We just don't see eye to eye about something."

Again that all-seeing look. "If I was you," said Lil, turning to me, "I'd stay here until hell freezes over."

"Oh, Lil, no!" Suzy leaned across the table, upsetting a Coke bottle. "Lil, you don't know what you're saying!"

Lil blinked. "Thought you said I was helping. But I get it now."

"Yes," Suzy said, "that's it!"

I wondered: What goes on in this place? Everyone seems to know what the other fellow is thinking.... "Let's play Twenty Questions," I said. "You two can win with two of 'em."

That eased things a little, and when the younger set whirled in and surrounded Lil, Suzy and I got up to leave.

Lil grabbed my coat. "You do what Suzy says. Suzy's got a mind of her own."

"Yes," I said, "I'm beginning to learn that."

The snow had ceased, the wind was gentle again, and the little tractor was back on duty. "I'm fond of that tractor," I said. "It's so damned faithful."

Suzy said, "Yes, it has a job to do. It probably would like to rest, but it comes out anyway. It has a job to do."

[*243*]

"You don't have to draw diagrams, darling. You're right, and I knew it all the time but I wouldn't admit it."

"Lil *did* help?"

"In a way, I guess. She was so honest about everything, and I have a hell of a time being honest about emotions. But the thing that counts is that I've suddenly realized my hanging around here won't make you happier."

She put her arms around me. "I knew you'd see it, Yack. Thank you for seeing it, darling! Thank you so much!"

We clung to each other, and it seemed to me that some of her strength—the strength I still lacked—went into me. Patients came by, and nurses and attendants, but they didn't matter and, strangely enough, we didn't seem to matter to them.

"I'm crying inside," Suzy said, "but I feel peaceful inside, too. Do you know how that is, Yack?"

I said, "no, but I'll try to learn."

At the gate to Eleven, Suzy said, "I don't care if they do boil me in oil. I want to be kissed."

A few minutes later I said, "I don't care if they pour molten lead on me. I want to be kissed."

We laughed together, and as we laughed the storm came back, whipping out of the north again, bringing sudden darkness at noon and raising a screen against any who might be watching.

the
THIRTY-FOURTH
day

I couldn't go to sleep last night. Neither could Len. He came into my room after the lights were out and we talked, but not about ourselves. I knew that he was feeling low because he had not heard from his family, but I said nothing. He probably knew, in a way, why I wasn't asleep, but he said nothing. It was one of those times when two men, no matter how close, sensed that there was nothing to be said.

Art came in finally and asked if we wanted some coffee. We followed him into the kitchen. It was bright in there and warm, and Art brought some home-made cookies. They were what we called "cry babies" on The Farm—molasses cookies with tear drops of white frosting. It must have been the cookies because, while Art and Len chatted, my thoughts drifted back to The Farm and my mother. I saw her putting the cry babies into the oven of the wood range, and I heard her saying, "Jacket (her pet name for me), the wood box is empty." And I remembered getting up, groaning, and going out to the woodshed. I was at that terrible age when all boys groan when any work is to be done. I groaned when I had to go out to the pump to fill the water pail. I groaned every

Saturday when I had to chop enough kindling to last a week. I groaned when I had to get up early to light the fires.

My mother was a beautiful woman, and I knew it when I was only six. When she went away on trips with my father, I cried for hours. When she returned, I rushed into her arms and cried some more, and she petted me and soothed me while my baby sisters stood by, puzzled but patient. In time my mother turned to them, but always I—the male child, the first-born—was the first to receive attention.

"That's it," I said aloud. "God-damned attention!"

Art and Len gave me surprised looks, then went back to their talk. I felt ashamed, but I drifted off again. I remembered how one day when I refused to chop kindling she burst into tears and ran out to the grove and flung herself on the ground. I was horrified, but I stuck it out for ten minutes. Then I went out to the grove and said I was sorry, and we wept in each other's arms. I thought, vaguely watching Art and Len and hearing nothing that they said: My beautiful mother, if only you had taken a horsewhip to me then.

I remembered the time my grandmother spanked me with a bedroom slipper; it didn't hurt, but I screamed bloody murder, and my mother came in and took my grandmother to task. And then made snow ice cream for me to make up for it. My beautiful mother, if only you had added a few extra whacks with that slipper.

Perhaps, I thought, the doctor was wrong in not going back to my childhood. On the other hand. I had gone back by myself and had seen my childhood as he might have seen it. Even a glimpse of it had been enough. Then he wasn't wrong; he was wise—patient.

I reached for a cry baby and drank some coffee.

"Ah," Len said pleasantly, "back from Mars?"

"No, just turning myself inside out."

Len said, "Keep this up and you'll wind up on Six sure as hell." But Art nodded as though he understood, and we went into a discussion of the Detroit Tigers.

Miss Brown, Miss Love, Bates, and Goodman spent most of the morning in the Colonic Room unwrapping presents that had arrived for the patients. They unwrapped the presents, inspected them for contraband, and wrapped them again. They left the door ajar and we peeked in now and then, as curious as children whose Christmas gifts have been hidden in a closet. Bates came out once with a handful of book matches.

"They were in a box from your sister," he said to me. "Sorry, but I got to put 'em away. You can have 'em when you leave."

"Go ahead and use them," I said. "You and the nurses are always running out of matches, anyway."

"I don't know why," he said, "but that reminds me that there's a letter in the office for you. Came in last night."

It was a letter from my daughter in California. She wrote that she and her husband wanted me to come out there. They had found me a cottage a mile from them, and it would be vacant in a month or so. In the meantime, they wanted me to stay with them. They didn't think I'd use them as a crutch; if I started to, she wrote, they'd sit on me good. Her husband Mac, she wrote, would drop everything when I was ready to leave and would meet me in Omaha and drive the rest of the way. She knew that I had never experienced mountain driving.

Here was a postscript that read:

Daddy, I'll never be able to say this to you, but I am so

happy that you are getting squared around about things. You have no idea what you mean to me and how much I love you. I just don't know what I'd do without you.

I showed the postscript to Len. I didn't think that my daughter would mind because Len and I were close, but I forgot that his own daughters had not written to him. He read it and his face quivered. "Son of a bitch!" he said and, handing me the letter, walked out of the Day Room.

He came back in fifteen minutes. I knew that he had been crying.

"You're a God-damned lucky guy!" he said.

I said, "Yes, I'm getting that idea myself."

"You going out there?"

"Yes. Made up my mind yesterday. Or had it made up for me. I'm glad I decided, though, before I got the letter."

"How's that?"

"Well, I wouldn't want to go out there on an emotional spree. I wouldn't want to do any leaning. I leaned too much on my other daughter."

"Women!" said Len. "God-damned women!" But I knew how he meant it.

I sat for some time thinking about California and my younger daughter and her family. It seemed to me that since I had been in the hospital I was always going back, trying to recapture something I no longer had. And then it came to me that I wasn't trying to recapture something—that I now could look back without tears, without reaching for the whiskey bottle. One psychiatrist had told me in Grand Rapids: "Forget the past. Start all over again. Get a hobby." But here they said, "Go into the past if you have to. Dig it up. See your mistakes. Admit them."

In the afternoon Art Ammidon asked several of us to help him carry Christmas presents from Center, where they were sorted. There were more than a dozen boxes for D-3, including two for me—one from California and one from a Grand Rapids couple. There also was a huge box for Len, bearing his wife's name and return address. I was glad for him and told him about it the moment we were back on D-3.

"About time!" he grumbled, but his face was a pleased red. "Any idea what's in it?"

"Thought you weren't interested in Christmas."

"Well, if she sent a box that means I won't get out before Christmas. Might as well be gracious about it."

I snorted. "Your being gracious! That I want to see!"

He was cheerful the rest of the day, and at supper he gorged on cherry pie. Len long ago had abandoned all pretense of living up to his diet.

"At my age," he said, "what the hell does it matter if a guy has a pot-belly?"

He spent several hours loitering near the Colonic Room and asking questions about his box. Miss Love told him that there was something in it that he liked.

"Not whiskey! My family wouldn't send me whiskey!"

"No," said Miss Love, making a face, "but it's strong stuff. It's limburger! And that's all I'll tell you."

He beamed. "That's enough. God, how I love that cheese!"

Miss Love said, "Our romance is off. I can't stand it." She turned to me. "Can you?"

"No. I don't like any cheeses. Guess I'm just a farm boy at heart. I like hot rolls, cornbread, pancakes, baked beans—just plain white ones—strawberries preserved in the sun. I do like avocados though, and farm boys don't get them—at least in the Middle West. I'll probably live on them when I get to California."

Miss Brown looked up. "You're going out there?"

"Yes."

"That'll be nice, I think. The doctor will be pleased."

"Why?"

"He wanted you to make up your mind to go there. Now don't go telling him that."

"The stinker! He didn't give me a hint."

"No," said Miss Brown, "the doctor is not the hinting kind."

Goodman and his wife had driven to California the winter before, and he offered me advice about routes and motels.

"I've never been in a motel," I said. "Always preferred hotels. But, of course, I never made a trip like this before—by car."

"You stay in motels a couple of nights," said Goodman, "and you'll never think about hotels. Thing to do is to pick out one you like on the western outskirts of the town where you decide to spend the night. Then you are all set to whiz out in the morning without bothering about city traffic. Get an early start and check in early in the afternoon; that way you'll be sure of getting accommodations."

I was suddenly enthusiastic about the trip. I asked Goodman about routes, and he suggested cutting far south to avoid the snow. Len said that was a good idea; he said that once I was out of Michigan and Indiana I should have smooth going.

"But my son-in-law wants to meet me in Omaha."

"Don't go that way—in winter!" Goodman and Len chorused. "If you think the snow's bad here, you ought to see it in Nebraska and Colorado," Goodman said.

"And you want to skip the mountains," said Len.

They argued about routes, and finally I went to Center, got the keys to the garage where my car was parked, and returned with a road atlas I had bought several months before when my wife and I were planning a vacation trip to California. That seemed long ago. What had prevented it? Oh, yes, I came down with virus pneumonia and was in a hospital for five days. On second thought, it wasn't a vacation trip; we were going out there to live. But while I was in the hospital my wife admitted that she didn't want to go out there to live. And the doctor said that I shouldn't attempt such a trip by car for two months, at least.

Why had I forgotten, or submerged thoughts of that planned trip? I had given in, and with good grace, I recalled, when my wife had said she was not eager to go to California. But I had resented it; I had resented it all the time until I went to Traverse City, and then something I had learned there had made me bury the resentment until, momentarily, I had even forgotten that it wasn't a vacation trip.

"Resentments!" I said. "Lousy resentments!"

Miss Brown said, "Yes, they can wreck one."

"Here we go again," said Len. "Class in psychology is now in session."

"I wonder," Miss Love said dreamily, "if liking limburger is a key to a man's character."

"Makes him a stinker all right," said Len.

I thought: I'm going to miss that man. I'm going to miss Miss Brown, Miss Love, Bates, Art, Goodman, the doctor. I'm going to miss Crispy and Lil. I'm going to miss the canteen and the dances.

I tried not to think about Suzy.

the
THIRTY-FIFTH
day

Because it was the day before Christmas, Miss Brown and Bates did not insist on the usual Monday cleaning-up.

"The place will be a mess tomorrow, anyway," Bates said, "what with opening the boxes and everyone munching on cookies and candies. You and Jacob'll have a real job tomorrow.

"What are you going to do when I leave?"

"There's always someone new," he said. "I don't think we'll suffer. I mean about the sweeping. By the way, I'm glad you decided on California. Sounds good to me. Change of scenery never hurt anyone. Why don't you advertise in the paper for someone to go along with you?"

"I thought of that, but I'm a lone wolf when it comes to driving. I get kind of nervous when someone else is along."

Bates said, "It's a long trip. Wife and I drove as far as New Mexico last summer. You need someone to talk to now and then on those long stretches."

"I follow you, but I think I'll do it by myself."

"Figured you would. But you can get lonesome as hell. And in your case...."

I said, "If I can't drive from Traverse City, Michigan, to Palm City, California, without getting in the dumps, then I shouldn't leave here."

He nodded. "Something in what you say. Just thought I'd mention it."

The doctor let himself in from the neutral space then, and we walked down the hall. I began to tell him about California, but Eloise appeared, too, looking nervously up and down the hall.

"We're taking off in a few hours," Eloise said. "You'll probably be leaving before we get back. I wanted to say goodbye."

"You mean you'll get to Indiana—on these roads—in time for Christmas?"

"Oh, this isn't too bad. Well, it was yesterday, when we wanted to start. But we'll make it."

"I wouldn't drive on the grounds even, in this kind of weather."

Eloise said that I was getting soft, that the winters weren't as bad as they were in the days of The Farm.

"You have snow tires and a prayer on your lips and somehow you get there," she said.

I said, "I haven't snow tires and I'll probably need a prayer when I leave. I don't know much about winter driving. Spent most of my winters in the subway or in taxis."

"Well, Merry Christmas and good luck."

"Merry Christmas, Eloise! And to Ina and Isabel, too. Thanks a lot for coming up. People appreciate a little attention up here (that word again!) but most of them don't get it."

When she left, I hurried into the Day Room, but the doctor was busy with new patients. I asked Bates to unlock my door

[*253*]

so that I could get my presents for Willie and Johnny. Willie was charmed by the box of gum; he held it up close to his eyes, and when he realized what it was, his hands shook with excitement.

"Well, say now, that's wonderful! That'll last me a long time. Thank you very much. You're a gentleman!"

But Johnny was not at all excited. He took one of the candy bars, bit off a piece, wrapper and all, chewed casually on it and dropped the rest on the floor. Teddy sidled up, his eyes as begging as a puppy's. Johnny smiled vaguely and wandered away, leaving the other candy bars for Teddy.

When the doctor finally got to me, I told him about my decision.

"That's fine," he said. "Wish I could go with you."

"I suppose I can go right after Christmas then?"

"Well, let's wait until after Christmas and see."

"My fatal charm doesn't seem to be working. You aren't suggesting that I stay here indefinitely?"

"No." He looked at me over his glasses. "What the hell; might as well be frank. I'd like you to stay until after New Year's."

"St. Patrick's Day is coming up, too. And then there's Decoration Day."

He chuckled. "I know it seems that we're putting you off, week by week, but we aren't. Point is, with a fellow like you, New Year's Eve and New Year's Day probably meant as much as Christmas. Like to get you over the hump, that's all. Stay until after New Year's and then I'll sign you out."

"You're the doctor!"

He said, "Yes, damn it! It's not always pleasant—being the doctor. But I've got a hunch you'd better stay for one more week."

When he left, I thought: That man's uncanny. He doesn't know a damned thing about what I did on New Year's Eve and New Year's Day, but he sensed it, and I've almost forgotten it.

No, I said on second thought, you haven't forgotten because on more recent New Year's Eves you've never failed to think about it.

It was vivid then in my mind. Each New Year's Eve my wife and I went to the apartment of a couple who had been married in our apartment. I chuckled as I recalled their wedding. We had a small apartment then, and it was not a cold day, but we had birch logs burning in the fireplace because all of us liked burning logs.

The living room was so small that the minister had to stand with his back to the fireplace and the poor man was scorched, where no man should be scorched, before he was through with the ceremony. And the kitchenette was so small that there was no room for the canapes. But our maid, Eva, who was as excited and pleased about the wedding as we were, solved the problem. She put the plates of canapes on the toilet seat and in the bathtub until the ceremony was over and she could enter triumphantly with them. In those days in New York many apartments had adjoining kitchenettes and bathrooms, and no one thought anything about it.

The first New Year's Eve following their marriage the young couple began their eggnog-mixing parties. Only my wife and I were invited. We worked for hours in the kitchen, mixing the stuff and, of course, sampling it as we went along. We poured it into big milk cans rented from a dairy company, and when the task was done we put the cans on the fire escape to chill. Then we went into the living room and listened to Victrola records. It was on those New Year's Eves

[*255*]

that I, the only one of the four of us without musical appreciation, learned to love Wagner. And Gilbert and Sullivan.

When Times Square went berserk at midnight we opened the windows leading to the fire escape and, with the milk cans sparkling in the glow of neon signs, we drank a toast to the next year. We never doubted that all of us would be together again next year....

It was impossible to climb the hill. Or I thought that it would be impossible for me. But I skirted it, thinking that Suzy, being younger, might have attempted it. There were no footprints leading up the slope, however, and I went on to the canteen.

The canteen was crowded with patients, and nurses and attendants, too, doing last-minute Christmas shopping. Queen Deborah was there flirting shamelessly with Len. Teddy was outside in the hallway, sulking again, and Len stopped his banter long enough to tell me Jeanne had given him a motherly scolding.

"She might have waited until after Christmas," I said. "He had a present for her and, I might add, not panties."

"Panties!" screamed Queen Deborah. "Who wants panties? Give me the good old-fashioned drawers!"

Len said, "You know what the kid did? He told Jeanne he had a present for her, but now he wasn't going to give it to her. He had a frilly handkerchief for her—but he's wearing it now in his coat pocket."

I wanted to go out and talk to Teddy, but I knew that it would do no good in his present mood. I got a crate and sat near the window by the Coke machine. When Suzy came in, I gave her the presents. She squeezed the box and knew immediately what it was. The candy was obvious.

"I wanted a little box so much, Yack! Shall I open it now?"

"Why don't you wait? It's more fun on Christmas morning. I never could understand Christmas Eve gift-openers."

She dug into a pocket and brought out her present for me. I, too, knew immediately what it was.

"A fountain pen! How did you guess what I wanted? I'm sick of the state pencils."

"So you can write to me. Write lots, Yack, please!"

I told her that I was staying until after New Year's and she said, "Oh. Darling, another week! We can be happy that week! We can have fun! I guess my prayers were answered."

"Your prayers?"

"I prayed that you wouldn't go away feeling that I made you go away. I didn't want that. I wanted you to feel that it was the only thing to do—the right thing to do. But I prayed, too, for just a few more days."

I patted her hand. I couldn't say a word. I couldn't tell her then how far away I *was* going.

Lloyd was checked out tonight. He was a voluntary; he wanted to be home for Christmas, and they couldn't talk him out of it. But those of us who knew his case realized that he would be back shortly. He didn't bother to say goodbye; he walked out with a pasteboard suitcase under his arm. Len said that he was smirking, but I thought that he looked frightened. His wife didn't come up to D-3 for him; she waited on the first floor.

"Just as well," I said. "I'm in no condition to have that woman giving me her thoughts."

Len said, "I'm in no condition. Period."

We avoided a session of bawdiness.

[*257*]

A group of Girl Scouts tiptoed timidly into the Day Room at seven-thirty and sang three Christmas carols. They sang vaguely, their eyes darting here and there, but for the most part fixed on Willie, curled up on one of the benches with his guitar folded in his arms. Something awakened him from his cat-nap—it couldn't have been the Girl Scouts' singing, for that was shy and reluctant. Willie sat up, carefully placed his guitar on the pillows, and pattered, unseeing, towards the Day Room doorway.

The Girl Scouts fell back in dismay. Willie, coming close to them and seeing them for the first time, halted and said happily, "Well, little angels on Christmas Eve!"

The little angels backed farther down the hall but bravely returned after Willie had disappeared to relieve himself. They hurried through the third Christmas carol and backed out, their eyes still bulging, before anyone could thank them and their leader.

Art and a patient brought in a bushel basket of apples and set it down near the center pillar. Usually there was a rush when there was an apple treat, but no one moved, not even the old men who liked to nibble the apples and spit the pieces of skin into the corners.

Larry had fetched his radio, and he turned it on, peering at the dials in the glow from the Christmas tree lights. He found a station that came in clearly, and sat back expectantly. It was "Silent Night" again.

No one moved, no one spoke until it was over. Then Larry buried his face in his hands. And the Day Room was filled with the soft sobbing of men—as the wind weeps when it passes through the pines.

the
THIRTY-SIXTH
day

Christmas or no Christmas, we were routed out at 5:30 A.M.
I had been up since four anyway, and so had Elmer and an el-
derly man we called The Frenchman who had the room next
to mine. It wasn't that we were excited about Christmas, but
for half an hour before we gave up and got out of our beds,
there had been a terrific din on D-4.

An attendant came down from there at five-thirty, and I
said, "I didn't know that the riveters worked on Christmas."

He said they had had a tough time with one of the patients.
I learned later that it was The Brat; he was transferred to Six
before I left and, like Pickerel, was not seen again on the
grounds or around Receiving.

While we were washing, I wished Elmer and The
Frenchman a Merry Christmas. Elmer growled the words in
reply, but The Frenchman, who had a violent temper, kicked
the swinging door to one of the toilets.

"Christmas? Why in hell didn't someone tell me it was
Christmas? God damn it, you can't get any service around
here!"

Two minutes later he was laughing with Teddy, who

usually provided fire for his pipe. But at intervals, all day, he burst out, "Why in hell didn't someone tell me it was Christmas?"

Teddy was still sulking, so far as Len and I were concerned, as though we were to blame for the failure of his romance. When I wished him a Merry Christmas, he didn't answer. Neither did Ralph. Johnny smiled and hung his head. I gave up then until Len and Larry came into the Day Room; they had greetings for everyone, but they gave up shortly, too.

"Cheerful little gathering, isn't it?" I said.

Larry was downcast by the lack of response to his greetings, but Len was feeling good. One didn't have to guess why; he knew, from the hints that Miss Love had given him, that his days in the doghouse were about to end. Limburger as a peace offering! I couldn't work up any enthusiasm, but I could understand it.

The sun was coming up as we went into breakfast; it was the first time in many days that we had seen the sun. But they kept on the dining room Christmas tree lights, and the women from C-3, serving behind the counters, greeted us boisterously. Only a few of us said Merry Christmas in return, and the women fell silent, as they probably had at home when their husbands were not in the mood.

Bates came in as we left the dining room. "Don't clean up now," he said. "Better wait until the presents are passed around."

So we went into the Day Room and waited, feeling strange that we weren't working. We watched the sun rise above the pines; we drank frequently from the fountain; and the old men, coming back to life with their bellies full, sampled the apples.

"Maybe it won't be so bad," I said hopefully.

It was ten o'clock before Miss Brown, Bates, and the student nurses entered the Day Room with our presents. They were stacked in a rubber-tired push-truck with canvas sides, used to shuttle laundry from floor to floor. We sat next to the walls, waiting, while Miss Brown and Bates sorted the presents and passed them to the student nurses to distribute.

At least a fourth of the gifts were for Ralph and Elmer. I was surprised that Ralph, the grumpy one, received so many, and Len was downright disgusted,

"They're from the women," he said. "Guy plays the piano all over the place and I suppose they think they've got to repay him."

"Well, he does play for them, and that makes them a bit happier for the moment. Look at those presents pile up!"

Ralph appropriated a table and stacked his presents there. He received cartons of cigarettes, handkerchiefs by the dozen, scarves, neckties, a pen and pencil set, cookies, candy—even a wrist watch. And a cigarette lighter which somehow had slipped through the Colonic Room inspectors, but which was promptly confiscated even as Ralph admired it. Ralph held court as the student nurses ooh'd and ah'd over his gifts; he even condescended to speak to some of them, but he did not offer any of them candy or cookies.

Elmer also was surrounded by presents from his family. Each had a little note attached to it, and when he read the notes from his children, he wept. Lewis had a box from his family, and he, too, cried as his fingers fumbled through it. Miss Brown and the students took turns trying to soothe them, but all the presents were distributed before they became calm.

Crispy staggered up to Len with his big box. "I think it's a Ford truck," she said.

[*261*]

Len tried to look unconcerned, but his eyes shone. "Better stand back," he said, unwrapping the box. "There's limburger in here.

There was limburger, all right, and there were a hundred and one other things: boxes of crackers for an assortment of cheeses, cans of sardines, cans of peanuts, cans of ripe olives, boxes of candy and cookies. There were oranges and walnuts; there were cigarettes and cigars. And, finally, there was a mechanical gadget for shuffling canasta decks.

A note was attached to the gadget, and Len read it to me. It said that the gadget would be nice "for us to use at the lake next summer."

"Well!" said Len.

"Is that the best you can do?"

He was pleased and excited—and so relieved. It stood out all over him.

Crispy came over, then, with my presents—three boxes. One was from California and contained a pull-over sweater, a carton of cigarettes, and a tin of chocolate cookies my daughter had made. The second was from one of my sisters: another carton of cigarettes (not my brand, but I swapped them at the canteen next day), linen handkerchiefs that I sorely needed, and candy. The third box was from the Grand Rapids couple and was envied by all. It contained an after-shaving lotion (at a premium on D-3) and three bars of toilet soap made especially for men. I thought: If anyone gave me soap on the outside, I'd be insulted, but here on D-3 I'm charmed.

The soap was the best present of all, counting even Ralph's wrist watch, for all of us—all of us who washed—dreaded using the stinging, husky bars of red soap supplied by the state.

Even Crispy was impressed. "They're so cute," she said. "My, they smell good." So she promptly was offered one, and took it, all the while protesting, "Really, I wasn't hinting!"

Willie got a box of home-made fudge from his school-teacher friend; he cried a little over it, but shortly he was doing justice to it, licking his fingers and smacking his lips.

"She sure knows how to make fudge," he said, offering me a piece.

The Frenchman received a pair of gaudy pajamas from a son. "What the hell are they for?" he demanded of Bates.

"They're pajamas; you wear 'em in bed."

The Frenchman beamed. "Well, now, what do you know about that?"

"They're a Christmas present from your son. This is Christmas, you know."

"Why in hell didn't someone tell me it was Christmas?"

Later he put the pajamas in his bureau drawer; they were there when I left D-3, and The Frenchman was still sleeping in his long underwear.

Bates told me that Franklin had received nothing from his family.

"That's a stinking shame!" I said. "Why can't Len and I fix up a box from our stuff?"

Bates said that it wasn't necessary; Franklin didn't give a damn. "We gave him a state box," Bates said, "but you can see he's not interested in it."

"What's a state box?"

"For each patient who doesn't get anything from his relations we fix up a box of candy, tobacco, and a pipe, supplied by the state."

"You mean to say that there are others besides Franklin who didn't get a thing from outside?"

"Plenty of them. Mostly those who have been here a long time. Their people just seem to forget all about them after awhile."

It was difficult to believe, but it was true, as I realized, looking around. Few of the old men had more than the state boxes. But they seemed satisfied. Perhaps, at one time, they had been disappointed, but years of disappointments and waiting had made them immune. How could their people forget; how could they be so heartless, no matter what the old men might have done before they were sent here?

Teddy received some presents from outside—and a tie from Jeanne. He was shamed-faced about it and sidled up to me to say he guessed he'd done the wrong thing yesterday in keeping the handkerchief.

"She's so noble," he said, "even if she won't marry me."

"Now you're talking sense, kid. Well, fix up the handkerchief and give it to her. She'll understand."

"Canteen ain't open today. I won't see her."

"Send it over to her ward. One of the student nurses will be glad to stop by."

He shifted from foot to foot. "Handkerchief's dirty." He pulled it from his pocket; he had wiped his mouth on it while chewing tobacco. "I was wonderin' could you let me have another dollar."

"You can't buy anything today; the stores are closed."

"One's open halfways down Front Street—a grocery. They got a tiny fruit cake for a buck and a half."

"She'd like that. So it's one-fifty now? But it was Christmas and I was still angry about the old men. "Here's the money, kid. Now I *am* broke. But don't you go down there without town parole."

"Miss Brown said it was okay—this once."

"Well that's different. Better scram now." He was off immediately without a thank-you.

When all the presents were distributed, Miss Brown got Ralph to go to the piano, but first he had to hide his presents in his room. Then he and Miss Brown played a duet, "Night and Day," which seemed a strange choice for Christmas, but Miss Brown said it was the only duet arrangement that Ralph had.

When they were done, Bates sighed and said, "Time to clean up, I guess."

Jacob and I went to work, followed by the moppers and then by Len with his polisher. Jacob and I had the real task, sweeping out the litter; it took us more than an hour, and by the time we were done the dinner bell rang.

Receiving's cooks did themselves proud once more. We had turkey with dressing, mashed potatoes and gravy, carrots, bread *and* butter, cranberry sauce, mince pie, and tea. I couldn't do the dinner justice; I had nibbled on too many cookies and pieces of candy. Franklin refused to eat and wasn't forced to. Jacob ate only the carrots and a piece of bread and butter, but he was happy because his sister sent him two cans of syrup.

Ralph outdid all the others; he had three servings of everything and added three more stripes of gravy to his much-decorated jacket. Teddy was runner-up with two servings; he worked up an appetite, he said, by racing down to the grocery for the tiny fruit cake which, by dinner time, had been delivered to Jeanne by a student nurse.

Half of the patients dozed off when we returned to the Day Room. The others sat listlessly, belching and holding their stomachs. When Boy Blue took his nap, Len stole his shoes and hid them under the Christmas tree. That was the only activity for several hours.

I managed to climb the hill and waited for an hour and a half. There was no sign of Suzy. But a squirrel, lured by the sunshine, sat at one end of the fallen tree, and I tossed some of the chocolate cookies to him.

When I was back in the Day Room, Larry brought out his radio and got a program on which servicemen in Tokyo talked to members of their families in the United States. It was a moving program; the words were the usual words of long distance calls, but there was a lilt to all the voices—and at times a quiver.

"How's Pop, mom?"

"He's fine. How are you, darling?"

"I'm fine."

A pause. "Mom, you still make those biscuits—with pork gravy?"

"Sure do! You'll have 'em when you get home, son."

"Gosh, Mom, that's swell!"

The student nurses came over, one by one, to listen. All but Crispy, who determinedly played ping-pong with a man she disliked.

I went to bed the moment Art unlocked the rooms. The last I remembered was The Frenchman demanding of no one in particular, "Why didn't someone tell me it was Christmas?"

Jacob and I had another hard round of sweeping, for the bedroom floors were littered with gift wrappings and pieces of candy and cookies. Ralph's room was the worst of all, and when Jacob clucked at the sight of it, Ralph flounced out, taking all his presents with him.

"My," said Jacob, "that's what comes from eating too much."

"Everyone ate too much yesterday—except you and Franklin. Well, anyway, we haven't hangovers?"

"You really don't know? Lucky man! A hangover is a combination of seasickness and birth pangs. It results from over-indulgence in alcoholic stimulants."

"Oh, my!" said Jacob. "I never took a drink."

"Not even a sip?

"Well, my sister wanted to give me some blackberry cordial once for my bowels, but I wouldn't take it. So she mixed in some kind of dessert and got it into me that way."

"No reactions?"

"I was all right until she told me. Then my bowels started up again."

Crispy came down the hall and Jacob moved away. She wore a dress and coat and I suddenly remembered that her group was to leave today.

"Came to tell you goodbye," she said. "Our bus leaves in half an hour."

"I'd forgotten. Gosh, Crispy, I hate to see you go."

"I'm not exactly elated. It's been interesting here—and different."

"Different is right. Speaking of which, you look different in those clothes. More grown up."

"Oh, dear!"

We rattled on, avoiding the clichés of goodbyes, until Crispy said, "Hell's bells, this is getting us nowhere! I'm going to say goodbye and thanks—for things."

"Goodbye, Crispy. And thanks—for many things."

We shook hands hastily, and I recalled that my daughters and I had often been stilted at partings. But I knew that I would not forget Crispy.

She hurried to the Day Room to say goodbye to Len, and I went back to my sweeping. I had to step aside for two attendants who were half-carrying Franklin between them. His eyes were glazed and his face was without color. I stopped at the office to ask what was wrong.

"They're taking him down to D-2," Miss Love said. "Easier to tube-feed him there."

"They're going fast, aren't they? Heilhitler, The Flash, Pickerel, The Brat, Franklin...."

"And pretty soon, you."

"Do you have to sound so eager?"

She laughed and slapped me on the arm with her keys. "Of course, when you go we'll all be in tears!"

I said earnestly, "I'm going to miss a lot of people here. It's something like parting from friends you've made on ship-board. Once I took a three-day cruise and met a fellow from Argentina. For some reason we liked each other, and we corresponded for three years. Then he stopped writing; I don't know what happened to him."

"I know. Many patients feel that way, and that's why they come back so quickly. I don't think you'll be coming back, though."

"No. For a visit, maybe, when I make my fortune."

"We'll put out the welcome mat. In meantime, if I may say so, Jacob is frowning something awful, and until you do make your fortune...."

"Yes, Miss Love. I mean, yes, Simon Legree."

After one day of sunshine, which made no impression on the drifts, the snow returned. But it was feathery snow once more; it floated lazily and never quite seemed to reach the ground.

I walked with the D-3 group to the canteen and exchanged a carton of cigarettes. Others were doing the same, but few did any buying. Their pocketbooks were empty and their stomachs were not, after yesterday's feasting. Even Queen Deborah shuddered when Lil ordered a hamburger "with everything."

When Suzy did not appear after half an hour, I went up the hill. My squirrel friend was there, flicking his tail expectantly. I searched my pockets and finally found a chocolate bar studded with peanuts. He did not care for the chocolate, but his tiny teeth unerringly found the peanuts and shucked them out. When one fell from his paws into the snow he dived after it, going completely out of sight but emerging triumphantly with it tucked away in his mouth. The peanuts disappeared rapidly, but the squirrel was not satisfied. He remained hopefully nearby, now sitting on the fallen tree in a begging attitude, now floundering through the snow, seeking a cache he vaguely remembered.

When Suzy came over the hill, he regarded her with alarm.

"It's all right," I said, but he was dubious. With an effortless leap he sailed into a pine and sat on one of the lower branches until finally convinced that three make a crowd. He left us, then, scolding us all the way back to his nest.

"Now it's my turn to scold," I said. "What happened yesterday?"

"I knew you'd worry, but my sister came just when I was ready to go out. And when she left, it was too late to go out. You're angry?"

"Good heavens, no! Relieved. I thought that maybe Christmas was too much for you."

"No, it was a nice Christmas—especially having my sister here. I hadn't seen her for six months. She brought presents from the family and we chattered most of the afternoon. I wanted to let you know, but no one went out from Eleven."

"Too stuffed with turkey?"

"Yes—and excited. Was it fun on D-3?"

"W-e-l-l...."

"I guess women like Christmas more. Or make more of it. Tell me about your Christmas."

We compared notes. While we talked, the squirrel returned, and Suzy tossed some walnuts to him. After that she was accepted; he remained with us through the afternoon, returning only now and then to his nest, probably to report to his wife that they wouldn't have to worry about a long winter after all.

I told Suzy about my plans for the California trip. She looked at me in a dazed way.

"California! I didn't think about California when you said you wouldn't stay here. I don't know why, but I didn't think about California. Oh, darling, that's so far away!"

It was my turn to look dazed. "I thought that was the idea. I thought we were agreed about that."

Her eyes brimmed with tears and she said nothing.

"Wasn't it?"

She buried her face on my shoulder and the tears came fast, mingling with the snow.

"Let's see now," I said, trying to pass it off lightly, "whose turn is it to cry? We always seem to be crying up here."

She sat up in a few minutes, wiped her eyes and blew her nose. "I'm sorry. I've said so many times I'm sorry, haven't I? But it kind of knocked the props from under me."

"I thought you knew, when I said I'd go, that I meant to California. I'll stay here at the drop of a hat, if you drop it."

"You know what I'd say to that." She began to smile again. "California's a wonderful idea. Don't you know, Yack, that women yammer for things, and when they get them, go into weeping orgies nine times out of ten?"

"Sounds like a believe-it-or-not."

"It's true, and I'm not proud of it. I'm not a bit proud about today."

"I'm not a bit proud about a lot of days. But let's stop belaboring ourselves, honey. There's only a little time before that blasted supper bell. Let's enjoy it."

"Now you're advising *me!*"

"Yes, and I kind of like it. New experience."

"You don't hate me?"

"Come closer and I'll answer that." It was a long answer.

"Very convincing," Suzy whispered.

the
THIRTY-EIGHTH
day

"You're going to the dance, of course?" asked Len.

"Of course. It's my last chance—if I leave right after New Year's. What I can't figure out is why they have what they call a New Year's Eve dance tonight. This is Thursday, and New Year's Eve isn't until next Monday."

"You got me. Art tells me the New Year's Eve dances are fun, though. They kind of let down the bars, and you can dance until ten instead of nine."

"No! That's real dissipation!"

"And they have punch—without any punch to it."

"Which means no hangovers."

"I can't remember a New Year's Day when I didn't have one." He made a wry face. "Shock'll probably kill me."

I put in my last day in Bath and wondered, as I sorted state clothes, how it would feel to have a bath whenever I wanted one. And use my own cigarette lighter. And ring up room service, perhaps, for a midnight snack. I wondered how it would feel to drive a car again, but I wasn't too happy about that. Unless a sudden thaw set in, the highways would be dangerous.

Taking his shower, Boy Blue moaned about the loss of his shoes.

"I don't know why you feel so bad," said Bates. "You wear 'em only a few hours a day."

"That's right," said Boy Blue, brightening and patting a few drops of water on his shoulders.

"Maybe Santa Claus borrowed them," I suggested. "Why don't you look under the Christmas tree?".... Informer!

Boy Blue cut his shower shorter than usual, which meant he was hardly damp, and dressed hurriedly. He was back in a minute carrying his shoes.

"Sure is funny how they got there," he said.

"Now that you've got 'em, put 'em on for Pete's sake," Bates said.

"Can't figure it out," said Boy Blue, wandering away, still carrying his shoes.

The laundry arrived while the men were in Bath, and I pounced on a pair of white socks of mine that had been missing since my arrival. There also was a white shirt, missing three weeks. A flannel shirt and a sports shirt never did come back from the laundry, but I didn't complain. Let the state have them; I certainly owed the state more than the $2.30 a day I paid. Many patients, going home, made terrific scenes, however. Bates said that one old chap refused to leave until they found one of his bandanna handkerchiefs. They finally gave him a state bandanna of much better grade, but he wasn't pleased about it.

Working in Bath was not exactly a pleasant job, but it was physical labor, and I had never done any physical labor, to speak of. I surprised myself by thinking that probably I would miss Bath, too—and the sweeping morning and night. Well, I'd have my own bungalow or cottage, whichever it was, to care for, but somehow that seemed different. I realized, then, the difference—I'd be on my own; no Bates to chat with: not even a Jacob to irritate me.

"I presume," I said to Bates, "that at one time you were a bachelor? How did you like it?"

The D-3 mind-reading technique functioned immediately. "Thinking of that, eh?"

"I was thinking that I'm going to miss Bath—in a way."

"Probably will. It's the routine. Bet you fellows felt kind of funny Christmas morning when you didn't clean up on schedule."

"That's so. Good old routine. Wonder if it'll take me long to get out of the habit of getting up at five-thirty?"

"That I doubt!"

When Teddy came in from his shower, I gave him a blue state work shirt.

"Gosh!" he protested. "I gotta look noble for the dance!"

I hunted everywhere but couldn't find a thing that he considered noble.

"Here," I said, "take this white shirt of mine. You'll probably have to wrap it around you twice, but it's got a noble collar anyway."

"Gosh, that's swell! Can I have some of that there smelly stuff you rub on your face?"

"Okay. You'll wow them tonight."

"Yeah. That nigger on D-1, he's goin' to give me some hair oil."

"Don't say *nigger*."

"Why?"

I started to explain, but Miss Brown beckoned me into the hall to meet the new group of student nurses. They were just as young and just as pretty as Crispy's group, but because they were new and shy, none of us warmed to them as we had to Crispy and the others, One of them was from Texas, and when she heard that I was through the Panhandle on my way to California, she sighed. "Now I *am* jealous. My, I'm so homesick. All this snow." She shuddered.

"They have bad storms in the Panhandle, don't they?"

"Not like the ones up here. And there are so many trees up here; you can't see anything."

Another example of routine, or habit, I thought. When I left New York I longed for months for the subway, the Battery, Brooklyn Bridge and strangest of all, for a tiny Portuguese cemetery on the Bowery, where I often sat during my lunch hour munching on a huge sandwich made of a loaf of Italian bread, spiced meats, and hot peppers. The sandwich was enough for three—and cost twenty-five cents.

The student from Texas missed the miles and miles of flatness of her Panhandle, and I knew that in California I would miss the Michigan trees, especially the pines and the birches. I never could work up much enthusiasm for palms. You're getting drearier and drearier, I said, and kicked myself back to work. Teddy had disappeared; we never did get around to the "nigger" question.

The auditorium was crowded for the New Year's Eve dance. There were many new faces, and Art said that a patient had to be a pretty bad actor to be kept from this dance. Lena was not there, and I felt sorry for her; I felt relieved, too, I had to admit.

"Does the three-dances-with-one person rule hold tonight?"

"Well, the recreation fellow who leads the orchestra usually keeps tabs on that, but I don't think he'll be very strict tonight."

"It's my last dance, you know."

"Go ahead. I'll speak to him if he says anything. But don't overdo it."

Suzy was gayer than usual. "I love New Year's Eve dances. They have a grand march, too. We'll have to save one of our dances for that."

"Art says we don't have to count them tonight."

"You mean we can have all of them together? How wonderful!"

"Well, maybe not all of them; he said not to be greedy…. You smell nice, young lady."

"Perfume my sister gave me. You smell nice, too."

"Shaving lotion. Also a Christmas present. But, if you'll pardon me, your slip's showing. About three inches."

"Oh, lord! It's new, too. Well, I'm not going to stop to fix it now."

After the first dance Suzy whispered to her attendant and they disappeared in the direction of what I presumed was the powder room, so I had the next dance with Jeanne while Teddy glowered. Jeanne said that she had been quite blunt with him, but that the matter would be settled in a week or so, for she was going on Family Care.

(Family Care is a system whereby "good" patients are sent into private homes or to farms, with the state paying for their upkeep. It gives them more freedom, and they may remain on Family Care so long as they are "good.")

"That's splendid, Jeanne. You've wanted that for a long time, haven't you?"

[*277*]

"Yes, and it took me a long time to get it. But they think I'm ready for it now."

"Wherever you go they'll probably want to dress you in pinafores and give you dolls,"

"Over my dead body!"

When Suzy returned, the slip was well concealed. "Safety pins," she said briefly. "I'll have to take a tuck in it—and I hate sewing."

I told her about Jeanne's good fortune.

"I'd like that, too," she said, without envy. "Or I think I would. On a farm. But I don't think—"

"Let's not talk about it—tonight."

"No, not tonight. Do you mind if I tell you I love you?"

"I can take it."

"I love you.... Did I ever tell you about my grandmother?"

I looked startled. "Whatever brought that up—and at such a moment?"

"The slip made me think of it." She began to giggle and we got out of step. "Grandmother was a tomboy when she was a girl and never quite got over it. Well, when she was eighty-two, a peddler came to the farm with cough syrups and things like that. Grandmother didn't like him a bit, but she was polite until he started to leave. I guess he was angry because he didn't sell anything and he kicked Grandmother's cat.

"Grandmother let out a yell that could be heard on the next farm. She hoisted her skirts—she had bloomers underneath—and made a running high jump at the peddler. She landed against his back, clamped both legs around his middle, held his throat with one hand, and beat him and slashed him with her fingernails with the other hand. He tore off down the driveway and tried to brush her off against a big oak tree. But Grandmother hung on, all the time screeching and clawing and hitting. When they reached the highway, she dropped off and gave him a good kick in the pants. We never saw him again.

"Grandmother stalked back to the house. We were in convulsions, but Grandmother didn't wear the tiniest smile, although we could see she was pleased with herself.

"'He was no gentleman!'" she said, and never mentioned the subject after that."

We had to stop dancing. I was laughing so hard that I could barely stand. Suzy joined in, and we leaned on each other, our shoulders shaking. Other couples bumped into us and glared, but we couldn't stop. Some of the attendants looked dubious at first, then they began to smile without knowing why.

"Suzy, darling, my stomach hurts!"

"Mine, too. If you could have seen her with her bloomers—black ones, of course—billowing in the wind!"

"Suzy, for heaven's sake, stop!" And we were off again.

I couldn't stop after I went back to the men's side. Len and Art caught the infection and began to laugh, too.

"It must be good," said Len. "What the hell am I laughing for?"

"I can't tell it," I sputtered. "I'd spoil it. Get Suzy to tell you some day."

I spent the next dance wiping my eyes and cleaning my glasses.

When Suzy and I thought it safe to rejoin each other, I asked why she had not told me the story before.

"Never thought about it until I fixed my slip. Didn't mean to give you apoplexy, darling."

We had three more dances before intermission and managed to keep in step. During intermission the attendants served punch and cookies, but even for refreshments the men had to sit on one side and the women on the other. Then came the grand march. Virtually everyone got out on the floor; women marched with women, and men with men, if they couldn't do better, and there was laughter everywhere.

As each couple passed the stage, they were given noise-makers. The next trip, ridiculous paper hats with rubber strings to fit under the chin. Then confetti and balloons. The auditorium rocked with the noise; the windows steamed from all the body heat; and the odor of powder, cheap perfume, and perspiration engulfed us. But only one patient found it too exciting—a gray-haired woman in a green silk dress, who threw herself on her back and kicked her heels in the air, revealing a black petticoat and pink panties. That ended the party for her.

Suzy and I had the last dance. We had had more than our share, but no one had objected. We were still chuckling at intervals but not saying much because one thought was with us—this really is our last dance....

the
THIRTY-NINTH
day

The alcoholics began to roll in in twos and threes today. The doctor said they were the result of pre-Christmas and Christmas celebrations.

"They try for a few days to get out of it—and then give up," he said. "Think drinking's going to bother you when you leave?"

"I don't think so, but I'm not going to boast that it won't. Did that too many times."

"Well, you should know enough now to stay away from it when you're down. And you *will* be down at times; you'll start to be the little boy of five again, but you can stop it now. I'm pretty sure of that."

He said that he would sign me out after New Year's. "Better take a day or so after that; you'll want to get your car out and probably buy a few things. I'll give you an order for your money and personal belongings; you get Dr. Sheets to sign it—and you're all set."

"I'm glad I'm not going today," I said, looking out the window. It was a sleet storm this time. The doctor said that sleet storms were hell, but he thought the roads would be all right by the time I was ready to go.

He knew Eloise, and I asked if she and her husband had made Indiana all right.

"They're home now, but she's still laid up. Got a new cold myself." He was coughing and his eyes were red. He seemed to want to rest, and his eyes wandered listlessly around the room.

I said, "You must be tired most of the time. And don't you get bored, too?"

"Tired, but never bored. Bad thing to be bored, even if the occasion calls for it."

I told him how often I had been bored in the past, and even cut off persons who bored me. He nodded.

"You got worked up over intolerance—the Dreyfus case, for example—but you were intolerant yourself if someone bored you. That's what boredom is—intolerance. Well, sermon's over."

He bore down on the alcoholics; some were repeaters, and they greeted him cheerfully but with red faces. Others, making their first visits, looked uneasy. New or old, he spared none of them; he didn't lash them, but goaded them. Apparently he could tell—or guess—from their reactions what was bothering them. He sailed into them as a group and left them gaping. Tomorrow he would take them, one by one. During my stay on D-3 I knew of only one alcoholic who never came around to admiring the doctor. All he wanted was to dry out and be released to go to the nearest tavern. He said that all psychiatrists were quacks.

Len grumbled about the doctor, but he admired him. Len grumbled about a lot of things he admired.

Despite the sleet, five of us elected to go to the canteen. Miss Love stood her usual guard until we were bundled up to her satisfaction, but no one protested. What we needed were oilskins to cover everything else.

Half-way to the canteen I remembered that I had not drawn my Friday stipend. I hurried back, and the others went on. Miss Love gave me my envelope containing the money.

"Imagine," she said, "anyone forgetting such a thing!"

"I thought they were supposed to pass out the envelopes here. They always have—until today. Saves us mentally retarded persons from concentrating too much."

"Do you wish to register a complaint, sir?" she asked sweetly.

"No. Feel too good today."

"She must have been nice to you at the dance!"

I said, as Miss Love let me out again, "It's not that. I feel good because of Grandmother and her bloomers."

Miss Love's pretty mouth fell open. "Are you all right?"

"Never better!" And left her to puzzle over it.

Near the canteen I heard Suzy calling me. She was behind me, running as fast as she could over the sleet-slippery path.

Her scarf trailed behind her, and her hair was tousled. One of her galoshes had slipped half off, making her limp as she ran.

Oblivious of others on the path, she threw her arms around me. "Oh, Yack, he said you were dead! He said you were dead!"

"Dead? Who said I was dead?"

She said, choking, "Teddy. He was outside the canteen. I asked him if you were inside. He said, 'He's dead, Suzy; he died last night.' I ran all the way over to Receiving, but they wouldn't let me go up to D-3."

"That dirty, no-good, stinking...."

Suzy looked up. Her face had been ashy, but the color was coming back. There were no tears—only tear-pain in her eyes. "He meant it as a joke, but he didn't laugh or anything. I didn't know."

"You stay here. I'm going in and getting that little bastard!"

Len met me at the canteen door and pushed me back with his big belly. "I've fixed it," he said. "I fixed him, too. No point in your adding to it. Anyway, he ducked out through Center; probably back on D-3 by now."

"I'll go over there and get him. Christ, Len, what he might have done to Suzy! This still could send her off."

"I know," Len said gently. "But I slapped him twice in front of everyone, including Jeanne, and that's about the worst insult you can give a seventeen-year-old, even one who's off his rocker as Teddy is. It was a stinking trick, but he just isn't responsible. You can't mop up the floor with someone who's not all there."

I had used the same argument when Len wanted to knock the block off The Brat. I calmed down somewhat.

"My slapping him took the starch right out of him," Len said. "He kind of took me on for awhile as his second pappy, you know."

"He'd take anyone on for a pappy if the guy had money," I said bitterly.

I went back to Suzy; she said that she didn't want to go into the canteen. "They'd all laugh at me."

"I don't think so. I don't think anyone is going to laugh at you—or play any more tricks."

[*284*]

I told her about Len. "Yes, that probably was the best thing to do. Len's grand, isn't he?"

"None better. I've never seen him drinking, but he'd have to go pretty far to sour me."

Suzy was herself again. She pinched my arm. "Yes, I guess you're still on earth, all right. You know, Yack, my first thought was that you had done something to yourself."

I was shocked for a moment; then I thought: Well, why wouldn't she think that?... "That's over, Suzy; I'm sure it's over. It'll crop up now and then, maybe—the doctor says it will. But that's as far as it'll go."

"I'm sure it's over, too. But just for an instant...."

We decided against the hill and walked along the paths. We crossed a little bridge over a stream that was fighting desperately to keep from being frozen over, and stopped in front of the garage housing my car. I lifted Suzy so that she could look through the window, but the sleet had glazed it and she could see nothing.

"It would be fun to ride in your car," she said. "What color is it?"

"Green, with gray upholstery. Suppose they'd let you go down town with me when I get the car?"

"Afraid not. I haven't town parole.

"I could kidnap you."

"That *would* be fun! Would you tie me up and beat me?"

"I don't think so. I beat only homely women."

She laughed to herself. "It wouldn't do for us to drive around the grounds, either."

"No. In fact, I'm surprised they haven't said something already about our being together so much."

"Well, they don't know about the hill—or that's what we

think. And lots of patients—men and women, I mean—walk together on the grounds."

I asked—and kicked myself for asking. "Will you go up on the hill after I leave?"

She looked at me in a puzzled way. "Why, of course. Why shouldn't I? I'll go up there, and I'll think of you, and when I come down maybe there'll be a letter for me."

"There'll be letters—many of them. I'll write every night on the way out."

"And tell me about everything you see? And about California? Are the orange trees pretty?"

"If you like orange trees. Give me cherry trees, blossoming or bent under their red clusters, any day."

Suzy said that she wouldn't be silly any more about going into the canteen. We went back and had grilled cheese sandwiches and chocolate milk. No one acted as though anything had happened. Only the bubbling Lil mentioned the incident, and we didn't mind her.

"My God," she said, peering at me, "death becomes you!"

the
F O R T I E T H
day

The young doctor called this morning, and we chatted in the
Visitors' Room until Boy Blue, carrying his shoes, interrupted us. He plopped into a chair and regarded us with interest.

"Sure feels good to sit down," he said for the millionth
time.

"The doctor and I are having a little visit—if you don't
mind," I said.

He said, grinning, "Oh, that's all right. Don't bother me
none."

There was but one language he understood. "Scram!" I
said.

He smiled sheepishly and got up. "And don't forget your
shoes."

"Thanks," he said. "Thanks a lot."

"He's a pest," I said, "but pathetic, too."

"Yes, I know about him."

"He's got a new habit now that's driving everyone
crazy—well, crazier. Beats his hands on the arms of a chair
or against the wall."

The doctor said, "He's given sedatives quite often, but

[*287*]

they don't seem to have the right effect. Well, I came up to see if you're ready for that dinner. How's about New Year's Day?"

I said that was fine and told him about California. He thought it a good idea. He was sorry to hear that my wife, whom he had met, and I were definitely separated. But he was glad, he said, that I seemed to be taking an interest in things, for I had chattered away about the patients, the hospital routine, and my plans.

"You certainly look and act differently than you did the day you came in," he said.

"I hope so! Wonder how I'd do with the Rorschach now?"

"Don't think you need one now. Well—about seven, say?"

"That means I can eat supper here and dinner with you, too!"

"I wouldn't advise it. We're having fried chicken."

"With biscuits?"

"Naturally."

"I've never eaten your wife's biscuits, but I ate tons of her mother's years ago. I'll be there promptly—and I won't touch supper here. By the way, how do I get out that time of night?"

"There won't be any trouble about that. Just say where you're going. You've had quite a bit of freedom here, haven't you?"

"More than I could use. After the first two days I never had the feeling of being in prison, which so many of the patients have. I can't say too much for the hospital, especially Receiving and its people."

He was pleased. "Nice to hear that. People outside get some strange ideas about state hospitals. They don't know the real conditions, of course, and believe everything they hear."

He had started to go, but we fell to talking about the fact that in Receiving the alcoholics and the mental cases were not separated. The doctor said the question had been discussed at staff conferences several times, and he wondered how I felt, having been with both types of cases.

"That's a coincidence," I said. "I thought about it—in fact, argued with one of the new alcoholics about it. He was horrified that he was cooped up with nuts, as he put it. But it seems to me that it's good therapy to have them together. Good for the alcoholics, that is; the others probably don't give a damn. When the alcoholic dries out and is able to look around, he's going to be impressed by the fact that he's comparatively lucky. I know that they smiled a little when I said that at staff—of course, I was new then—but I still believe it. Well, I *have* been sounding off, haven't I? Want me to take over your job, Doctor?"

"The consensus at conferences had been that the two should be separated," he said, laughing. "But I think you've got something. Well, I'm really going now."

When he let himself out, Teddy was waiting in the neutral space for someone to open the door. Apparently he had been helping in the dining room. When he saw me, he ducked his head and scuttled between the doctor and me and down the hall.

"Training for a marathon?" asked the doctor.

"That's Teddy, a young so-and-so. We had a little run-in yesterday, and he feels slightly uneasy in my presence."

Teddy avoided me the rest of the day, but I saw him talking to Len several times. Each time Len was laying down the law.

I went to the canteen in the morning—another Saturday had rolled around—to get cigarettes before the noon closing. Red was there, clean-shaven and trim in a white pullover sweater.

"Got off Six yesterday," he greeted me happily. "In one of the cottages now; got ground parole and everythin'. Doc sure came through."

The transformation in Red was remarkable. All the bitterness seemed gone; he spoke hopefully of going home in a short time and said that he was itching to get to work.

"What the hell happened, Red? Did they give you a miracle pill or something?"

"Naw. Like I told you, I just got wise to be myself, that's all. Kicked out some God-damned things what was makin' me go haywire."

"Like the Marines?"

A shadow crossed his face. "Mebbe. Other things, too. Kinda peps you up, don't it, to get 'em out?"

"You're telling me!"

We had Cokes, and I told Red the news of D-3 until Len came in. Then I didn't have much chance. I got my cigarettes—I had been too generous with the Christmas cartons—and walked over to the hill. But it was glazed by the sleet; one could come down all right, but I doubted that one could go up. I had letters to write, so I returned to D-3. When Len came in, he said that Suzy had not come to the canteen.

"What do you know—that Red guy?"

"Sure has changed, hasn't he?"

Len said, "You know, maybe there's something to all this crap they sling around here."

"Hold that pose!" I said. "Camera!"

"Hell," he said, "a guy can change his mind, can't he?"

After dinner I saw Suzy outside the rear entrance to D-3. I hurried down.

"I've a chance to go down town," she said. "One of the attendants is taking three of us. I didn't want you to worry."

"I wasn't worrying. We couldn't get up the hill, anyway. Maybe I'll go down town, too."

"Will you bow if you meet me on the street?"

"That's about as far as I could go on Front Street, don't you think? I *could* wink, though."

"How wolfish! Darling, I have to run; there's the attendant. We'll take a long walk tomorrow."

I went down town an hour later for lack of anything better to do. It was dull in the Day Room; I had written my letters, and I had read all the books the doctor had lent me. Half-way down I regretted my decision, for the going was slippery. By the time I reached the business section I was tired out and uncomfortably warm. A sign caught my eye and, after looking carefully around, I entered the store.

This probably will ruin my reputation, I said, but I took the plunge—and ordered a chocolate ice cream soda.

On the way back I met Suzy and her group. I bowed, and then I winked as wolfishly as I knew how. Suzy cast down her eyes, thereby stealing the scene, for I had to snort with laughter. They passed on, with the three other patients giggling and the attendant looking back with a puzzled expression on her face.

After supper Art asked me to help him sort Johnny's belongings.

"Is he going home?"

"Not Johnny. They're moving him to Thirty-two. He can do a little light work—if he will. Might help a bit."

For some reason I was upset. I hated to think of Johnny in Thirty-two with no Miss Brown, no Miss Love, no Bates to gentle him. On D-3, although he ignored everyone, he must have sensed that the older men were fond of him. And he would miss his seat on the ping-pong table.

We wrapped his few extra clothes in a sheet, and Art went to the Day Room to fetch Johnny. I had a chocolate bar and some gum, and I offered them to Johnny, but he shook his head. He wasn't sulking; he simply wasn't interested. When Art told him that he was being transferred, he smiled vaguely.

"We'll miss you, Johnny," I said. "All of us will miss you." But he was staring at something over my head, and I doubted that he even heard me.

An attendant from another floor came to take him to Thirty-two. Art was on D-3 alone and couldn't leave. I tried to shake Johnny's hand, but he pulled away, startled. Then the attendant gave him a little push, and he went out the door into the neutral space, not looking back nor answering our goodbyes.

the
FORTY-FIRST
day

I had my name put on the going-to-church list, thereby pleasing Miss Brown once more.

"You hitting the sawdust trail?" demanded Len.

"That's a slight exaggeration. I want to say goodbye to The Reverend. He hasn't been up here since Christmas."

"Oh, yes, he has, but you're so busy outside these days that you've missed him a couple of times."

"I'll probably be busy outside, as you so prettily put it, until I leave. So I'll say goodbye where I know he'll be. The Reverend's been damned nice to me."

In the auditorium I found myself, as before, next to The Financier. I told him that I was leaving in a few days, and he said, "Glad you wangled your way out. Going to Detroit, by any chance?"

"No, California; but the way I drive I might wind up in Detroit after all."

"Better not. Dangerous town, Detroit; extremely dangerous. I think," he said, as though he had any choice in the matter, "that I'll stay here through the summer. They tell me it's real nice."

After The Reverend's sermon, which was brief, I went to the stage and said goodbye.

"California, eh?" he said. "Well, you'll probably be glad to see some sun, but I rather hoped you would settle in town. There are a lot of people there who remember you."

"No one here seems to agree what I should do," I said. "Guess that's why I had to choose for myself."

"Yes. Well, that's wise. Make your own decisions, my boy."

Other patients crowded up with their little offerings; The Reverend and I shook hands, and I found my way back to the D-3 group.

I walked with Curly, who suddenly said, "Say, I talked with her last night."

"With whom, Curly?"

"My wife, of course, " he said impatiently. "They let her come in and we had a nice long talk. Say, she looked pretty."

"I didn't see any visitors last night."

"Oh, you was in bed. They let her in about midnight. Say, they ain't so bad here, after all."

He rattled on, telling what he said and she said and how she was dressed. He was so happy about it that I asked no more questions. Poor Curly. Really over the brink now.

And yet, later, I wondered if it was a case of poor Curly. Lord, he's happy now, at least, and he wasn't happy when he was staring out into the night. Perhaps this way is more merciful. I recalled how many times I argued with doctors in favor of so-called mercy killings, and how righteously indignant they were and how intolerant of a layman's opinion— even if the layman only wanted to hear himself express his opinions. Well, no use going over all that again.... But I stopped thinking of Curly as "poor Curly."

In the afternoon I met Suzy outside Eleven, and we strolled—skidded, rather—along the paths branched off from Center. We didn't talk about ourselves, except to chuckle briefly over the down town meeting. We talked mostly about books we had read; about dogs and cats; about church sociables (Suzy went to many of them when she was small, and so did I); about beach picnics; about the old general stores in the rural areas. And, finally, we argued placidly about a man called Eisenhower.

I was limping when we arrived back at the gate to Eleven. "Long walk yesterday; long walk today. I'm not young any more, Suzy."

"It was worth it, though, wasn't it? So close and so—calm. I feel good—no, better than good. Contented—that's how I feel."

"That's a word few persons can use honestly. I feel that way, too."

We parted without saying more.

In the evening Len and I went over my road atlas, and he plotted a route for me. Down the shoreline of Michigan, into Indiana and Illinois, then over to St. Louis. Through the Ozarks, into Kansas for a few hours, Oklahoma, Texas.

"Ever been in Texas?" Len Asked.

"Once—when I was a cub reporter. Got a job in Fort Worth. My father financed the trip—and it *was* a trip in those days—and gave me fifty bucks to tide me over the first week. The second night there, a block off the main street, someone slugged me and took my wallet. I beat it for home as soon as my father came to the rescue with a telegraphed money order. I don't think my mother ever forgave me; she thought I should have stayed and become an oil millionaire.

[*295*]

I should have stayed, instead of running home, but I don't know about the millionaire part."

"Still counting your mistakes, huh? Well, then you hit New Mexico. You go this way and you won't have too many mountains. Then Arizona, down through Tucson and Yuma, and you're almost there. Cinch."

"Yes, just a little matter of about 2,500 miles."

"Ought to make it in five days."

"What do you think I am—a hot-rod kid? I never drove five hundred miles in a day and I don't intend to start now. Three hundred miles, at the most, and I'm pooped. And it's not a matter of life and death; if it takes me two weeks, I guess my family can endure it."

"Bet I could do it in four days. I drive like hell."

"I daresay. Drunk or sober?"

Len said, owl-eyed, "Why I wouldn't think of driving with a snort in me!"

The new alcoholics, sitting nearby, chuckled. They were drying out and the world looked better, but all they could talk about was the binges they had been on and the dire prospect of spending New Year's Eve on D-3 without a drop to give a man courage to face another year.

"I remember one Eve," said a man from Chesaning. "I really got looped, but I had enough sense left to know I'd need a coupla eye-openers next day. So I got me a bottle and drove home. My wife, she knew all the hiding places, so I went into the back yard and hid it under the snow. Well, next day I sure did need it, and I went out and pretended like I was shoveling some paths. But it snowed all night and, by God, I couldn't find that damned bottle. Betcha I cleaned the snow outa that whole backyard."

He sighed as though it hurt him. "Know what? Looped

like I was, I turned the wrong way coming outa the garage and buried the bottle in my neighbor's backyard! He found it a coupla days later and was tickled as hell. What could I say?"

That started them off, and their stories *were* funny. An alcoholic is never more humorous than when he is telling a joke on himself.

Shortly, however, they became maudlin about their binges and their hangovers. Len and I quietly left and took a constitutional up and down the hall. As we passed Mannie's room the second time, he beckoned to me.

"Say, wouldja help a feller again?"

"A letter?"

"Yeah, I got one from the wife and I wanta answer it right off. The wife," he said proudly, "reads and writes." He showed me the letter; it was only a note:

Dear husband, why didn't you send us no Xmas presents? We had a good Xmas anyways. How is the weather up there? The kids is OK. Well, will close. Your wife.

Mannie said, "Now you think of something to say. Like why I didn't send no Christmas presents."

"Well, what was the reason?"

"Didn't have no money. The wife, she didn't send me no money."

I did the best I could, explaining Mannie's financial dilemma, discussing the weather, and sending Mannie's love to the children, his wife, his mother and father, and two aunts.

"That's wonderful," he said when I read the letter to him. "That'll make her sit up." He hesitated, then went on, "Say, I

[*297*]

wanta ask you somethin'. Last time the wife was up here she talked with Doc, and when she came back she was cryin'. She wouldn't tell me nothin'. I can't figure it. You got any idears?"

I knew the answer. After writing the first letter for Mannie, I had made some inquiries about him. His wife was crying because they wouldn't let him go home; they were afraid that car door might swing open again. They might never permit him to go home.

I pretended to ponder. "Seems to me, Mannie, that she was crying because you wouldn't be home for Christmas. Women are like that, you know—always crying over some little thing."

He leaned back on the bed, relieved. "Say, I never thought of that. Sure, that's why she was cryin'. Women ain't got no guts, have they?"

"Babies," I said. "Cry-babies, Mannie."

"Yeah."

Going to my room, I thought: Of all the lies you have told, here is one you needn't regret.

the
FORTY-SECOND
day

When the Monday cleaning was over I began to think about packing. That was one characteristic the hospital hadn't changed. Throughout my adult years, whenever I went on a trip, I prepared days in advance. When I left The Farm to go to Grand Rapids as a cub reporter, I packed, unpacked, and re-packed a steamer trunk my mother had given me. I did it for two weeks, and when I finally left, I was in such a state that my mother had to pack it all over again.

In the New York days, whenever I was sent on an out-of-town assignment, I arrived at LaGuardia Airport or Grand Central station at least an hour ahead of time. My city editor once bellowed at me because I was fifteen minutes late arriving at the office, and everyone in the place laughed at him. It was the first time I had been late in fifteen years.

The habit remained with me on D-3. I asked Miss Brown if she would unlock my room so I could sort things out. And, please, could I have my bags?

"Why, you're not going for several days." said Miss Brown. "And you haven't even been signed out. As for your bags, you have to go to Storage for them, and you have to have an order to get them."

"Well, could I have my car keys? I'd like to see if the darned thing will start. It's been standing a long time, you know."

"I don't think you'd better have the keys. Why don't you get the garage key and just look the car over? Might make you feel better."

"I feel all right. I don't want a last-minute rush, that's all."

Miss Brown smiled patiently. "You'll have plenty of time. Now run along and look at your old car."

"It's new."

"Well, look at it anyway." She considered. "If you want to take some of your clothes over to the car, that's all right."

Larry, standing nearby, begged to go along. Miss Brown nodded. "Then maybe I can get some work done," she said.

Larry and I collected the soiled linen in my room and tied it in a bundle. Then I got a spare suit from the Clothes Room, wrapped half a dozen shirts and some ties in a newspaper, and debated whether to take along socks and handkerchiefs, too.

"I'm kind of short on socks," I said. "Better leave 'em here."

Larry was as excited as though *he* were going away. We marched back to the office and I asked for the garage key.

"That's at Center," Miss Brown said. She told me which office the key was in, but suggested that I see Dr. Sheets first.

"Shouldn't I have my fingerprints taken, too? And put up bond?"

"Scram!" said Miss Brown, startling both of us. But she laughed as she let us out. "You two look like old-clothes men," she said.

A mild rain was falling as we left Receiving. I found it hard to believe. Snow, sleet—and now rain. We'll probably have a dust storm by the time I leave, I thought. When we reached Center, the rain was coming down hard; the spare suit was beginning to take on a bedraggled look, and Larry and I could barely see through our glasses.

I settled Larry in a chair in the main hallway of Center, piled my belongings on him (he *did* look like an old-clothes man then), and went into Dr. Sheets' office. When I asked about the garage key, he understood at once.

"Getting a little itchy? Natural. Of course you may have the key. Better not take the car out, though. Wait until the day before you leave, say."

"No chance of taking it out, Doctor. Miss Brown has the car keys—and she's hanging on to them."

"Sensible person, Miss Brown," he said smiling.

"A grand person. They're all that way on D-3."

We talked about the hospital in general and D-3 in particular; then Dr. Sheets took me to the office where the garage keys were kept. A woman secretary who had charge of them was a little anxious.

"You'll return the key as soon as you're finished?" she asked.

"I promise."

Larry and I went through Center, down some stairs, and through the corridor that led by the canteen. I looked in, but Suzy wasn't there. Lil was, however, and promptly demanded, "What's up? Ain't leaving already, are you?"

I told her what was up, and she asked if she could come, too.

"Of course. Make a party of it."

We splashed through the puddles already forming on the

icy paths, crossed the little bridge and, coming up to my garage, no. 8, were met by Suzy.

"Surprise!" she greeted us.

I said, "Don't tell me that you knew all the time we were coming here."

"No, I'm not mind-reading today. I wanted to see the car, and I thought the rain would clean the windows—so here I am."

"Just in time," I said, "for the unveiling."

We got the padlock open, kicked away the snow and ice, and opened the doors.

"Ladies and gentleman," I began. Then I peered inside. "Good God, that's not my car!"

But it was, because the license plate said so. I never would have recognized it otherwise. It was streaked with dirt, all the chrome was rusty, and the windows were as pock-marked as those of a Bowery saloon.

Lil was the first to recover. "It's nothing," she said. "You picked up all that stuff driving with snow when you got here."

"Yeah, but all that sand and gravel was underneath. And that stuff they put on slippery roads—that's what's taken the shine off the chrome. Hell, a little wash job and she'll be pretty again."

I took Lil's word for it, but it looked like a hopeless task to me. We stowed my clothes away, and then I went through a big cardboard container in the trunk. I found fistfuls of sticks of chewing gum, but had no memory of putting them there. We divided the gum, also more fistfuls of soft lead pencils, absentmindedly taken home from the office in various pockets. Larry sputtered over a sheaf of typewriter paper, and I gave it to him. There were some paperback mystery books, which Lil happily clutched to her ample bosom.

"It's your turn, Suzy. Take your pick."

She was reluctant even to look into the container, but when I came up from the bottom of it with a face towel, she exclaimed, "Oh, I'd like that! I'd like a towel for myself."

I found another one, but she insisted that it go to Lil. Then I found a package of chocolate bars, and we fell to munching. But I was perplexed; I remembered putting the chocolate bars into the container, but I had no idea where the face towels came from. You *must* have been in a state, I thought. What other surprises are in here? There were no more. But chewing gum and face towels....

"Let's take a ride," said Lil.

"Can't. I don't get the keys until the day before I leave."

"Hell, let's pretend to take a ride."

So we got into the car. Larry scrambled into the front seat with me. I started to protest, but Suzy shushed me and got into the back with Lil.

"Let her rip!" yelled Lil. "Give her the gas! Give her— what else do you give her?"

"It's customary to turn the ignition, but that's out. We'll just give her the gas. Here we go!"

We leaned back and pretended. "Hell of a draft back here," said Lil. "Close your window."

Larry reached over and timidly tugged at the steering wheel. His hand slipped and landed on the horn button; he jumped, bumping his head against the top, but he was entranced. He pressed one finger on the button and kept it there until I said, "Gently, Larry; we don't want the fire department swooping down on us."

I could see Suzy in the mirror. She was mildly interested in the chocolate bar, but one hand caressed the face towel. I felt a wave of tenderness for the three of them. And then a wave of hopelessness, for I could do nothing for them. Nothing more than I was doing now, sitting in a motionless automobile and pretending as we used to pretend on The Farm in a horseless buggy....

Suzy must have guessed my thoughts. She said, still pretending but with a shade of anxiety in her voice, "If you'll please let me out at the next corner.... It's nearly dinner time."

We locked the car and the garage door, and went out into the slanting rain.

Ten of us went to the movies in the auditorium. Five were habituals; they went every Monday night. But the other five, including myself, joined them as a gesture. It seemed almost indecent to sit in the Day Room on New Year's Eve.

We saw a Donald Duck cartoon and a terrible war picture in which the hero was in danger, for thirty minutes, of being blown up in a powder magazine. The film broke three or four times, but there was no clapping of hands; there was no stamping of feet. Again, that curious restraint among people presumed to be unrestrained.

We were back on D-3 and in bed at 9:05. Len peered into my room a few minutes later.

"Some cheese and crackers? Art's making coffee."

"No thanks. I'm exhausted. Can't take this night life."

In bed at 9:05 on New Year's Eve! No one ever will believe it, I said, and went to sleep.

the
FORTY-THIRD
day

Unlike the people outside, we received mail on New Year's day. All hospital mail was sent to a post office box, and we weren't dependent upon the mailman. I had a letter from my sister telling of her family's Christmas vacation in Florida and of their swimming on Christmas day. "We wished that you could have been with us," she wrote.

Looking out a window, I wished so, too. The rain had stopped, but the thermometer was dropping steadily and a stiff wind was blowing off the bay. The sleet storm left a glaze; the rain, freezing over night, coated everything with ice. Perfect, I thought, for starting a trans-continental trip.

Len, trying to be casual, pulled up a chair. "If this keeps up, I'll have to get a bulldozer to dig out a road to the cottage."

I tried to be just as casual. "You contemplate a change of residence?" I knew damned well what was coming because I had seen Miss Brown give him a letter.

Len said, "I won't beat you out of here, but I'll be leaving this week for sure."

"All right, mystery man. Take that sappy look off your face and let's hear the news."

"Well, my wife's closing up the house and going to the cottage. One of the daughters may come along, too. We'll kind of camp out there for awhile. Spring's just around the corner."

"I can see that you haven' looked outside. If you did, you couldn't see anything—you're that starry-eyed.... To hell with that! Len, you old bastard, I'm tickled to death!"

"I'm not exactly moping."

"If you were a peacock you'd be strutting. I bet you're going to have easy sailing from now on."

"Maybe so. Wish you had something more definite in sight."

"Don't worry about me. I'm the professor; I'm the philosopher."

We were light; we were timid, as are most men, about saying what we really felt. Len looked off into space, and I knew that he was making plans: have to get the road open, have to get some firewood, have to have the phone turned on. Watching him, I felt a stab of envy. I had no plans to make.

Len and I went out after dinner, but the canteen was closed because of the holiday. Len wanted to look over the car, but there was no one in Center to give me the garage key. And we risked falls with every step we took on the paths.

"I'm going to have a hell of a time getting over to the doctor's tonight," I said.

"You going to Doc's?"

"To another doctor's. For dinner. Fried chicken and biscuits."

"We'll probably have hash," he said gloomily.

I loitered near the gate to Eleven, and Len pretended that

he didn't know why. But we saw no sign of Suzy, and finally we went back to Receiving. We stopped at D-2 and rapped on the door. The attendant said that we could come in to see Franklin and Frank.

Franklin was in bed. He looked much worse than when he left D-3, although they were tube-feeding him. He hadn't been shaved for days, and a terrible odor came from his mouth. He recognized us but wasn't interested. There was no talk of electrocution; no talk about his sins. He lay there looking at us, yet barely seeing us through the torture in his eyes. I had to leave, but Len was made of stronger stuff and he talked to Franklin awhile before joining me in Frank's room.

Frank seemed much better. He beamed at us and motioned to Len to open the top drawer of his bureau. It was well stocked with candy, and both of us ate too many chocolate covered cherries. Frank had the Rose Bowl game on his radio, and we listened for half an hour. Next year, I thought, perhaps I can watch the Rose Bowl game. Next year....?

I told Art about my invitation to dinner, and asked—if there wouldn't be any kickback about it—if I might shave.

"Sure," he said, and got the safety razor, the brush, and a tube of cream I had used the day I went to staff. That seemed years ago.

"I'll leave the door open," I said. "And Len can hang around if you're busy."

"Feel like you might cut your throat?"

"Hell, no!"

Art laughed. "Close the door then. Otherwise you'll have the whole gang watching."

I shaved quickly, despite the dull blade, but there was

something wrong about the lighting and I cut down my moustache to Hitler size before I realized it. When I turned in the razor to Art, he said, "Take a shower if you want to. After all—chicken with biscuits."

"You've been talking to Len."

Art said, "He's drooling. He loves his victuals, that man."

When I reached the doctor's—after falling only twice while covering the two blocks to his house—I was ravenous. They didn't keep me waiting long; dinner was served after I met the three small sons and the even smaller daughter who, I was glad to note, were not fed first, but sat at table with us and joined in the conversation—when they had the chance.

I ate too much and doubtless talked too much, too. But there was so much to eat: fried chicken (not plastered with flour), mashed potatoes and gravy, biscuits ("Better than your mother's," I said truthfully), salad with Roquefort dressing, ice cream and strawberries.

"They'll die a thousand on D-3 when they hear about this," I said.

And there was so much to talk about: the days on The Farm when my hostess, who lived nearby, was about three; the long enchanted summers when we lived only for swimming and tennis; the long enchanted winters when we skated across the bay or coasted down Howe's hill. We talked of Miss Davis, who taught the first four grades, and of Mr. Wilcox, who taught the others. We talked—and then we talked some more. The doctor was nice about it, but he must have felt left out.

When we ran down, the doctor took me to the basement and showed me the skeleton of a sailboat he was building. I was a good audience because, since I was old enough to pick up a hammer, I longed to build things. But I was utterly without skill; anything I built either collapsed if one breathed on it or shamed me with its Rube Goldberg absurdities.

I was in the doctor's home and not his office, but I couldn't resist saying, "You must subscribe to the hobby theory. A psychiatrist once told me that I *had* to have a hobby. I tried everything from finger painting to studying the migration of birds, but I never found a hobby that lasted."

"Hobbies are a great help," he said, "But there's no point in groping for one. Your work probably used up most of your physical and mental energies. I wouldn't worry about a hobby, if I were you."

"I'm not worrying, but I know that if I could build a sailboat in my basement—if I had a basement—I'd be more elated than if I won a Pulitzer prize."

The evening went by quickly. The three boys were taken down town by their mother for a movie spree. When the movie was over, the oldest boy telephoned, and their mother prepared to drive down for them. I wanted to stay on, and I was urged to, but it was after nine.

"Hospital routine's got me," I said. "If you'll drop me off at Receiving, I'll drive down with you."

They understood. During the evening they understood many things without my explaining them.

The doctor's wife let me out in front of Receiving, forgetting that it was against the rules for a patient to use the front entrance. I stood on the steps until the car disappeared down the driveway, then took the path that led to the rear entrance.

As I rounded the first corner of Receiving, a clump of bushes suddenly erupted and a figure, vague in the darkness, jumped at me. I jumped, too—but backwards. One foot skidded on a hummock of ice and, with arms beating and feet kicking, I plopped into a snowdrift, breaking the ice crust and sinking at least three feet.

From the bushes came a gurgle of laughter that wasn't vague.

"Suzy, you fiend!" I sputtered, digging snow out of my mouth and eyes, "Get me out of here!"

I couldn't move; I might as well have been in a strait-jacket. Suzy, still gurgling, came out of the bushes; she grabbed my hands but couldn't lift me from the trap, and the more I floundered the deeper I sank.

"Get a good hold of my ankles and pull," I said. I was beginning to laugh, too, but I was thinking: This would be a fine time for an attendant to come along.

Suzy got the hold and she pulled. I came out of the drift slowly, but I came out. I got to my feet, shaking the snow from me and feeling some of it melting down my back. Suzy was trying to look apologetic and was getting nowhere. So we let ourselves go as we had over Grandmother and the peddler.

When we were back to normal, I said, "And now, young lady, what in hell are you doing outside at this time of night?"

"I've been chasing fireflies, sir."

"Of course. This is their mating season; snow and ice bring out the beast in them. Suzy, you didn't just sneak out?"

"No. My sister was up in Petoskey after Christmas, and she had to come through here on her way home. So she came to the hospital, and they let me go down town with her for dinner."

"Sounds like an alibi in an Agatha Christie mystery. So?"

"My sister brought me back in a taxi, and then I thought you might be coming back pretty soon, so I waited—in the bushes. I wanted to see you, darling. I didn't see you yesterday; they wouldn't let anyone out yesterday because of the weather."

"Next time would you mind standing in the middle of the driveway? No more Moses-in-the-bulrushes. Suzy, I do love you so, you worm!"

"I can go home now," she said, her voice soft and glad.

We held hands and went around another corner of Receiving and along the path to Eleven. It was not until I came and climbed the stairs to D-3 that it struck me.... Suzy had said, I can go *home* now.

the
FORTY-FOURTH
day

They took down the Christmas decorations today. The cards on the center pillar were distributed to their owners or thrown into the trash can. Miss Brown supervised removal of the Santa Claus posters and hovered nearby while Larry, the new student nurses, and I took the trimmings from the tree, which was shedding its needles as if in haste to have it over with. Once the trimmings were taken away, it seemed to crouch in its corner in forlorn nudity.

Miss Brown carefully packed the trimmings in a cardboard container and said cheerfully that they would be all right for another year. I wondered: How many of these men will be here next Christmas? Will Miss Brown and Ralph play another duet? Will Boy Blue lose his shoes again? I went down the list, thinking a question about each....

I missed Willie and asked about him. Miss Brown said that he had been taken to the dentist to have two teeth pulled. He was back in a few minutes, holding one hand to his cheek but saying proudly, "I took it like a man."

The doctor gave electros, and it was late in the morning when he got around to me.

"All set?" he asked.

"All set."

"Well, here's an order for your money. Here's another for your bags. Miss Brown will give you the car keys. I won't say goodbye now; I'll see you this afternoon and we'll go over things."

Miss Brown gave up the keys without a murmur. "So you're really going?" she said. "Well, Jack, you've been an easy patient."

"I think I'll have that put on my tombstone: He was an easy patient."

"Oh, go along with you! That's meant to be a compliment."

I told Miss Brown I would like to leave a present for the D-3 staff and asked if there was anything they needed for their kitchen snacks.

"You don't have to do anything like that," she said. "But we do need some coffee cups—the kind that won't break. You shouldn't do it, though. You save your money."

"That's all I have been doing for forty-four days."

I took my orders to Center, but they said in the accounting office that Dr. Sheets would have to sign them. He scribbled his initials on them, shook hands, and wished me a good trip. I tried to thank him for all that had been done for me, but I couldn't find the words.

"I'm grateful as hell," I finally said. "That isn't prettily put, but it's what I mean."

He walked to the door with me and we shook hands again. Then I went to the accounting office and drew my money and the personal belongings I hadn't been permitted to keep on D-3. These included a dollar watch, stopped at 1:30, and an Indian head penny, which I presumably had carried for years in my pocket without knowing it was there. But the accounting office had found it and carefully listed it.

I got the garage key, again promising the anxious secretary that I would turn it in during the afternoon. There was a soft snow falling when I left Center, but by the time I reached the garage the sky darkened and the wind came up, and I knew that another storm was on its way.

The car responded immediately. It choked a few times, sputtered, then settled down to a peaceful purring. I patted the steering wheel. "This is only the beginning, pal" I said. "We've got a long way to go."

I left the car in a down-town service station to be gassed, oiled, greased, and washed, and went shopping. In a hardware store I found some coffee cups that wouldn't break. They were made of plastic and resembled beer mugs more than cups, but I thought they would do for the D-3 kitchen. I also bought a large fruit cake, to the surprise of the grocer, who said, "Thought I was stuck with that, the holidays being over."

I wanted to get something extra nice for Suzy. I went into a jewelry store and looked at rings, bracelets, and earrings, but they seemed cold to me. Next, I toured a department store but couldn't make up my mind. I settled, finally, for three cakes of soap that had the scent of gardenias, and three velvety face towels. Strange presents, but I knew that she would like them more than rings or bracelets.

The car was not ready when I returned. I walked to Washington Street and tried to locate our house. I was certain that I was at the right corner, but the house wasn't there. Where it should have been was a ranch-type house. Well, what did I expect? It was in 1917 that we lived in the house on Washington Street. Houses don't last forever.

Down town again, I looked for Wahl's, where we ate hamburgers and banana splits after the high school dances. But Wahl's was gone, too. I walked for miles, it seemed, trying to find a familiar landmark, but there was none. On Union Street I saw a name on a sign over a tavern-restaurant that brought back memories of a classroom sweetheart. I went in and had a sandwich and a glass of beer. Her brother was behind the counter, and I knew him at once, but he didn't recognize me. When I told him who I was, he took off his apron, called to a young man in the kitchen to take over, and perched on a stool next to me, firing questions and insisting that we have drinks of Old Grandad. I had two and felt that at any moment I might float up to the ceiling.

I asked about his sister, and he said casually, "Oh, she's in the state hospital. Been there for five years."

"I've been there for forty-four days," I said. "I'm leaving tomorrow."

"Is that so?" he said. He got off the stool and wrapped his apron around him. He put the bottle of bourbon back on the shelf. "Well, it's been nice seeing you," he said.

We shook hands. I could *feel* his eyes in my back as I walked out. The Flash knew what he was talking about, I thought, recalling his warning about Main Street's sly curiosity.

The car was shiny clean and seemed eager to be on its way. It was a shame to take it out, for the snow was sweeping in from the bay, and it had the feel of snow that scorns the feebleness of flurries. The car skidded three times on the way to Receiving; after the third time I got the feel of it and had no more trouble.

Miss Brown and Bates liked the coffee mugs. I bounced one on the kitchen floor, and they were even more pleased.

"We'll christen them tomorrow morning." Miss Brown said. "We'll have coffee and fruit cake and anything else you want. You have breakfast with us."

"That'll be fine," I said, but I didn't feel that it would be fine. I ached inside, and I pretended that I didn't know why—but I did.

I walked to Center and returned the garage key. The anxious secretary was relieved and grateful. Then I went out the back way to the canteen. No one I knew was there. I went out and started for Storage. A block away, I saw Suzy waiting on the front steps. I had the soap and the towels with me and I gave them to her. I had thought that I would make a joke about them, but I didn't say anything. Suzy only glanced at them.

"What's wrong, darling?"

"Nothing. Not a damned thing."

She said cheerfully, "I'm glad everything's all right."

Pretending, we went into Storage and I collected my bags. Still pretending, we went to the canteen, which suddenly was crowded. I bought for the house. Hamburgers, hot dogs, coffee, chocolate milks, and Cokes were passed around, but the bill came to less than five dollars.

Len sat with us at the table. He and Suzy ordered hamburgers, but they didn't touch them. They sat there looking at me, until finally I burst out, "For Christ's sake, stop trying to hypnotize me!"

"Better take it easy, pal." Len said.

Suzy said nothing, but she reached across the table and put her hand on mine, not caring who looked on, and I realized how childishly I was behaving.

"All cured," I said, with the ache still inside me, and we went on pretending for the rest of the afternoon.

When I left Suzy at the gate to Eleven, she said that she would be on the hill early in the morning.

"I want to say goodbye there," she said.

I told her that I planned to leave about eight, "Can you get out that early?"

"I'll get out if I have to burn down the building!... My darling, please don't look so sad!"

I kissed her and walked quickly away, back to Receiving, counting my steps. One, two, three...where's this new man business?...four, five, six...thought you were grown up... seven, eight, nine...do you want your mamma, little boy?

It was like having a cold shower. The ache was still there, but it was different. It was a clean ache.

I thought I had missed the doctor, but Miss Brown said that he had given up to the cold or flu bugs and was in bed. I was disappointed that I couldn't say goodbye to him, but I wrote a note and left it with Miss Brown.

I went to bed early. Art came in as I was drifting off. "You'll be gone before I come on tomorrow," he said. "Happy landings!"

I told him, "I'll always remember that first night, Art. Happy landings, yourself!"

Just before lights-out, Larry tiptoed into the room and pressed a folded piece of paper into my hand. Then he tiptoed out. I got up and opened the paper near the door where the hall lights struck it. It was a penciled note that read:

Jack, my wish for you is that you will take the Lord Jesus Christ as your Saviour, for there is none other name whereby we may be saved.

The little June bug, I said. The sweet little June bug.

the LAST day

I was up at four and packing my bags when Teddy came in, young and ungainly in his long underwear.

"I wanta apologize," he said. I knew that Len had sent him, because *apologize* wasn't in Teddy's vocabulary. "I done wrong," he said. 'I didn't mean to."

We hadn't spoken to each other since the day he frightened Suzy. He was twitchy; he didn't know what I would do.

"It's all right, kid," I said. "I guess you've learned a lesson."

He said eagerly, "I wanta do somethin' for you."

"You can be nice to Suzy after I leave. You really want to do something? All right, sweep the snow off my car. I know it's buried in the stuff." I had left the car outside.

"Gosh, I'll do that! I'll get her all slicked up. I'll go down right now."

"Better wait until Miss Brown comes in. She'll let you out, I'm sure."

"Okay. Gosh! Well, okay!"

I had a piece of toast and a cup of coffee for breakfast. When we filed back from the dining room, I automatically went to the Utility Room and got out my brush. But Bates said, "Your successor is ready to go. No more sweeping for you. Elmer's taking over."

"Oh, Lord," I said, "that'll kill Jacob. He says Elmer isn't any good. Doesn't get into the corners."

"We'll get by," Bates said.

At 7:30 Miss Brown called me into the kitchen, and we had coffee and fruit cake. I was disappointed that Miss Love and Goodman were off duty. The coffee mugs were a success except that, for some reason, the heat of the coffee penetrated the handles.

"You'll have to use mufflers on them," I said. "Or [leering at Miss Brown] rubbers!"

When the coffee was gone and there was no excuse for lingering, I said goodbye. Then I went into the Day Room and circled it, shaking hands with the men. Willie kissed my hand and cried; he probably didn't know why. I thanked Larry for his note, and he shuffled along with me. Some of the old men were confused and shook Larry's hand, but he didn't try to explain.

Ralph was at the piano. I waited until he was through. It was *Night and Day* again.

"So long, Ralph," I said.

He ignored me and began playing *Rhapsody in Blue.*

"I'm leaving, Ralph," I said. "Just want to say goodbye."

He went on playing. Len shouted across the Day Room, "Don't bother with that bastard!" Larry and I moved on.

I got my bags and went to the office. Bates said he would take me to the ground floor and check me out. Len walked to the door with me.

"Well," he said.

"Well," I said.

We shook hands. "Son of a bitch," Len said. "I can't get anything out."

I said, "Son of a bitch; I can't either."

We shook hands again, and Bates opened the door into the neutral space. We waited a long time for the elevator, and when it came it was crowded with women from C-3. They noticed my bags immediately.

"You're going home!" said one. "Oh, Jesus, he's going home!"

They murmured to themselves, darting glances at me as their attendant herded them into C-3. Bates and I rode down to the first floor, and he checked me out with the telephone operator. It never occurred to me to ask why the telephone operator had to know that I was leaving.

Bates walked with me to the front door.

"Hope I never see you again!" he said.

I knew how he meant it.

Teddy was waiting beside the car. He had brushed off the snow, but it was piling up again. I arrived here in a blizzard and I'm leaving in a blizzard, I thought. What does that mean—if anything?

"Thanks, kid," I said. I gave him a dollar bill. He looked so young—and eager.

"Now, beat it back," I said.

I went up the hill. I was panting when I reached the top. It took me several minutes to get my breath. When I did, I said vaguely to Suzy, "The squirrel isn't out."

"No," she said. "Just crazy people. What's that song?"

"*Mad Dogs and Englishmen*?"

"That's it."

I said, "Suzy, I can't talk. I want to go—or stay. Shall I stay, Suzy?"

"No, Yack. Kiss me, Yack—and go. Go quickly."

We didn't say goodbye. I pressed the red mittens, and then I went down the hill. I got into the car, backed it, and got into the driveway. I turned down the window and looked up the hill. But the snow had blotted out everything; there was no hill there; there was no one on the hill. Even the pines had disappeared in smothering whiteness.

Traverse City Record-Eagle
Friday, May 2, 1958

J.D. Kerkhoff Taken by Death

Grand Rapids, MICH., May 2
—(UP)—Grand Rapids relatives of Johnston D. Kerkhoff reported that the former Grand Rapids Herald news editor died Wednesday while on a trip to Tijuana, Mexico.

Kerkhoff, a native of Oak Park, Ill., had been living in Imperial Beach, Calif., where funeral services will be held.

He began his newspaper career on the Traverse City Record-Eagle, joining the Herald in 1919. Later he served on the staffs of the Detroit Times, New York Journal-American, Philadelphia Record.

In 1942 he returned to Grand Rapids as the Herald's news editor, a post he held until 1948 when he left and later joined the staff of the New York Post. He was the author of three published books, the best known of which was "How Thin the Veil."

MORE FROM MISSION POINT PRESS

STORM STRUCK:
When Supercharged Winds Slammed
Northwest Michigan
By Robert Campbell; Foreword by Bob Sutherland
Photography by Northwest Michigan Residents
and Visitors

POISON ON TAP:
How Government Failed Flint and the Heroes
Who Fought Back

A Bridge Magazine Analysis

BLOOD ON THE MITTEN:
Infamous Michigan Murders
1700s to Present

By Tom Carr

AN UNCROWDED PLACE:
A Life Up North and a Young Man's
Search for Home

By Bob Butz

INSIDE UPNORTH

A Guide to Traverse City, Traverse Area
and Leelanau County, 2017

Made in the USA
Columbia, SC
07 June 2021

39280489R00202